Epistles from Pap

Letters from the man known as 'The Will Rogers of Indiana'

Assembled by

J. Frank Durham

Edited by

Douglas Hay

TM

Guild Press of Indiana
Carmel, IN 46032

Dedication

To "Munny"—Aura May Sawyer— and "Pap"—Andrew Everett Durham—small-town lawyer, farmer, Hoosier politician and father extraordinaire of son J. Frank and daughters Mary Joanna, Sarah Jane, Margaret, Ann Drew and Aura May.

Introduction

The writer of these letters, Andrew Everett Durham (1882-1954), was a well-known figure in his day—an Indiana State Legislator, railroad lobbyist, small town lawyer and banker, part-time farmer and livestock-raiser, public orator, occasional newspaper correspondent—and prolific writer of letters.

Andrew's son, J. Frank, still lives in Greencastle, Indiana, the place where Andrew made his mark. For years Frank had wanted to "do something with Pap's letters" in the way of publication, but, as a practicing attorney and busy man in his own right, felt he needed some help. He tried to enlist his sister, Joanna, once an Associated Press feature writer, New York Bureau, who now resides in Milford, Pennsylvania. She was one of my columnists when I was editor of the weekly Pike County Dispatch, in Milford. However, Joanna felt she could not take time from her own obligations to assist on Frank's project, and asked me to help.

Frankly, I wondered at first whether Andrew E. Durham's letters would arouse much interest in these days of globalization, the Internet and a pop culture centered around sensational audio/video special effects, but I agreed to at least look at a few. Soon an Express Mail packet arrived with the first of hundreds of pages of yellowed onion-skin copies of typewritten correspondence, most of it dating from 1913 through 1954.

It wasn't long before I cracked my first smile over a clever turn of phrase used to describe a domestic scene. The first good laugh followed not long after that, upon reading how a former governor colluded with a livestock speculator to run up the price of breeding bulls. An account of a disastrous summer theater production was downright hilarious. Then I found myself nodding soberly in agreement over witty but forceful arguments about the need to balance the budget and restore fiscal responsibility to government—an argument that could have been made yesterday, except that the deficits quoted were only in the millions, not the billions. Finally, there was a story about an ill-fated love affair of an old bachelor brother that produced a lump in my throat.

I quickly discovered that Andrew Durham had a great wit, an irrepressible sense of humor and untiring interest in his surroundings —the people, the politics, the commerce of everyday life—all of it studied thoroughly and recounted energetically with a homespun irony akin to that of other humorists of his era, such as George Ade, Mark Twain and Will Rogers.

In his day, Andrew was much in demand as a public speaker. A brittle newspaper clipping included with the letters revealed that at a reunion of his college fraternity, in 1929, he shared the podium with legendary baseball manager Branch Rickey and prominent Chicago attorney Roy O. West.

As demonstrated by his letters, Andrew was an irrepressible story-teller who could not resist a jest even when ordering parts for a stove. When writing in pursuit of a payment on an overdue note at the bank, he would ease the bite by asking the debtor's "help" in paying for a daughter's wedding. Andrew wrote incessantly. I suppose everyone wrote more back then, when telephone connections were often poor and always expensive, but stamps cost only 2¢. Letters were also a form of entertainment in those pre-TV days.

Much of his correspondence was business-related, and Andrew was evidently a very busy man. But he could still find time to type out a five-page, single-spaced letter of advice to the son of an old friend who had landed in jail. He had never even met the young miscreant. In that and other instances, Andrew's prose took on new energy, stressing the therapeutic value of character and principles, as well as a good laugh.

Long before I stopped reading that first day, I was hooked. This stuff is priceless. Some of it might appear exotic or dated, particularly to non-agrarian folks who do not know what it is like to live off the land or reside in small towns where everybody knows everybody else— but even satisfied urbanites may be interested in reading about a different way of life. And they surely will see similarities to their own situations in the many stories about eccentric relatives, surly waitresses, guileful politicians, child-rearing and money woes. Far from being outdated, I decided, much of Andrew's material has a timeless quality—it addresses standards and values, family and community foibles, human dignity and folly—universal themes that still exist, even in our electronic age.

Editing the letters was the easy part. Frank and I never did decide how to organize them for publication. His "Pap" had corresponded with hundreds of people about a multitude of personal and professional topics; several diverse activities and interests would often be recounted in the same letter, sometimes as they occurred but often in retrospect several years later. We finally decided to present the correspondence in chronological order, so as to best reflect the flow of Pap's life, including his memories as well as his latest observations. I found it great reading, and hope you do also.

Douglas N. Hay
Mill Rift, PA
April 22, 1997

Some background on 'Pap'

"Pap"—Andrew Everett. Durham—was born May 3, 1882, the youngest son of James V. Durham and Sarah A. (Black) Durham, of Russellville, Indiana. His paternal grandfather, Jacob, had emigrated from Kentucky to become one of the early settlers of Russell Township—a farmer, store-keeper, state legislator and mover and shaker in his own right, as described in one of Pap's papers.

Pap's father was also active in local affairs, and supplemented his farm income by starting a private bank in Russellville along with Pap's older brother, Ernest. The Russellville Bank stayed in family hands for about 70 years. Pap was fond of recounting how, as a youth, he got his start in business there—as janitor, for $2 a week. He eventually worked his way up to chairman of the board. The bank survived the Depression in fine order and declined to join the FDIC, which Pap publicly denounced as a sham designed to subsidize poorly-run banks at the expense of well-run ones, with the public footing the bill.

While maintaining their Russellville interests, Pap's parents moved to nearby Greencastle in his youth. After graduating from high school, he was sent to Western Military Academy, Alton, Illinois, to "straighten out" after his strict Kentucky-bred mother discovered that he had been hanging around the local pool parlor. He graduated from the academy in 1899 with high honors, and continued his education graduating from Indiana University in 1903 and from Indiana School of Law in 1906.

On Thanksgiving Day, 1910, he married Aura May Sawyer, of Muscatine, Iowa. The wedding took place at the retirement home of the bride's parents, in Milford, Pennsylvania. The union eventually produced five daughters and one son.

Pap began his political career with election to the Indiana House of Representatives in 1913, following in the footsteps of his grandfather. His politics emphasized conservatism, low taxes and self-reliance. He was re-elected to the House in 1915, and then elected to the State Senate in 1917 and 1923. It is noteworthy that all of his victories came as a Democrat, although most of his constituents were registered Republican.

Pap was not only good at wooing Republican voters. He was also generally effective in gaining bipartisan support for his legislative undertakings. But he was not loath to take resolute action, if required. When it appeared that a Republican gerrymandering bill would succeed, Pap, as Minority Leader, had his Democratic delegation go into "hiding" across the state line, preventing action on the reapportionment bill by removing a quorum. It also froze all other legislative activities. The Republicans finally agreed to withdraw the objectionable bill, and the "runaway" Democrats returned.

His growing family necessitated a larger income and after a gubernatorial run failed to materialize, Pap retired from the Senate, in 1929. He devoted more time to his law practice and became a lobbyist for the Indiana Railroad Lobby Assn. In such capacity, he continued to monitor his former peers, and had the reputation of having attended every Legislative Session from 1913 to 1951.

Throughout his life, Russellville was a continuing source of gratification to Pap, and also provided a wealth of material for anecdotes of small-town life, which were incorporated into his public-speaking and his voluminous correspondence.

The family farm just outside the village was also a valued source of income, as well as sustenance, and Pap took a personal hand in its operation, spending more and more time there as he grew older.

Andrew E. Durham passed away at home in Greencastle, July 23, 1954.

Glossary

Pap was an inveterate inventor of nicknames, applied mostly to his family. Some of the letters in the collection contain the following references:

"Annabelle Lee" (Mrs. Ralph Weinrichter of Menlo Park, California) has a daughter, Kathryn, and a son, Ralph Weinrichter II, also of Menlo Park.

Deceased daughter Sarah Jane (Mrs. Robert Anderson) had five children: Heather(deceased) Scott, Roderick, Jennifer (now Mrs. William Amon of Fairfax, Virginia) and Cathy (Mrs. Richard Sandler, also of Fairfax.)

Joan's four include William McGaughey, Jr., and Andrew D. of Minneapolis, Minnesota, David P. of Rochester, New York and Margaret Durham McGaughey Isaacson of Brunswick, Maine.

In addition to the two sons mentioned by Frank (George and Andrew) he has two daughters Stephanie (Mrs. Stephanie D. Burton, of Winter Haven, Florida) and Madeleine (Mrs. Keith Thomas of Shelbyville, Indiana.)

Aunt Margaret – sister, Margaret D. (married name, Bridges)

Franklin Pierce, a.k.a. Frankfurter—son J. Frank

Francisco – daughter-in-law Frances (nee Haberkorn)

Ira – Ira Flauer, hired hand on the family's Russellville farm

Jane – daughter Sarah Jane (married name, Anderson, now deceased)

Joan, a.k.a. Jonie Bonie—daughter Mary Joanna (married name, McGaughey)

Margaretta—daughter Margaret (deceased)

Munny, a.k.a. Munny-Bun – wife Aura May (nee Sawyer)

The Old Brakeman—Walter J. Behmer, retired Gen. Supt., The Pennsylvania Railroad

"Red" Purnell—Fred Purnell, Congressman from Indiana

Sugar Foot, a.k.a. Footser—daughter Aura May

Uncle Ernest—brother J. Ernest Durham

About the Co-Author

J. Frank Durham, who compiled this anthology of his father's letters, was born in Greencastle, Indiana, October 3, 1915. He went to work early, as a newsboy carrying the *Indianapolis News* and local paper, and then began his education at the legendary Dan Beard's Boy Scout Camp, in Pike County, Pennsylvania. He was subsequently a member of the Phillips Exeter Academy Class of 1934, obtained an AB degree from hometown DePauw University in 1937 and LLB from Indiana University in 1941.

Frank's budding law practice was interrupted by World War Two. He enlisted in the U.S. Naval Reserve, graduating from bomb disposal school and serving on Guadalcanal, where he received a field promotion to the rank of ensign. After being released from active duty, Frank chaired a committee that secured the only captured German V-1 Rocket ever put on public display in the United States. A unique war memorial, this "Buzz Bomb" rests atop a solid limestone V-shaped base at the southwest corner of the Putnam County Courthouse, in Greencastle.

In 1944, Frank married Frances M. Haberkorn of Detroit, Michigan. They had four children, Andrew H., George B., Stephanie and Madeleine. During a 1975 tour of the Pacific, Frances suffered a fatal aneurysm. In 1979, Frank married Elaine Eide Moe, of Sacramento, California, who is not only a gourmet cook but an active jazz band pianist.

Although he never developed his father's intense interest in politics, there are similarities. Frank was elected Prosecuting Attorney of the 64th Judicial Circuit for two terms, and then Greencastle City Judge for two more terms. He still practices probate law; was a trust officer of the Russellville Bank for 25 years, and a former bank vice president.

For recreation, Frank runs a bulldozer and backhoe on the family farm near Russellville, continuing to actively participate in its management, like his "Pap" before him. The farm also has the hangar and airstrip for Frank's Cessna, which he enjoys flying when not engaged in his law practice or farming. He first soloed in 1935. In 1971, he was a guest of the Canadian Government, helping celebrate the 100th anniversary of the Northwest Territory by flying with a small group down the Mackenzie River. He has flown a small plane to Alaska and back seven times, and was a guest writer in a published book by Loren McDonald, "A Very Private Pilot." On another occasion, Frank and a friend took his young sons on a float trip down Alaska's Porcupine River, using kayaks they built themselves from kits in an Eskimo village.

At age 82, J. Frank Durham is a worthy scion of his very active lineage.

Acknowledgment

Acknowledgments and thanks are long overdue to Elaine, my lovely spouse, who is largely responsible for the success of our marriage; my sister Aura May Durham, for all the proof-reading and telephone-answering; my sister Ann (Mrs. Ralph Weinrichter of Menlo Park, CA), for her research and help; my sister Joan (Mrs. William McGaughey of Milford, PA), for her editorial assistance and continued interest in this book, Indiana University Chancellor Herman B Wells, who steered me to Nancy Niblack Baxter, president of Guild Press of Indiana, the book's publisher; my lifelong friend Maurice Smith, former newspaper, radio and TV pundit at Fairbanks, Alaska, for his practical and constructive suggestions; my Delt fraternity brother Loren Sylvester McDonald, who had a similar undertaking in his recently published book *A Very Private Pilot*; my neighbors Jack and Marian Cook, for their continued assistance, suggestions and interest; and last but most noteworthy, the distinguished writer-editor, Douglas N. Hay, of Mill Rift, PA, for appropriately handling the epistles from Pap. Without his sure and steady hand, they would probably have been permanently entombed in trunks and boxes in Pennsylvania, Indiana and California.

J. Frank Durham

Chapter I:
Early Years 1899-1911

As a boy of 17, Pap was considered somewhat wayward by his strict Kentucky-bred mother, after being caught hanging around the local pool parlor. He was also out of favor with his father for daring to criticize the latter's rather conservative attire. So to help him "straighten out" and prepare to become a useful citizen, he was sent to Western Military Academy, Upper Alton, Illinois, in 1899. He graduated from that institution with high grades, but the endeavor to reform him was nevertheless only partly successful. Enrolling at "Old Asbury" (DePauw University, Greencastle), he promptly got in trouble with the Methodist administration for organizing a dance at "The Delts," his fraternity house. About to be suspended, he beat the administration to the punch by transferring to Indiana University, where he went on to undergraduate and law degrees.

Pap subsequently met and fell in love with Aura May Sawyer (better known as "Munny" to the family). The couple eventually married and Grandfather Sawyer gave them a generous start in life by financing a house in Greencastle, but not before being satisfied with Pap's credit-worthiness.

First taste of the outside world

(Pap's earliest surviving letters were written at Western Military Academy, Upper Alton, Illinois, the first to Mitch Taylor, a Civil War veteran, the other to his mother.)

Upper Alton, Ill.
March 9, 1899

Dear Uncle Mitch,

　　I am over here in Illinois going to the Military Academy. This is the damndest place I ever got into. They are terrible strict. They make me get up at a certain time in the morning (6:30) and have the meals at a certain time. They make us go to bed at 9:00 and have the lights out at a quarter after nine. If we do anything wrong we have to carry guns and walk. For smoking the penalty is five hours hard walking. If we wear a dirty collar we have to walk an hour. They make us have our rooms unlocked so that they can come in at any time. They require us to make our own beds and if they are not just right they report us and that means two hours walking. This is a damn sight harder than ground-hog hunting. How I wish I was back. . .

　　Don't forget our spree down the creek next summer. While I was writing just now I heard the whistle of the steamboat on the Mississippi. We hear several every morning. . . From what I know now I shall be home about June 7 or 8 and we will get right to work on the boats.

Yours Truly,
Andrew E. Durham

Upper Alton, Ill.
April 6, 1899

Dear Mother,

　　After going to so much trouble to get a declamation it is not going to do me any good. Instead of having a preliminary contest in which we all could speak and then having some good elocutionist decide those who were the best speakers, the teachers here allowed each fellow to vote for anyone he pleased and the three boys getting the highest number of votes were elected to speak. . . And I cannot even get to try. . . There was nothing fair about the thing at all. . .You see, all the officers here work for each other. . .They just got up and nominated each other and that was all there was to it. It is very hard on me coming in at the middle of the year and have just barely gotten acquainted. Nearly all of the Senior Class are officers and I am a private, and being as there are so many officers it is nearly impossible for a private to get anything.

But there is one thing that I didn't get left in and that was Scholarship. They have here what they call the Upper Ten. That is the ten students who have the highest grades in the whole school. These ten get their names put in the school publication. I was fourth on the list of ten out of 84 scholars, and first in the senior class . . . My general average was 95 percent.

Are you taking care of my shotgun? Have you had it cleaned out? Where is it? . . .

Help the kids start out but don't hurry them

(Andrew and Aura May Sawyer had a prolonged engagement. The reason becomes clearer upon reading this letter, written surreptitiously by Pap's future father-in-law, F. P. Sawyer, of Muscatine, Iowa, to Pap's father, James V. Durham, in Greencastle. This is not one of Pap's own letters, but is interesting nevertheless for what it says about family values)

Muscatine, Iowa
February 17, 1909

J.V. Durham
Greencastle, Ind.

Dear Sir:

I suppose as is quite natural, you are giving some thought to the approaching happiness of Andrew, as we are to that of Aura May; so you will understand my motive in writing you direct, and without the knowledge of either Aura May or Andrew. . .

I think you probably know our suggestion as to building a moderate house to rent to them, but as we have never boiled it down to exact conditions (only the general idea), you may not understand just what we contemplate.

You are unquestionably as mindful of what your son does, as we are as to ours; but the boys are expected to "look out for themselves" more than the girls; yet had it not been for my father's help, both as to judgment and moderately financially in the way of a gift at majority and loans to help me start (which I later repaid) I would not have been able to succeed or don't think I would—as I have. And the gift of $500 after the wedding from my father-in-law was not without big appreciation on my part. A few years later, when I was building a moderate home on a lot bought with part of the $500, which my wife had not invested in special furniture, and some I had saved, he gave us $2,000 more to help build the home. I certainly appreciated it, and put the home all in her name. Later, after we moved and it was sold, I returned the money to her and she still has it.

My own experience and observation convinces me that the best time to help young people who show qualities . . . is when it will do them the most good, which I think is when they are starting out, and not after they have slaved along and shown their ability to take care of themselves (though it does often bring out their best qualities quicker, but they don't need the help so much then). I don't mean that one should go so far as to lessen their realization that they must "support themselves", but the first three or four years are hard for young people who have to make it all without some help.

But I don't believe in hurrying such a move. First, they should wait to see if their love for each other promises to be what should exist to insure the desired future, and secondly, 'til they can feel fairly assured that they can be self-supporting or are willing to live as the husband can reasonably afford.

In this generation, what were luxuries to us in younger days are to a degree necessities to those who have been brought up with them, so that the problem is not exactly as it was in the pioneer days, when good health, no debts, a job at $1.25 per day, three economically furnished rooms and enough to pay the preacher were all that were required. . .

I explained to both Aura and Andrew a couple of conditions I thought advisable before I could approve their setting the day. First, satisfaction that they had not, or were not apt to change their minds as to each other, and secondly, that he should have demonstrated his ability to earn or have in sight an income of $1,000 per year. I did not think this high, but wanted them to know they must expect to live economically, and that I expected them to depend on their own resources. The limitation I named was more theoretical than arbitrary, though they both think I still hold to that; but it depends on where they are to live whether this is above or below what they would need for the first year or so. They are becoming restless, and I don't blame them, and to carry out my plans as to a house requires some little time if they want it ready for their first home—as I would like to arrange it if advisable.

This has led me to write you, feeling that you and Mrs. Durham should be consulted, and know just what Mrs. Sawyer and I contemplated, and to have your approval; also that you think they are not taking an unwise step, from your point of view, as you know much better what Greencastle presents as a permanent home for them, and Andrew's present situation, and what he can reasonably expect in the near future.

Aura May has various pieces of furniture which have been given her from time to time, and her first piano, which she thinks will be all she needs for awhile . . . so that it is not the original outlay that need perplex them. As to the house, I will try and briefly explain.

I contemplate putting up a seven-room house, with . . . living room, . . . dining room and kitchen for first floor; three bed rooms and bathroom for second and one room finished in attic. They would not furnish the smallest bedroom, but use it for sewing room. . . I don't want to exceed $6,000, including ground, as they don't want to carry a load, and I don't feel that I can tap my estate too heavily when out of business and depending on income only. . . I propose to rent this to them at the rate of $200 for first year, payable monthly if they can do so, and 'til they can from their income increase the rent to bring me equal to 3% per year and taxes and insurance, for a period of five years. . . At the end of five years I would expect they would be able to make it more if I or my estate needed it, or that they would buy it at just what it had actually cost me.

If my estate will permit me to do so at that time, or any earlier time if they wish to buy it, I would expect to give Aura May at least $2,000 of the value. . . In case of my death I would so arrange that the whole investment would go to Aura, as part of her share in any of my estate. . .

I do not expect any guarantee beyond their own ability to do it. So I am not referring the matter to you for any part in it; but so that you may let me know if you feel the plan would be beyond expectations from what you know of matters there, or probability that his position is not calculated to develop so as to be able to keep up his end or remain in Greencastle. I do not know how much he is making now, or if you expect to aid him in any way, and feel that such matters are, and should be, just as a father may be willing, or can afford; and I always feel that parents must first consider each other and the needs for advancing age, no matter how kindly they feel toward their children. . .

But it occurred to me that it was certainly due you that if I calculated on doing anything which might look as if it would directly or indirectly put a burden on Andrew and overload him, you should have an opportunity to judge. . .

Also that you should know what was intended before you might approve such a step and possibly have in mind some plan for them of your own, with which mine might conflict.

Or that perhaps you would advise something different, in which I could cooperate with you. . .

There has been a little hope on their part that there could be a June wedding; but I know they wish to be governed by your and my approval. At least from Aura May's remarks from time to time, I feel that they are perplexed as to whether they would be considered rash or unwise to even set the time at all, particularly as it appears they have not come up to my second stipulation as to his income. I used it about 18 months ago, when he asked for my consent to their engagement, and I have not been asked to change, so I guess they placed more stress on it than I intended; but before I modify it, if that is the greatest barrier, I concluded to write you, as to your approval of my plans, and your judgment.

As a matter of fact, we all know that what it costs a young couple to live all depends on their health and their inclinations. Aura May is exceptionally practical, and with no heavier expense for rent than my plan contemplates I think if Andrew has the prospects of moderate living expenses, it is putting them to rather hard lines if they are waiting to meet my early stipulations.

But I don't want to do anything to hurry them if you feel with your knowledge of conditions there that my plan or their marriage this summer sometime (perhaps as soon as a lot can be secured and house built and ready for them) is not wise. . .

I have read the above to Mrs. Sawyer and she approves my sending it and joins me in good wishes . . .

Very Sincerely,
F. P. Sawyer

(*The reply made by Pap's father is not known, but the house was not built that summer, and the wedding did not take place for almost another two years*)

Chapter II:
The Will Rogers of Hoosier Politics
1913-1930

Pap was developing a successful law practice, but this was not enough to satisfy his extrovert nature. He decided to go into politics. And it became a long-term commitment. Between 1913 and 1951, Pap attended every session of the Indiana Legislature, either as a member or a lobbyist. He was elected to the House in 1913 and 1915, following with two six-year terms in the Senate. In 1927, he was Minority Floor Speaker for the Senate. He was never defeated in any of his races for the Legislature, which spoke well for a Democrat running in a predominantly Republican district. Pap's bipartisan equanimity as well as his developing sense of humor was reflected in a letter of recommendation on behalf of a young Republican who had the good sense to vote Democratic.

Public speaking goes with politicking, and Pap developed a flair for this too. He was much in demand as a speaker before service clubs and other organizations, and his light-hearted, homespun populist style was even compared to that of the great Will Rogers. Anecdotes of life in small-town Russellville figured large in his material. The letter titled, "Hazards of Trying a Comeback" is an example—this lengthy epistle was by way of an apology for not being able to appear in person before a group, but a version of it was undoubtedly spun from a podium or two on other occasions.

Pap's sense of humor, generously tinged with irony, found other outlets as well, including a gibe at a company that was making a big deal over a small bill. But he could also be serious, such as when he wrote advice to the jailed son of an old friend.

As the years went by, Pap found politics and public speaking more time-consuming and less-rewarding, particularly when faced with the obligations—financial and otherwise—of raising a growing family. He did not choose to seek re-election upon the expiration of his second Senatorial term, in 1929.

Proof of fitness

Greencastle, Indiana
March 29, 1915

Honorable John W. Kern
Washington, D.C.

My dear Senator Kern:

In behalf of Joseph R. Lloyd, of this city, who informs me you suggested that he get his Representative (among others) to address you concerning his desires, I am taking this opportunity to make a plea that you recommend him for admittance to the U.S. Military School at West Point.

You know, Senator Kern, I sometimes wonder if a letter of recommendation is a knock or a boost in these days of wholesale recommendations, they have become so easy to obtain. . .

However that may be, there arise occasions where it is a real pleasure to recommend deserving young men . . .

As proof conclusive he cannot go far wrong after setting himself right this early in life in the face of adverse precept and precedent, I can only say Mr. Lloyd comes from one of the largest and most influential Republican families in Putnam County, and yet, last Fall (his first vote), he voted the straight Democratic ticket from top to bottom.

I am sure you will agree with me: If all the above be true, and our young friend is unable to meet the full requirements of West Point for admission, . . . the Academy should be abolished.

Who's wasteful now?

August 13, 1917

My dear Mr. Sawyer:

. . . I am very much obliged for the invitation out, but I can't get away. We will have a special Session of the Legislature, it now seems almost certain. . . The coal situation is acute in this State, and it is for relieving that situation the reason is given for calling a special session. . . I'll venture a guess, it won't be for the purpose of coal legislation, but on the other hand we will have to fight out again Governor Goodrich's pet Excise Tax Bill, and for additional appropriations for state institutions. The former I'm opposed to; the latter I am not. Only the latter comes with ill grace. Goodrich, in his opening campaign speech, which was delivered in Greencastle, charged the Democrats with criminal wastefulness of the state's money, especially in the maintenance of the state institutions. And he made his whole campaign on that one issue—Economy. Now I learn from Dr. Edenharter, Superintendent of Central Hospital for Insane, that for the first time in his experience as Superintendent during a period of 26 years, there is a deficit—and a large one—in his maintenance fund for that institution. The real reason is obvious: things have advanced so in price. I forgot to say too, that our appropriation this time for The Central Hospital was larger than it ever was. All in all, our General Appropriation Bill was $1,250,000 larger than it was two years ago, and our Specific Appropriation was $250,000 larger. I know, because I was on the Ways and Means Committee both years. It all goes to show that what a fellow uses to get in on don't always turn out to be just as he would have you believe. . .

Senatorial aspirant

June 20, 1918

Mr. Sam D
Wingate, Ind.

Dear Sam:

Along with a vast concourse of other office seekers, I attended the Democratic State Convention at Indianapolis yesterday, and got my hide again saturated with Jeffersonian and Jacksonian doctrine. . .

Of course, I called around on the Montgomery County Delegation to allow them a chance to give the "once over" on what they were reasonably expected to cast their franchises for State Senator for this Fall. As I told you some time ago, I'm a candidate for State Senator from Montgomery and Putnam Counties, and the Lord knows I want it and need it. Want it even more than Noah T_____ wanted to be J.P. at Veedersburg.

Some time when I'm over in your bailiwick, I want to look you up and get a little advice if you won't mind giving it to me. Don't suppose you'd mind doing that.

Every once in a while I make an inquiry about "Red" Purnell and they all say he's doing fine. He sure is a mighty loyal friend. His job never swelled him even so much as a urine ant bite would. I want to go over to see him one of these times, and see just how long it would take me to find the Capitol building.

He and I took our first trip to New York City together. We got the roofs of our mouths sun burned. . .

As ever,

Embarrassing moment

April 16, 1921

Chicago Tribune
Chicago, Illinois

Gentlemen:

It happened only recently during the warm spell. I was in St. Louis, and by chance, met an old school friend who I had not seen since we were boys in Military School together. With him were the female members of his family, and a large part of their feminine acquaintances it would seem. After introductions and felicitations all around, it so happened another former cadet of the same Correctional Institution was passing in an auto when my friend hailed him and called my attention to the fact that a brother Shriner whom I ought to know was approaching. Imbued with the spirit of the Order, I stepped to the curb at the point of highest visibility to my pedestrian party, and started a most elaborate and obsequious salaam—when suddenly and without warning, the posterior warp and woof of my trousers gave way into a jagged 14-inch Maltese Cross with the suddenness of the dam at the Johnstown Flood.

If the remuneration for submitting this is in proportion to the humiliation and mental pain and anguish suffered, the Tribune Corporation will pass its next quarterly dividend.

Respectfully,

Pap's Class of 1899 in all their glory. Pap is in the back row, first left.

Andrew E. Durham as a young boy. Pool playing would soon get him into trouble and marching to a different drummer—at a military school.

Mrs. Sawyer, Pap's mother-in-law, had puzzling shipping methods, but kept the railroads busy.

Mr. Sawyer, Pap's father-in-law, was sympathetic, but did not want to spoil the children.

Aura May Sawyer, Pap's future bride, had an early career as a poster girl for Friends' Oats, later merged with Quaker Oats.

Pap's gift for theatrics as a public speaker was nurtured during his college days. Here he is center stage in a minstrel troupe.

Pap's change of address notice during his residency at Western Military Academy, 1899.

Pap and Munny's wedding party at the home of the bride's parents in Milford, Pennsylvania, on November 24, 1910.

Pap is front and center in this photograph of the Indiana University Law School Class of 1906.

The 75¢ Mystery Bill

March 3, 1922

The W. H. Anderson Co.
524 Main Street
Cincinnati, Ohio

Gentlemen:

I am just in receipt from you of a statement for 75¢ prefixed with "Balance as per Last Statement", and underneath and to one side of the figures is a sort of Odd Fellows hand with thumb extended parallel to the open fingers, and "if you please" inscribed on the palm thereof.

For the life of me I don't know what that balance is for. The only thing I can remember having bought from you was away back there about the first time Bryan ran, it seems to me. I ordered, and paid cash at the time of purchase, a set of Watson's Works Practice and Forms. Part of the set was to be delivered at once (and it was) and the balance in a short time thereafter. Well, time wore on, the horse was supplanted by the automobile, congress shoes were relegated to the attic. . . Sometime during this time, which we will call the "Elizabethan Period" of this transaction, to my utter consternation, I received another volume of this important Work. I was delighted, as the clear and fresh blue of the volume brightened up the general drab of those other volumes that had come to me long before. . .

Again, time wore on. Grover Cleveland and his Memorial Day fishing trips were discussed less and less by adverse politicians, . . . telephones came into universal use, Cole Younger was released from the Stillwater Prison; . . . George Blake, one of our local inventive geniuses, set in motion in his downtown basement his perpetual motion machine, that when once got in motion was only stilled when it disintegrated and tore out his east brick wall and scattered cogs, wheels and shafts over a radius of two blocks; . . . when, lo!—another and last volume made its appearance, making my set . . . complete. What more could I ask, except to fervently regret that they all did not get here before mine eyes were dimmed, mine step halting, and my hand palsied?

But, I see I have become reminiscent, as old men will. . .

What I wanted to ask in this letter is for information about what this bill is for? If it had been a *remittance of 75¢*, I would presume it was accumulated interest at 2¢ per decade on my original investment in the set paid years ago, and that you had relented and were quietly paying me off in a depreciated currency, with the hope I would accept it and say nothing.

But it is a *demand*, and I am therefore at complete loss to account for it. It might be for the postage on that set extending through all these years. On the other hand I do not believe it is that for two reasons: I dimly recall when I bought the set, and paid cash in advance, that covered all charges; and second, if it were for postage, the accumulated interest I would owe you by lapse of time would be in an amount far in excess of the 75¢ demanded.

Please enlighten me.

Respectfully,

To the Committee on Sky Lights?

December 6, 1922

Honorable Emmett F. Branch
Lieutenant Governor
Martinsville, Indiana

My dear Governor,

I have your "epistle to the Corinthians" of recent date concerning committee assignments for the coming session of the Legislature,

and desire to thank you for the opportunity of suggesting my prefer-
ence.

I had read in the Indianapolis paper where the Messrs. C_____,
H_____ and C_____ had met with you for the palpable
purpose of putting us down-trodden and foot-sore Democrats where
we could do a minimum of harm, and so I went over yesterday—the
State Committee was scheduled to meet—for the purpose of interviewing those delectable gentlemen to see if I were not scheduled as the
ranking Democrat of the Committee on Sky Lights and Ventilation.

The sessions I was a member of the House, I was on the Ways
and Means, Railroad and Banking Committees. . . My fitness for the
above committees is striking. The expenditure of money always ap-
pealed to me, as I have had little of my own to expend, and naturally
those of us in that class like to see the other fellow's go. As an authority on railroads, I met the 5 o'clock p.m. train at Russellville regularly
for years and years; not that I expected guests, but it was the custom of
the town, so I have an intimate knowledge of the stopping and starting of trains. I was "connected" with the Russellville Bank from the
ages of 8 to about 18 ("Connected" has a variety of meanings. "Red"
Purnell, now in Congress from the 9th District, and I roomed together
during a part of our college careers at I.U. I heard much of his "girl"
back at Veedersburg, whose father, Red freely confessed, was "connected" with the Cloverleaf Railroad. Some years later, I learned the
good man was Section Boss at that point). My "connection" with
Russellville Bank was spent principally in a janitorial capacity, and the
balancing of pass books.

And so, in the full knowledge there are 33 of you and one of me,
but that I have truth and justice on my side, and my trust is in the
Lieutenant Governor, I must stay where you place me and be content,
except that I do hope the Committee on Swamp Lands is full to over-
flowing . . .

Very respectfully,

Waxing poetic over first love

November 24, 1925

Ithaca Gun Company
Ithica, New York

Gentlemen,

I am sending you by parcel post the barrels of an Ithica hammer-less shot gun, No. 29438, I must have bought 30 years ago or more when a very small boy. . .

It was the pride of my younger life. I have slept with it in sheer delight, and for fear it would be stolen. For years not a pin point of rust marred its gloriously shining barrels; the stock shone as does the throne of Allah from being gone over hundreds of times lovingly and tenderly with silk and wool, oil and polish. Its shooting prowess—it made the fur fly out of unsuspecting rabbits before Bryan built his crown of thorns and cross of gold; it sought the tender spots in ambitious fox squirrels when automobiles were as scarce as we Democrats are now; it has shot at everything from a beer bottle to a chicken-thief, and never failed or refused to respond.

The number of this gun was burned in my memory so unforget-tably that today it came to me as doth the lamb the ewe. And while I do not know when the Magna Charta was wrung from King John, yet this numeral remains with me—yesterday, today and to the ages.

But evil days are come. The unrelenting grip of time has forced a finger-hold. Disintegration shows, for the first time, its hydra-head. When it happened, or how, I do not know, but only today, in remov-ing it from its case preparatory to a hunt on the morrow, I found the rib split at the muzzle—and so, I must forego my biennial hunt.

Look it over and fix it up. You will probably have a bill for ser-vices. Send it on and if I haven't gone into bankruptcy keeping kool with Coolidge during these most damnably hard times, I'll try to splice enough money together to meet your demands. . .

Respectfully,

Advice in a custody battle

May 19, 1926

Mr. J_____,
Hot Springs, Arkansas

Dear Sir,

I have given the matter of the custody and control of your boy some thought. . . In Indiana the general rule of law is that the father of a minor is entitled to the custody of his child or children . . . even as against the child's legal guardian—which happens to be the fact in your case. As I understand it, Mr. A_____ was appointed guardian of your boy in this court. Your letter pretty positively asserts that you never at any time, either verbally or in writing, released such right.

I find that the courts have pretty generally taken the view that the welfare of the child is the paramount matter. If it can be shown that the father is not a fit or suitable person or not able financially to support such child, then the courts will step in. As I understand the situation, neither of these affect you adversely. . . To me it seems, under the circumstances, most deplorable, or rather unfortunate that the A_____s have taken such a fancy to the boy, and are unwilling now to give him up. He is a very fine boy, I am told, and will make a fine man. But I cannot see their position, and fail to get their angle.

In the event that you determine to bring a writ of habeas corpus proceeding for your boy, you must make good preparations in advance. You must be prepared to show the court most forcibly that you are a fit person to keep him; that your wife is anxious to have him, that you are amply able to support and school him; that you are not financially cramped, and all that sort of thing. It will take witnesses, and good ones. . . As a tip I might say that Mr. H_____ of this city is somewhere in Hot Springs now, in one of the hotels or sanitariums, I presume. I would say absolutely nothing to him about the trouble over the boy, but I would make a special effort to have him out to the house and let it get to him that your people are good people and financially able, and that you have a good home, and favorable surroundings, etc. Make a friend of him, and later we might use him advantageously. The B_____s go down there in Arkansas somewhere. Keep an eye for the Greencastle people, and if convenient let them all see how you are fixed. You know what I mean.

I sympathize with you in your trouble. If such a condition came to me I would be fighting mad. But we must absolutely refrain from showing any anger. That weakens a man's case.

Respectfully,

No charge

Greencastle, Indiana
March 16, 1927

Honorable F. Harold Van Orman
Lieutenant Governor of Indiana
Evansville, Indiana

My dear Van:

I am just in receipt of a copy of your "epistle"...

I want to move that the latter part of your fifth paragraph be made more specific – that part pertaining to the extension of the hospitality of your hotel. Does that mean with or without remuneration? And whether or not it means the invitee's family? A favorable construction on your part might lead to the culmination of our going en masse next Summer on a pilgrimage...

Finally, I would advise you that we are safely ensconced at 309 E. Seminary Street, this city, and in your seeking the Primary suffrages of the Putnam County and Greencastle constituency for Gubernatorial preferences, we would urgently convey the knowledge that our palatial home is in the exact center of the City and a house to house canvass can be most advantageously made, using our manse as a radius—with our compliments (Meaning, in the vernacular, "no charge").

As ever,

The costs of public office

December 21, 1927

Mr. James D. Wilson
New Richmond, Indiana

My dear Mr. Wilson:

I am in receipt of your very considerate letter. . .

It is a satisfaction to hear now and then that one has the approval and support of the people who gave him his job—especially in a legislative way. . . It is so much harder to oppose money spending than it is to support it—so much more difficult to fight the creation of new boards, commissions and bureaus than it is to aid in bringing them into existence. And the crowd or lobby or whatever you call it who are fostering these expenditures always on hand during the Session to make it hot and unpleasant for anyone who opposes them, while the people who have to pay most of the bill are back home so busily engaged fighting clods, weather and pests, in order to get enough money ahead to pay these additional taxes, they haven't time to be loafing around a Legislative Session. . .

As to my being a candidate for re-election again, I doubt it, although I most sincerely appreciate your offer of support. That is what elected me—Republican support. But the truth is, as much as I like Legislative work, . . . if I continue in politics, I ought to try for an office that pays more money. I am in very moderate circumstances, financially; have a family of six children, five of them girls, and the oldest a girl ready for college next year, and you probably know what that means. Some think I was grandstanding and getting ready to run again, when I sent that $292 back to the State. But it wasn't at all. I sent it back simply because it was absolutely and unqualifiedly un-Constitutional, regardless of what our State Supreme Court says; and for the further reasons that I was elected knowing my salary would be $6 per day, that I had opposed salary increases during the term of office all my legislative career and could see no good excuse for exempting myself from that rule, and for the further reason that our agricultural interests were in such a deplorable condition they couldn't be asked to stand any salary increase—however much I needed, or would have liked to have it myself. And I hear that by reason of my having sent the excess salary back I have incurred the displeasure of a considerable number of my Democratic colleagues, who expect to try to see to it that I am not re-elected Dem. Floor Leader next Session. And so it goes. . .

Most Respectfully,

His opinions carry weight

(Excerpt from a letter sent by Indiana State Forester R. F. Wilcox to Charles Barnaby, of Greencastle, March 11, 1929)

The Senate passed our LaFuze Bill which appropriates $100,000 a year to this Department for our nursery program and acquiring land for state forests. This means great things for the future lumber industries of the state, and of course all of the citizens of Indiana. . .

During the discussion, when the boys were getting away off the track, pro and con, Senator Durham demanded the floor and made a statement which carried more weight than all the other arguments put together. He said that Charlie Barnaby had been in the lumber business for 40 years and probably knew more about hardwood trees than anyone else in the country. . . He said you wrote him that this positively was a good bill and they had better take your advice and pass it.

Senator Durham discriminates very closely, I have noticed, in the matter of legislation. . . and I have noticed that the other members of the Senate give his opinions serious consideration. You are to be congratulated on having such a splendid man to represent you.

As good as Will Rogers

(*Excerpt from the* Service Club Grenade, *newsletter of the Service Club of Indianapolis, Feb. 16, 1929*)

We confess our inability to make even a pretense of reporting the talk given the club last Monday by Senator Durham. It was understood that the senator hailed from Greencastle, but this was an error. His home is in Russellville, where according to his own admission, there "ain't a golf ball or a pair of pajamas in the whole damn town."

Senator Durham is one of "God's Chosen Minority," as he himself admits. Invitations to speak before this club and that led him to believe for a while that he was an orator, but he finally came to the conclusion that demands for his public appearance were made because, as a Democrat, he was quite a curiosity.

Give Senator Durham a wad of gum and a rope, and he would be as good as his fellow Democrat, Will Rogers. He entertained the club, had everybody in an uproar, for a full half hour with his tales about the characters in his home town.

Those who stayed away Monday missed one of the most enjoyable meetings we have had in a long time, even if the Lincoln Hotel lost no money on the lunch.

The hazards of trying a come-back

Greencastle, Indiana
July 2, 1930

Mr. Claud F. Fix
Shelbyville, Indiana

My dear Mr. Fix:

I received your very kind letter of May 30th, relative to a proposed oratorical "come back" on my part before a Shelbyville audience. I say "come back" because I was the alleged speaker of the evening with the Shelbyville Rotary Club in May of this year. It may happen you have heard of that disaster, and are charitably giving me an opportunity to redeem myself in the eyes of Shelbyville people. Your surname indicates such. . .

Experience has taught me a repetition is generally more dangerous even than a first offense. It is in law, and it generally is in other things. Let me illustrate from my own experience.

Years ago, my home town, Russellville, Indiana, had a home talent company. In fact, we have had many of them. The town and community was surfeited with them. The epidemic would break out, die down, and then break out afresh. Warner Kinkead was the cause of most of it. Warner was our self-imposed "leading man" on all and every occasion. For one thing, he was a bit older, but his principal claim to "stardom" was due to the fact he had spent two years away from Russellville, and was therefore more sophisticated and worldly-wise. The rest of us had ventured no farther than an annual pilgrimage to Crawfordsville for the County Fair. . .

Warner's parents had emigrated to Kansas. The second year the grasshoppers "took them," with the result they all came back to Russellville, and along with Warner came a "make-up" box which he had in some manner acquired, together with a yearning for a theatrical career. Therefore, he was an actor, none could successfully dispute. He had the evidence. Warner put on many home talents, advertised under the auspices of the Rathbon's Sisters, the Mt. Pisgah Aid Society or other neighborhood organizations.

From a comparatively modest beginning, we aspired to greater things—harder plays and more cast. Warner soon learned the more there were in the cast, the more doting fathers and mothers, aunts and uncles, would turn out in the audience to see and admire his uncanny histrionic abilities.

Eventually, we assayed a tragedy—an unavailing struggle against fate. "Sea Drift" was the name of our first—and last—tragedy. The climax was to come in the 8th or 9th Scene of the 10th or 12th Act, when in point of actual time it would be after midnight and our remaining audience (those who, of necessity, had to stay to take 95% of the cast home in time to help with breakfast or the milking) either somnolent or clear "gone."

The script went like this: The heroine is stranded on a bit of driftwood far out on the storm-tossed sea. From the lighthouse the startling cry rings out: "A fair maiden in dire peril in the sea beyond the breakers! Oh, Oh! Who will save her?"

"I will save her, or lose my life!" responds the hero (Warner), who thereupon hurls himself into the angry waves from a beetling cliff. A fearful struggle ensues between man and watery elements (ably aided and abetted by several bucketsful of real water from the wings). The maiden is rescued and brought to shore, but for some reason known only to the author the effort is too much for the hero. With a choked and exhausted murmur, "Call her Sea Drift. She is God's gift from the sea," he then and there expires from overexertion and exposure.

This called for an ocean scene—a considerable of an ocean scene—and none of us had ever seen it. But we had read geographies and seen pictures, and Uncle Bud Nichols had several stereopticon views of the ocean at its worst. The Clodfelter girls sewed long strips of sheeting together and Jess Carrington, our local barn painter, painted the result of their labors to look like what he, in his artistic mind, thought the sea ought to look like. We borrowed two hand-power blacksmith's bellows from Fred Fink's blacksmith shop to put at either wing, and under the loosely-laid sheeting. The bellows pumped air underneath, thus causing undulation after undulation, making what we though was a most realistic semblance of the ocean in active operation. My particular part, among others, in this theatrical venture, was to operate one of these bellows, and operate it like "hell," as Warner said, at the proper time.

A few of our props and effects are worthy of mention: the lighthouse was built from four round old time banana shipping crates fastened end to end, with a lantern from the livery stable hanging cheerily in the top. . . David Henry Burton, local inventor, hooked up immense quantities of old baling wire to some sort of wooden structure representing the driftwood the heroine was to cling to so perilously, in such a way that when Jude Glover, concealed beneath the ocean, turned the handle of a lop sided grindstone, the "driftwood" and beautiful maiden clinging thereon would bob up and down. A hand corn-sheller shelling corn into a tin bucket emitted most of the noises we thought an ocean would make on an occasion like that.

Shep Wilson, who could bark like a dog, and who, it was said, did go with a show one whole summer in that capacity, and who, concealed in the corn field out alongside Hebron School House, did scare the little girls almost into hysterics one afternoon, lent us generously of his caninal talents.

Eventually, we eventuated into the Big Scene—the maiden was adrift, the cry of alarm rang out.

"I will save her or lose my life," quoth Warner, in a voice that sounded like an auctioneer at a farm sale. Jerking off his coat, he plunged into the raging sea. Buffeted by the angry waves, he crawled to the fair maiden. He grasped her tenderly and started for the shore. Midst the noise of the corn-sheller, the barking of the dog, the efforts of the bucketeers and bellowsmen, and encouraging cries from on shore, his foot caught in a seam of the sheeting, ripping up about two yards of the ocean. The air we had so industriously pumped in, rushed out at the rent. The sea collapsed. The corn-sheller ceased shelling. The barking dog and frenzied shore cries were hushed. A dead silence fell until some sacrilegious individual in the audience whispered loudly, "It's a miracle boys; he's walking on the sea." . . .

Some good Samaritan finally got the curtain down.

But what I started out to illustrate was the mistake we made—I mean the big mistake. We had advertised "Sea Drift" for two nights, thereby giving our second night's audience an opportunity to get ready for us—which they did in due and ancient form, as will be quickly sensed. A shame, since as a whole, the show probably progressed more smoothly the second night—up to the Big Scene—which was never finished.

Later on, the male part of the cast met on the bench in front of Sam Brown's meat market to talk it over, and inquire of Warner how he was getting along. His talk was short and much to the point: "Boys, we're not appreciated, and they needn't never ask me to put on a play in this town again. . . I didn't mind the tomatoes, or the potatoes – much—or even the eggs—could see 'em coming and dodge 'em. But I would like to know the SOB who threw that china door knob."

I presume you see my point by this time concerning a second effort in Shelbyville—oratorically.

Seriously, I . . . shall have to refuse your very kind offer. My father-in-law has been very low for months. He lives in Pennsylvania. My wife was called to Pennsylvania by the family, who thought the end was about come. . .and I shall have to hold myself in readiness to go at any time.

Respectfully,

Swamped

Greencastle, Indiana
Oct. 2, 1929

Mr. D. Ray Higgins
937 Illinois Building
Indianapolis, Indiana

Dear Sir,

I have your very kind letter inviting me to make the talk before the Shrine Club. . . I should be delighted to make whatever talk I could, but the truth is I am sort of swamped in a small way with things of that nature. I am having some important cases tried this month, and I just *must* get ready for them. . . There must be an epidemic of Masonic meetings, or rather dinners, just at this time. I had a call yesterday from Terre Haute for a similar purpose, and last Saturday one from Logansport.

Now the truth is, and I told the other parties this same thing, I am more than rusty on Masonry. . . What talks I make are nearly always directed toward the Legislature, or some sort of politics, and are more in the nature of fun along those lines than serious stuff.

Mr. Cooper, whom you know, has very kindly put me on the program at a National Meeting of Insurance Men for the 10th, and the Lord knows I don't know anything about insurance, except to pay the premiums when I can get the money scraped together.

And so if you will kindly excuse me for the present, and then, after consulting . . . on my real inability to make an interesting Shrine talk, if you all still want me, perhaps we can get together at some other time.

Respectfully,

Advice to a young prisoner

Greencastle, Indiana
Oct. 1, 1929

Mr. Harold M_____, #6347
Washington State Reformatory
Monroe, Washington

My dear Harold,

The writer of this letter may be unknown to you, although the chances are you know, or have heard of me. Anyway, your mother and I grew up together, girl and boy. I knew your grandfather and grandmother – fine, fine, old pioneer folks. . .

I am not only the boyhood friend of your mother, but have also probably done all her legal work here. And so, in view of all of this, and for other reasons, I am quite naturally interested in you and your welfare. . . I have tried to find out the facts in your case, and probably have them fairly straight. . .

Now, Harold, of course we both realize you have done wrong – very wrong in fact—and you are paying the penalty to society for that wrong doing. But do it like a good sport—like a good loser—and not be a whiner or welcher. . . Do not imagine that I am a maudlin and mouldy old lawyer, or that I am magnifying the error you made, because such is not the case. I come in contact with this sort of condition all the time. I realize that what you did will be done again and again in the future by others. What I *insist* is that it shall never again happen to *you*. I know there are those associated with you now who are fools enough to maintain an air of bravado about them, and pretend they have been wronged by society . . . and they go about here and there telling what they are going to do when they get out, and how they're never going to get caught again. That type is hopeless and utterly worthless, but their greatest trouble is that they lack brains. They prate about this and that rich man breaking the law and getting by with it; or this and that bootlegger or what not, has a pull, or has the authorities bought and paid for, or is too smooth to get caught. All of which is 90% bosh. Confirmed crooks are never smart. They invariably . . . get caught. Why? Because there are smarter and shrewder men after them than they are, and so, the smarter man wins.

And all the time, the crook is a restless and furtive fugitive, never feeling safe and secure . . . and never knowing what the next hour will bring; never having any peace of mind; and never having any respect for himself.

I am not talking about the boy who, due to youth and inexperience, or stress of circumstances, or in a spirit of half excitement, picks a pocket, or sells some hooch, or steals a watch. . . You come of the right stock. The big thing for you, or anyone else who has made a mistake, is to get the right mental attitude toward that mistake. When a fellow finds he is wrong, reverse then and there. Don't wait and don't try to "bull it through". . . and make friends, not enemies, of the reformatory authorities. You will be surprised, yes, amazed, to learn how badly they want to be friendly with you. . . Show by your actions and attitude that you realize your mistake, study hard to fit yourself for life after you get out, don't whine or complain, don't sulk or slight your work. Brighten and cheer up. And for God's sake, prove you're a man and not a coward, because all confirmed criminals are cowards, without exception. . .

For your information, and to play square with you, I think within the year I shall write your warden or someone, asking how you are getting along and what sort of young fellow you are, because he will know, and I hope and trust my good opinion of you will be verified.

And so, why is it, Harold, that I am taking my time away from my business, and writing you this long and rather rambling letter? Surely, I can have no motive of personal profit in it. No, it is to let you know that not only me but thousands of people all over this big, free country are interested in you and anxious for you and those others of you who have made a slip, all of us hoping and trusting and many praying for your welfare. So don't think you are friendless or forgotten, or ostracized. And each day and every hour and conscious moment, never lose sight of the fact that your coming away from there with the right attitude, the correct vision, and firm determination of rectitude of future conduct, depends solely on you.

Write me sometime.

Sincerely,

A long way from home

July 17, 1930

Hon. Harry N. Quigley, General Counsel
C.C.C. & St. L. Railway Co.
230 E. 9th St.
Cincinnati, Ohio

Dear Sir:

I was in Houston, Texas, about two months ago on some business with the Humble Oil Co. An old Chicago lawyer named Hait or Haut or something like that had business with the same company. . . It was the time Houston was celebrating the fact they had come to be the second city in size in the South—a gain of over 100% in ten years. Parades. Newspaper head lines. Everybody talking "Houston, Houston." We outsiders got a bit tired and bored with all the talk. One of the vice presidents of the company took us riding and to see his country home, all the way out talking up Houston, and occasionally giving the old man a little peck about Chicago lawlessness, racketeers and gunmen.

We saw the house and flower gardens and then went to see his bird collection. Our host took us to a big cage and pointed out a long-necked bird of brilliant plumage, and said: "That is a Bird of Paradise. What do you think of him?"

The old lawyer replied: "Well, I think he's a hell of a long ways from home."

It was a knockout.

Respectfully,

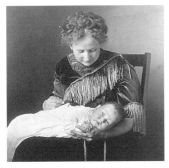

Munny and Mary Joanna.

Pap and his firstborn child, Mary Joanna (Joan.)

Pap as a young man.

Pap spent a good part of his early years digging for votes as a state legislator.

The children received an early riding lesson on ""Old Mame." (l-r, Jane, Margaret, Frank and Joan)

Pap put on a dignified pose as a member of "God's Chosen minority," the Democrats.

Pap's mother, Sally Durham, escorted by his older brother, J. Ernest Durham, ("Uncle Ernest"). She put a damper on Ernest's romance with a "female cigarette distributor."

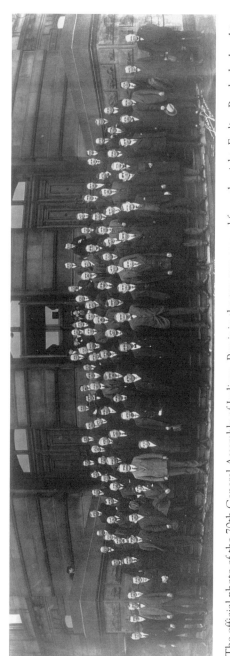

The official photo of the 70th General Assembly of Indiana. Pap is in the top row, second from the right. Earlier, Pap had taken his flock across state lines on a "strike" to prevent a quorum, thereby keeping the majority party from passing any legislation, particularly the gerrymandering bill that would have damaged the Indiana Democratic Party.

Pap wrote this letter to Munny while the Democrats were "on the lam" in Ohio to prevent passage of the Republican gerrymandering bill. He returned from his exile in "Grand" style.

An early "political family portrait" Pap and Munny and (l-r) Joan, Frank, Jane, Ann, Margaret. *The Indianapolis News* headlined: "If Pap Goes to Congress."

The Democratic 'strike' of 1925

One of the most colorful escapades in the political history of the Hoosier State took place in 1925. Pap, who represented Putnam and Montgomery Counties in the Indiana State Senate, was an enthusiastic and imaginative participant.

The spark was the proposed "Penrod Bill" (named for the Senator who introduced it) which, not unlike legislation offered from time to time even today, contained a hidden provision.

The bill (S.B. 300) proposed the transfer of a central Indiana county (Lawrence) from the Third U.S. Congressional District to the Second. The invention was to make sure there would be sufficient Republicans in that district— Senator Penrod's—to insure his election to Congress. Naturally, his good fortune would have come at the expense of the Democrats.

The Indiana State Senate in 1925 was almost totally controlled by the Republicans, but there was one small hitch. Unless a quorum was present, no votes could be taken and no legislation could be passed—not just the offending Penrod bill, but any business at all. And there were just enough Democrats to threaten such a "political blockade."

As expected, the Republicans presented the Penrod Bill of Feb. 25.

The Democrats were prepared. Hastily, all fifteen of them who were present (two others were ill and absent) "bolted their legal confines and took refuge in the neighboring state of Ohio. Most of the "bolters" made the trip in a bus rented ahead of time. They wound up in Dayton, where they took up residence in a hotel owned, curiously, by Hoosier Lieut. Gov. Van Orman, a Republican. In a "spirit of bipartisanship," the latter telegraphed the runaways to "be my guest."

Another Democrat, Senator Harrison, left the next day secluded in an Overland Moving Van. Pap's transit was courtesy of his railroad pass. The train deposited him in Cincinnati, and he went on to Dayton from there.

The Minority Leader, Senator Joseph M. Cravens of Madison, Indiana, halted the escape bus briefly on its way to Ohio to order a barrel of apples to be forwarded to the Indiana Senate, accompanied by a note—"Compliments of the Minority Members." The erudite Senator Cravens (known informally as "Uncle Joe") was the bachelor scion of perhaps the most distinguished and aristocratic families in Indiana at that time.

The Indianapolis Star and other newspapers had a field day covering the Democratic "bolt," which brought official undertakings to a complete halt. Photos of all the "strikers" were printed side by side almost as if they were fugitives in a rogues' gallery.

A poignant victim of the escapade was the official "Doorkeeper" of the Senate, one Jerome K. Brown, who was ordered by the Senate leadership to go to Ohio and serve warrants for the arrest and return of the vagrants. Poor Doorkeeper Brown protested against going it alone, but to no avail. He arrived in Dayton 11:45 PM on the 25th and served his warrants on the "bolters' in their rooms at the Gibbons Hotel. The warrants were ignored, but Brown was invited to join a poker game in progress.

The Ohio governor and attorney-general pronounced that Indiana arrest warrants were without official standing in Ohio (which coincidentally was under a Democrat administration at the time.) The governor furthermore invited the Hoosier "strikers" to stay on in Ohio "without being molested" as long as they wished.

Senator Cravens accepted the invitation "with great pleasure—until the Penrod Bill is withdrawn."

Senator Penrod countered firmly that nothing of that sort would take place.

Thereafter the shenanigans increased as the plot thickened.

The Republican Majority in the Indiana Senate set about trying to find a hale and hearty Democrat on Hoosier soil who could be legally compelled to resume his seat. Pap's eldest daughter was accosted on her way home from school in Greencastle by a friendly pair of men she had never seen before. She thought it a bit strange, but all Hoosiers were unrestrictedly friendlier those days. They got around to inquiring of Pap's whereabouts. When the fifteen-year-old reported the conversation later at home, her mother explained that Pap was "just hiding out somewhere with his Democratic friends."

Senator Cravens' adroit public comments expressed regret for the legislative drought, but noted, "The Democratic Minority in the Senate has from the beginning done its best to aid in the passage of every constructive and economic measure brought before that body. . .in the hope of benefitting the overburdened taxpayers of the state. Our only regret is that there have not been more measures of economic and constructive character to vote for. . ." He took the opportunity to expound on party grievances.

The Republicans threatened to call out the state militia and place the matter before the Marion County Grand Jury, which they said might fine the runaways $1,000 and imprison them. Such threats and the clumsy attempts to serve warrants or "kidnap" a Democrat backfired, however, and became targets of public hilarity.

The papers made light of the fact that the Marion

County Horse Thief Detective Association was sworn in "to watch for Senators who might attempt to sneak back home to Indiana without being detected."

Faced with becoming a legislative laughing stock, the Republican Majority capitulated to the Democratic Minority, making a prophet out of Pap, who had predicated in a letter home that a "truce' would be arranged in a day or two.

The Indianapolis Times carried the banner headline: D.C. STEPHENSON BEHIND MOVE WHICH BROUGHT 15 ABSENT SENATORS BACK; REPUBLICAN POLITICAL BOSS ASSURES DEMOCRATIC FUGITIVES *MEASURE* THEY ARE OPPOSED TO WILL BE DROPPED.

The runaways were also given promises of immunity from arrest and the quashing of any indictments against them. Thus, having thoroughly enjoyed their rest and recreation, they cheerfully returned to their seats on the afternoon of Feb 27.

The saga of the "Democrats who bolted' in order to make their political point perfectly clear (and effective) became an oft-told tale in Hoosier political circles.

And Pap received his just political reward.

Shortly thereafter, he was chosen as successor to "Uncle Joe" Cravens as Minority Leader in the Indiana State Senate.

Chapter III:

Family years, bull breeding and good credit—1930-1940

While continuing to attend legislative sessions, Pap did so in another capacity. He put his considerable oratorical and literary skills to work lobbying his former peers and Congressional representatives on behalf of some lucrative new clients—the railroads. The improved income situation also allowed him to devote more time to his growing family, and to write about the comedy and crises of domestic life: A relative's eccentric shipping practices, a daughter's distress at being blackballed by a sorority. As the decade progressed, the older children were flying the nest, going on to higher education and finding mates of their own.

Aside from domestic duties, his law practice and lobbyist activities, Pap became more involved running the family farm and in other agrarian pursuits, including the purchase of Hereford bulls. The livestock provided grist for his pen on more than one occasion, including a memorable account of some thoroughbred price-fixing. Pap even started thinking like a bull (or as he imagined one of his prize studs would feel after the animal was struck by a train).

He also found time to champion small and solvent independent banks like the family-owned Russellville institution against onerous government "reform" regulations during the Depression; to promote his old alma mater, Western Military Academy; and suggest a hospital tighten up its security after he fell victim to thievery.

Pap wrote some family history—a poignant account of a chair that was an heirloom, and a satirical account of his grandfather's attempt to create a new county with Russellville as its seat of government. That effort may have failed, but Russellville still wound up with good credit at the Waldorf-Astoria during daughter Joan's wedding.

Outraged over sorority power

Excerpt from a letter Pap wrote to his mother-in-law, Mrs. Sawyer, sometime in 1930.

. . . Joan has triumphed overwhelmingly and unequivocally.

A college sorority in my way of looking at it is a very small matter. In college circles, it is a thing of momentous magnitude. It is ridiculous—utterly ridiculous—that sororities should have the hold they have and should wield the power they do . . . and the heartbreaks they cause or bring about. . . This letter is to be read by you and by no one else. And then it is to be destroyed, and its contents divulged to no one. Because I am actually ashamed that my daughter could be so influenced so permanently by so small a thing as anybody's college sorority. . .

It happened at the time Joan entered college. As is customary, at high school graduating time, the sororities look over the girl graduates with a view to bidding them admission to the several sororities. Joan was invited to a great many – among them Kappa Alpha Theta. Kappa Alpha Theta was founded at DePauw probably 50 years ago. It was among the first of all sororities. I had a cousin, now long since dead, who was one of the founders. In fact, I think she was probably the most active of all of those founders. All of my people, except Sister Margaret D. Bridges and one cousin, were naturally Thetas. Mrs. Bridges did not go to DePauw, but went to a girls school, Oxford, where they did not have sororities, so that let her out. . .

Joan asked me which was the best of all. . . I told her that Theta was best, and I felt sure she would get a proposition from them, . . . that if I were she, I would belong to Theta or nothing. And of course I meant it, and for that matter mean it now. Well, that sort of talk fortified her to refuse others, and therefore I was to blame indirectly for what happened afterwards, because I am inclined to think if I had said nothing that she would have joined another. . . And I did not know what heartbreaks were in store for her. The Thetas invited her to their "rushee" party, and things looked well. Then something happened. I do not know what it was, but she was dropped and never bidden into Theta . . . and so she became a barb—that is a non-sorority girl. She was ignored so far as parties were concerned. She did not get into the social life of the college scarcely at all. The fraternity to which I had belonged invited her to two or three things, and then sort of dropped her because she had no sorority to reciprocate with. . .

In spite of this social handicap she began in a small way to make herself felt in college circles. It became noised about by the faculty what a fine scholar and girl generally she was. It came to me from a thousand sources—or almost a thousand. Some of the other and lesser sororities came to her and asked if she would consider a proposition. By that time, she had her back up, and she declined universally. But many is the night during these two years when she was studying in the dining room that she would say that this one and that sorority or fraternity were having a big dance, or something along social lines. Blue, of course she was blue. And discouraged and humiliated. But she is a thoroughbred. She never disclosed it away from home. Just went about her daily college business. Kept her scholarship and head up, however she might be hurting inside. . .

Last Tuesday the lightning hit. The Thetas called the house . . . and they asked her to come to the Theta House for supper. And after supper, they asked her to join. And she did. And that night came home with the colors on. She is a happy, happy girl. Things have changed overnight. The leading college man, or at least one of them, called the Thetas and openly congratulated them on getting her. Hundreds have congratulated her, and all this makes her very happy.

I have told you all this to sort of try to explain what she had undergone. It makes me hot under the collar to write it, and to even think about it. To think that a thing of that character could so get hold of a college and of college students to make them or break them at the whim of this or that fraternity or sorority is an outrage. But it is a fact nevertheless. And so I am glad for her eventual triumph. But at the same time, I am humiliated to think that such things exist in a free country. And the more so because membership in any organization of that character is not based on ability or scholarship but is based, on a large measure, on the whim of the individuals who happen to belong in the organization at the time the individual is proposed.

I must stop, or you will not get this all read.

PLEASE DESTROY IT AT ONCE. . .

As Ever,

Andrew

Daughters adorned like unto Cleopatra

Greencastle, Indiana
Nov. 17, 1930

Dear Sister Margaret:

Joan and Sarah Jane went to the Theta big party last Saturday night, and I'll tell you they both looked mighty pretty, at least they did to me. "Not because they are my daughters," as Charlie McWethy says, and all that sort of thing. But I'll say this, they looked mighty pretty to me. Sarah Jane had her hair waived and screwed on some ear rings that hung on small chains about six inches long, and I'll be dad burned if she didn't look like the advertisements you see for perfumes and things of that sort in the Ladies Home Journal. She was so highly colored by reason of the excitement she didn't need any artificial color. Her necklace I think was Joan's, maybe one that Grandma Sawyer gave Joan—looks something like an old fashioned hammock in shape, made of brilliants or imitation diamonds set in black, and she walked out looking like Mrs. Stuyvesant Fish's favorite daughter. And Joan looked just as well, all trigged up for the occasion. Her greeting to the boys when they came was that of a young woman perfectly confident in herself. No stammering or anything of that sort. Sarah

Jane was not so free in her conversation, but she'll get over that. She is a great deal like Ma, only she has more nerve in speaking out. . . Both of them had their hands and nails smoothed up and shined up and tapered down like unto Cleopatra herself.

That night they got home shortly after midnight. The boys just brought them to the front door and about a minute after the door closed I heard the shoes flying here and there. I heard both of them say their feet and legs ached so bad they were numb. They talked it all over and I went to sleep.

Andrew

Christmas chaos and amazing freight

Greencastle, Indiana
Dec. 26, 1930

Dear Sister Margaret:

Yesterday was Christmas Day. Of course we had far too much of everything: two big crocks of oysters, about 150 biscuits, a 24-pound turkey, and so on—you know how Aura does things—so we will have a hard time getting things eaten before they get too old and dry.

We spent the day mostly at home. The children all got a good many presents. Grandma Sawyer has been sending things for the past month or two. She has the world beat. She actually sent about a peck of apples all rolled up in a mattress, or feather tick. First we get a head and foot board of a bed; then she finds out she forgot the rails, and they come separately; then in a few days the slats come on independent; then we find they are the wrong slats, and also that one of the rails sent belongs to another bed back there. . . She sent a sort of tea wagon—that is she first sent the frame part with the glass imbedded in it—it was one she had in one of the houses and one fine morning decided that Aura should have a tea wagon. That came through in enough crating to make kindling for two or three months. In about two weeks, here came another crate with the greater part of the balance of said tea wagon. But on careful investigation and splicing, we found one wheel gone and also one handle. She had retained the one wheel to get it fixed, so in due time, it came. Later the missing handle was located and sent. And all the time, these various parts and pieces come by parcel post, freight and express, as the spirit moves her. By some strange coincidence the freight invariably comes over different railroads. We will get the main parts, say via Big 4, the slats via Monon and the rails by way of the Pennsylvania; then a "cunning" little dinky that Grandma saw in a shop in Middletown and figured would match the wheels of the tea wagon so nicely, will come by parcel post, and so it goes. The freight men at the various depots have come to look on me and my consignments of freight in amazement. . .

We had a terrible time getting to sleep last night. Since Frank has been home, things have been going along pretty smoothly. The girls were glad to see him, and he to see the girls. But it couldn't last. I saw Jane and Joan getting their heads together a good deal yesterday afternoon, and finally Schweet Babe got in it. Frank and I were playing casino. The girls were upstairs, then went out to a picture show or something. Frank was a little nervous. Finally he went upstairs and came back after a long absence and said that Joan had put soap chips all through his bed. He had cleaned it out, and had filled Joan's bed full of nut shells. Then she came home looking suspiciously, eased upstairs evidently to learn if Frank had found out what had happened to his bed. She found hers and had to take everything off and shake the covers, and then it started. No great noise, but much shutting of doors, running here and there, low whispering, giggling—and everything except going to bed. I stayed out of it, and in the wee small hours of the night, the house settled down and everybody this morning was too sleepy to get up for breakfast. So that is the way it goes.

Andrew

Name change needed

Greencastle, Indiana
July 13, 1931

Mr. J.P. Austin
1005 White Bldg.
Seattle, Washington

My dear Pony,

I needs must forego your wonderful party. . .There is nowhere on Earth I'd rather be—not even in Hoover's shoes. . . Not long since, I was in Russellville, my old home town northwest of here—the town where all the good folks come from, and a town I have consistently and persistently advertised in the local legislature for the past 15 years. We were reading where Hoover had, among other places, visited the Virgin Islands. George Potter, our local wit, was listening to the account. Finally George commented thus:

"If Hoover did to them islands what he's been doing to us people out around here, they'll have to change the name of the islands to something else" . . .

As ever,

Taking chances

Greencastle, Indiana
Dec. 14, 1931

Mr. R. W. Buckworth,
Crawfordsville, Indiana

My dear Mr. Buckworth:

Several days ago I received a very kind and thoughtful letter from you concerning a proposed forensic effort on my part to be attempted before the Crawfordsville Rotary Club. . .

I realize the Stock Market is undergoing a terrific upheaval and people are taking chances who otherwise and under other conditions, wouldn't think of such a thing, but for you to take a chance on me appearing satisfactorily before your Rotary Club is the wildest gamble I have heard of to date. Nothing more hazardous comes to me just now, except, perhaps for the public to take a chance on Democratic Party next year. Then, anything can happen.

And so, in half-keeping only with Senator Watson's classic on his "sugar" speculations—in explaining his having given his note for the stock, he dismissed the whole subject with: "The stock is no good, neither is my note. Therefore the whole transaction is now even"—I therefore here and now accept your invitation before you have to re-scind it—and may God give you all strength to hear me out.

Very Respectfully,

Plight of the railroads

March 11, 1932

Mr. Courtland C. Gillen
Member of Congress
Washington, D.C.

Honored Congressman:

I was just about to preface this, my first epistle to you, with "Honored Congress*men*," because, for what reason I know not, an all-wise, beneficent and just Providence has seen fit to inflict me with not one, but two, Congressmen—you and Red Purnell—thus causing me to bear a double cross. Please catch the awful potentiality of those last two words, "govern yourself accordingly and look to the southwest" as Thomas Taggart of hallowed memory would say. . .

I want to call your attention to the railroad situation. As you have long known, I am what might in a spirit of braggadocio be called "of counsel for the Big Four," carrying with it a pass to Indianapolis and return, and elsewhere about the lodge as the worshipful train-master may direct. You also know I was in several sessions of the Indiana Legislature—now also of hallowed memory. I have seen railroads kicked and cuffed by legislative bodies, and I have seen their securities descend from the highest point in the way of safe, sound investments to about the lowest. . . Railroads are in a hell of a fix. And it is not the fault of the railroads by a long shot. Among the principal reasons for their present condition is the unfair competition in interstate hauling being indulged in by busses and trucks. There are bills now pending in Congress designed to regulate this unfair bus and truck competition, and I think Senator Couzens of Michigan has one. . .

Railroads, being of a public character, should be regulated reasonably, but it seems to me they are just about regulated to death. That probably accounts in part for their present condition. Did you know the B&O couldn't run an excursion from Chrisman to the Russellville Horse Show without the permission of the Interstate Commerce Commission, at a round trip fare to be fixed or approved by the Commission, and not until after giving notice? . . .

Above in this letter I have used the words "unfair competition" when speaking about busses and trucks. Let me illustrate. Considerably over a year ago a contract was let in Chicago for additions to the Field Museum, I think it was. The contract called for the use of Indiana Limestone running into over 100 cars. Mr. Curry was instrumental in getting the contract for a contractor friend. No sooner had the contract been let than an independent hauler living in Chicago approached this contractor and offered to deliver the stone from the Bloomington and Bedford districts on the job as it was needed, for exactly the Interstate Commerce Commission's fixed railroad freight rates from the various sources along the Monon to the Chicago terminal—thus saving the contractor the haul bill from the terminal to the job, a sum running into a considerable figure. It was all that everybody concerned from the Monon's view point could do to keep that contractor from accepting the independent hauler's offer.

Now let's suppose that contractor had accepted the offer. What would have happened? That independent hauler would have manned his fleet of Illinois trucks with Illinois drivers; they would have had their trucks overhauled by Illinois mechanics before starting; they would have filled their enormous tanks with Illinois gas so as to have made the round-trip without having to stop for gas; the drivers would have taken their Illinois-filled dinner buckets; and down concrete State Road No. 41 they would have probably come. Turning east on No. 36 at Rockville, they would have intercepted a barred rock hen and 11 chickens in front of Ab Shalley's at Bellmore to the utter annihilation of the interceptees. In an unguarded moment some driver would have removed Zephus Burkett's mail box and distributed it and its contents consisting of a Kitselman Brothers Fence Catalog, the *Farm and Fireside*, and a pamphlet telling how to make hens lay between there and Hanna's Crossroads, where they would or would not have made the turn safely down No. 43. Frank Hathaway's thoroughbred calf would have been "out" at his place and heard of no more; Paul Tucker's bay mare been soon describing a parabola with a radius of three miles. And the left hind wheel and end gate of Professor Ogg's spring wagon would have been removed quickly and efficiently directly in front of your house at Bloomington and Walnut.

On to Stinesville, Bloomington or Bedford they would have trekked their stately way, probably taking more than a good half of the highway. Loaded up, they would have made the return over Indiana paid-for concrete highways in impressive massed procession, just fast enough to keep Indiana taxpayers from passing them. . .

What would Indiana or Indiana people have got out of this all-summer cavalcade for the use of its highways, or for the sustenance of its citizens? Unless there had been a breakdown too serious for roadside repairs, or a truck had accidentally run out of oil or gas, or some driver had seen fit to buy a Babe Ruth for his sweet tooth, Indiana and Indiana people would not have received a damn cent for the use of their $60,000 per mile concrete highways.

Now what would the Monon—the largest purely Indiana Railroad have received, or paid, or how would it have fared in the deal? It would not have received the job of hauling that stone because its rate was fixed by law and it couldn't hack prices; it would have continued paying its men, upkeep, expenses and taxes just the same. . . It owns and maintains its own right of way; also all rolling stock and equipment of all kinds and character, and pays taxes on same – regularly. It stands there ready and anxious to receive all business it can get, not only for today but for tomorrow, next month and next year. It can't crank up, call the dog and leave jurisdiction and unpaid debts at 3:01 a.m. on any given day. It does not ask a monopoly. It only asks fair treatment, and that bus and truck competitors be put on a competitive basis by being required to pay a fair return for the use of the public highways, or else buy, build, and maintain those of their own; that they shall maintain regular scheduled routes, rates, and service in winter and summer, sunshine and rain, fog and clear weather; and otherwise submit and qualify for regular continuing business, just as railroads are now required to submit and qualify.

Now, in return for this splendid thesis, I want to ask my Congressman some favors. Will you please look into bills now pending before you on this subject, and tell me wherein you favor or disfavor them – and why? Perhaps I am wrong in the attitude I take. If I am, I want to get right, and I know of no one better able, or more willing, to inform me than my own Congressman.

Respectfully,

Wet, dry or moist?

Greencastle, Indiana
April 11 1932

Mr. James G. Smith
Alamo, Indiana

My dear Mr. Smith:

I have your inquiry about Court Gillen, and I shall answer to the best of my ability. . . . He is a man of ability, a lawyer, a decent man and surely is entitled to another chance in Congress. . . I do not know that he is particularly dry. I do not know that he is particularly wet. . . He may be a trifle moist, and he may not be. He has never been known as a radical on anything, within my knowledge. I have heard some criticism against him on his so-called dry vote, but I have also heard that anyone with any sense, under the same circumstance, would have voted exactly as he did.

For that matter, he will not be beaten by the "lady candidate". If my information is correct, she got into this race simply and solely on account of the one vote Gillen made on the Prohibition question. . . Now, if that is the case, she might be characterized as a radical "wet", obsessed on that one question, and forgetful and more or less incompetent on everything else. And I am saying to you right here and now that there are other important questions pending except "wet" and "dry." . . .

You know, it is a very easy thing to sit or stand around and "cuss" those in a legislative body for what they did or did not do. . . If everybody had all the information, and had given a question the same study and attention as the one who did the voting, there would be less criticism than there is. . .

Let me illustrate how these things go. I was nominated as Representative from Putnam County in 1912. I was young and inexperienced. A day or two after my nomination, Colonel Matson, who had been in Congress for years, and was a lawyer here at the time and almost retired, gave me some advice: "Find out where the coat racks are, where your seat is, and when the Legislature assembles take your seat and keep still. There will be times when you will think that you have the exact solution for whatever is being debated. When you feel this coming on you, get up and get your hat and walk around the State House, then come back and sit down and keep still. If you will do that, they will not find out how ignorant you are. . . I don't want to hear of you taking any part in the debates your whole first term, I don't want you to introduce any bills. I just want you to be on the job every day and every hour, and attend your Committees, and above all else, keep still."

I followed that advice, I think absolutely, or nearly so.

But there was another side to the matter. . . After the Session was over, I met a farmer friend who had worked hard for me, and I asked him if he were pleased with the way I had conducted myself. He was not. He said: "I thought if we sent a mouthy young lawyer to the Legislature, he would get some laws through, and we would hear from him, and he'd be up there doing something. I never saw where you even made a speech."

Time went on. I served in 1915. Then I went to the Senate in 1917 from Montgomery and Putnam, and again in 1923. Some time shortly after either the 1925 or 1927 Session, I met this man on the streets here in Greencastle. He came up to me beaming, and said: "I'll take it all back. You are the best Senator we ever had. . . I can't pick up the papers without seeing your name strung all over it. . ."

People jump at conclusions, and sometimes they jump wrong unless they know all the circumstances. . .

Cordially,

A damaged bull story

The following exchange of correspondence occurred after a prize bull on the Durham farm near Russellville was struck by a railroad train.

May 31, 1933

Mr. Andrew E. Durham,
Greencastle, Indiana

Dear Mr. Durham,

Our mutual friend, Mr. Byers, has sent me your most touching letter of May 27th, relating to the unfortunate usurpation of the B&O right of way by your pet bull. Fortunately, however, the incident does not – at least so I assume—extinguish your "line". Naturally, the distinguished bull was a thoroughbred, and in this respect he has nothing on our train, as it is also a thoroughbred, and when thoroughbred meets thoroughbred something *must* happen. . .

It may be necessary to have our representative call upon you and the bull to ascertain your respective incapacities as a result of the collision. I regret, however, that under the laws of the great State of Indiana, your own mental pain and anguish is not an element of damage and, so far as I know, there is no way of proving that of the bull other than by hearsay, which of course is incompetent.

Very truly,
Frank J. Goebel
Assistant General Solicitor

The reply of "the bull."

June 3, 1933

Honorable Frank J. Goebel,
Asst. Gen. Solicitor
Baltimore & Ohio Railroad Company
Cincinnati, Ohio

Dear Sir:

I am told I am a Hereford bull. . .I was supreme on the Durham farm, and lord of all I surveyed—that is, until recently. . .

For years I had noticed some sort of animal or monster wend its way shrieking and rumbling across our land, always going along the same trail without variation. In daytime its head emitted black smoke and a terrific noise with its rattling body trailing back, slender and long like a snake. At night it had an enormously bright eye in the center of its mammoth head, and belched forth fire sometimes. . . We got used to it, and finding it to be totally unsociable, we adopted the wise policy of ignoring it—that is, until recently. . .

I was grazing along what my owner says Ring Lardner would laughingly call a fence, and just stepped through, or on, or over, it to where the grass looked greener. And then I went on and up to where there was less grass and more gravel, and some ties and rails. . . Then something happened, and I went winding down and down. Oh, the pain!

My owner . . . has said more nice things about me and my good qualities and worth since I got hurt than he ever said in all the years gone before. . . He said to some men who came out to see me after I was damn near killed: "Did you ever in your life see so good an individual bull, any where, any time? Look at that head. Imagine what it looked like before he got hit. . . I wouldn't have taken a thousand dollars for him before he was hurt. No. I wouldn't have taken two thousand dollars, nor there isn't a man among you who would have taken five thousand for him if he had been yours". . . Then my owner said: "It's confidential, of course, and I know you men well enough to know you'll keep it to yourselves. Ex-Governor Warren McCray had a man down here secretly to buy him at $10,000—to head his herd."

"Now," my owner says, "what would you appraise him at? I want to be fair with the railroad. . . You and I are farmers, and everybody knows a farmer has a hard time, and all farmers should stand together, but at the same time be fair, of course, to the railroads. Naturally we all know that railroads are not fair, and are big rich corporations, paying great high salaries to presidents and lawyers, especially lawyers, for sitting around in swivel chairs, milking the public, fixing mythical valuations to base freight rates on, and then eternally asking for rate increases when they are so high now nobody can ship anything over them. . . ..

Still, I want you men to be absolutely fair with the railroad . . . ..

I don't know what happened after that because they moved off toward the house. . . They say the chances are that I will live, but I wish I were dead. . . Pain, pain, ever since. My head is swollen to double, my sight in one eye may be gone. I still bleed at the nose. . .My mental anguish is unbearable. I know that which I had in abundance and have ample living proof of is gone from me, never to return. I have lost my social standing in the community in which I reside and my wimmen folks are laughing at me – and at this time of the year. . . Oh, grave, where is thy sting. . .

If you care to apologize for your hasty remarks about bull mental pain and anguish, you may address me as:

Respectfully,
The Bull

Stamp out small banks?

June 3, 1933

Honorable Virginia Jenckes
Member of Congress
Washington, D.C.

My dear Madam:

I should appreciate your sending me a copy of H.B. #5661, (the Steagell Bill) as re-written by the Senate. I am informed the Senate struck everything out of this bill after the enacting clause, and substituted a bill of their own—probably the Glass Bill, with some amendments.

If the bill as passed by the Senate reads as I am informed it does, I am very much opposed. . . It would drive all small country banks out of business at least for the one reason that it requires a capital of not less than $50,000. Small country banks cannot stand a capitalization of $50,000 and pay dividends on any such amount. Small banks have small ways, limited deposits, limited territory—and consequently limited earning powers. . .

I desire to say I have been connected in one way or another with a small country bank, the Russellville Bank, of Russellville, Putnam County, Indiana, since childhood. I was sort of raised in that bank. I own the majority stock in it. I worked in it for years. It represents the life work of an older brother, now dead. It has a capital of $15,000 and a surplus of $47,500. . .

In times like these, all proposed bank legislation should be carefully considered—to say the least. There are not so many of us left, and those that remain deserve some consideration for having weathered what we have.

I am cognizant of the fact that something serious ails, or has ailed, the banking business. . . I am also aware that banking, with its attending care, custody and handling of other people's money, takes on a public nature that some other businesses do not have. . . And please do not form the opinion that I, in the slightest degree, desire to block sound, reasonable, safe and sane banking legislation. Absolutely the contrary. But . . . I insist that a small community is entitled to a small bank for its small business in the same arithmetical ratio that a large or populous community is entitled to a large bank. . . Viewed from the angle the Senate seems to have, I should think it would be better to fix a minimum of capital and surplus combined (for as far as security to depositors is concerned, there is no difference between capital and surplus) for a maximum of deposits.

Suffice to say, I am utterly and unqualifiedly opposed to an arbitrary fixed minimum capitalization of $50,000 for small banks. . . To me it means mighty, mighty few banks in towns of less than 2,000 people.

If that is the intention, then the bill is perfect—in that respect.

Very Respectfully

A fan of the old school

July 8, 1933

Mr. Lee Tracy
Metro-Goldwyn-Mayer Studios
Hollywood, California

My dear fellow Cadet:

This is not a "fan" letter. . . I probably recognize ten or fifteen actors and actresses at sight. Yesterday I saw a movie magazine. You were telling about yourself. I saw the name "Western Military Academy" in print and that galvanized me. I read the article from start to finish. I was tremendously pleased at the kindly treatment you gave "Western." Hence, this letter—the first I ever wrote an actor or actress. My God! Mother taught me a theater was the Devil's work-shop.

I graduated Western in 1899. . . I had arrived at the age where I was reluctantly permitting the "old folks" to reside in our home. The local high school eventually granted me a diploma in order to make room for students. "Western" was father's answer. . .

Everybody has a hobby. Some good, some not. After about 30 years of worldly experience, "Western" and its welfare is probably mine. There was where I first learned a small town banker's son might later on in life meet some noticeable competition. . .

"Western" needs favorable advertising and plenty of it. I cheerfully do what I can, but of course my field is tremendously limited. Just what you said in your magazine article about yourself is what "Western" needs. Only more of it. Last evening and today I learn you are one of the best known men of your profession. You evidently have thousands of admirers. Some time, some where, some how, some of them will have a boy here and there of the proper school age. And the fact those parents hold you as they do, if they can only know you went to Western, will be the deciding factor where those boys will go to school. Get me?

I am not a sentimentalist. I don't ask any one, and especially a stranger, to spend either time or money on me and my hobby for me alone. Honestly I don't. I'm pretty tight myself. Maybe I have to be, and I'm that way by nature anyway. But without any expense of course to you, if you would drop the hint to the Metro folks that you have an idea a newsreel of an up-to-the-minute Military school, at say, Commencement time, would have an appeal to the public, and especially to the younger feminine public, and that "Western" is the school to "shoot", or whatever it is you call it, and Metro would agree, then we might get somewhere with publicity for Western. . .

I do not ask or expect a reply. I think I know what you are up against in the way of correspondence. I was in the Legislature for 16 years. We have Legislative "cranks" here, just like you have movie "fans" there—only not so much so. Now I'm a railroad lobbyist whenever the Session meets. Furthermore I'm a Democrat. As a waggish local constituent puts it, I've "gone from bad to Hell."

Be that as it may, if sometime I should learn a newsreel was showing W.M.A. in all its glory of flags, pennants, brass buttons, and an inset of Lee Tracy as its most distinguished alumnus, I can assure you I'll dismiss the help, unbait the trap, lock the door, call a frightened and bewildered family, and hie us away to Indianapolis, or wherever it may be showing, there to carefully explain to disgusted adjacent seat holders, that I—I the erstwhile conservative country lawyer—am also an alumnus of that greatest of the great boys schools, and thus get a bit of reflected glory. . .

Respectfully,

P.S. To whoever reads this. Please give me a break and show this letter to Mr. Tracy. I've never bothered him or you before, and I promise I'll never bother again.

Considerable difference

January 22, 1934

In re: Estate of Charles A. D_____
Hon. Isaac Kane Parks
Inheritance Tax Administrator
231 State House
Indianapolis, Indiana

Dear Sir:

I have your letter of direction concerning the above inheritance tax matter. . .

I am a trifle confused . . . on whether you want an exact copy of the federal estate tax return as we filed it, or whether you desire a copy of the return as was finally accepted by the government. . .

"There was considerable difference."

The above quotation happened years ago at Russsellville (my

home town) when Bill Goodwin was section boss on the I.D.&W., and Milt Kinder, a pretty good old man—but terrifically profane—worked on the section under Bill. The crew was laying rails down west of town near Brumfield's trestle. Milt was driving spikes and missed one and hit his foot – and the air was blue, and it looked like Indian Summer down that way. They rushed Milt to a doctor and patched him up.

In due course, a long four-page questionnaire came to Bill from the main office in Cincinnati: "Full name of injured employee? Age? Years of service? How did the accident happen? When? Where? Who saw the accident?" etc. etc. And on the last page, about two thirds of the way down, was this one word. "Remarks?", the rest of the page left blank.

Bill, the section boss, sat up about all night making it out – painfully and laboriously. At last he came to the "Remarks". He was puzzled and confused (something like I am about the return you ask for)

Finally, under that heading he wrote the following: "Now about them 'remarks'. Do you mean Milt's, or do you mean mine? There was considerable difference."

Respectfully,

Columbia no place to go to school

June 8, 1934

Hon. Frank L. Littleton, Atty.
Big Four Building
Indianapolis, Indiana

Dear Sir,

I have just returned from New York and Joan's graduation in Columbia... My Gosh, but that is a big school! On Tuesday they gave out between 4,000 and 5,000 diplomas. Had the exercises outdoors in front of the library. Must have been 15,000 or 20,000 or more people there. The crowd looked a bit like the Speedway races... Between my seat on some bleachers and where the diplomas were given out were numerous flights of steps, a sort of sunken garden, some four or five tennis courts, a wide blocked-off street, and a football field the short way. And between were the graduates and visitors, in camp chairs and on bleachers as thick as they could be packed. They had loud speakers, but not enough of them for me to hear from the seat I occupied. It took over an hour for the graduates and faculty to march in from four entrances. There surely must be over a thousand in the faculty. Anyway, I made up my mind then and there that Columbia was no place for an undergraduate to go to school. It is too big. The students have practically no campus life. A great part of them are from the City of New York and surrounding cities, and they room all the way from the Battery to the Bronx. Endless numbers of them never see or know one another. . .

As Ever,

Richard Fairfax—A bull story without peer

July 20, 1936

Mr. B.C. Byers
Macatawa, Mich.

My dear Mr. Byers:
I haven't been in Indianapolis since I started the two little girls up into Maine to a girls camp, so unless I succeed in cooking up something, this letter will be a fizzle for news.

In May I bought a 16-months old Hereford bull, Hugh Fairfax by name, at the McCray Sale at Kentland. Since that time I bought a McCray-bred Fairfax Hereford bull from a Mr. Dillman at Waveland, and also traded an old Woodford Hereford bull to the Indiana State Farm for another McCray-bred Fairfax Hereford. So you see I am slightly in the bull business.

For your information, you knowing nothing about anything except railroading and good looking women, Mr. Warren T. McCray got his big start in Herefords after he acquired Perfection Fairfax, a Hereford bull that afterwards won the International Championship, and was acknowledged generally to be the greatest sire of his day. He started the "Fairfax" fashion.

In getting the pedigrees of these last two bulls straightened out, I made four trips to Kentland. The trip prior to the last one found the ex-Governor in a petulant frame of mind. He called me "Senator" very formally, was easily irritated and gave this and that as an excuse for the delay. The truth is, I think, that his herd books have been kept in about the same condition as Joe C_____ kept his desk in the Senate Chamber.

But my last trip was different. When I got there the old boy was in his office selling a Hereford to some young fellow from the north part of the state—I hope Lake County, because anybody from Lake County needs a trimming. I stayed outside and eventually they came out.

"Why, hello, Mr. Andy," said Warren T. "How are you this fine day?"

It was hotter than Tom B_____ ever got in a poker game.

I knew the old fellow had had a good breakfast, and that he had no doubt spliced me up a pair of pedigrees of some sort or other. I just sort of imagine that when a herd book gets slightly mixed up, or time has elapsed and a given bull's heredity sort of lost in the hazy past, that those fellows quietly sit down and whittle out a pedigree that sounds about right. . .

Let me tell you a bull story about as he related it to me last Friday. This is Warren T. speaking:

"About 1902 or 1903, I wanted to branch out bigger, buy more land and become a Hereford leader for sure. . . Mr. _____ was showing Herefords in Indianapolis. He had by far the best bull I had seen or heard of. His name was Perfection Fairfax, and he had a pedigree that read like the Lees of Virginia. . . The only way his owner would part with him would be to sell his whole herd of 37 cows too—

for $17,000 cash. I brought him home to Kentland. He won the International Championship and we both became famous in the Hereford world. The Fairfax strain took the country by storm. His sons and daughters were sensations. He lived until he was past 17 years old, and was a virile breeder to the day of his death."

"Look up yonder on the knoll past the machine shop and the big barn. See that cement column up there? The boys here at the farm erected that monument, and old Perfection Fairfax lies right under it. He died in 1918. Old Perfection made breeders millions of dollars. Look up there on the wall to my right. See that oil painting? That is Perfection Fairfax. I had a famous artist paint that. See that long picture over there on the wall east of old Perfection? That is a picture of 32 of his sons I sold at one time to one breeder down in the Argentine. We had that picture taken the day they left the farm. They made me some money."

"What is the highest price, Governor, that you ever got for a bull?" I asked.

"The highest price I ever got was $25,000."

"Holy Nellie, " said I. "Isn't that the highest price anybody ever got?"

"No," he said. "Do you want me to tell you about that? . . .It's a pretty long story but interesting. Along about 1915 Perfection Fairfax was getting old, and I decided I'd go out again and buy the best young Hereford bull on Earth. As I traveled and asked, I kept hearing about a Richard Fairfax, one of old Perfection's calves—a calf I had raised, and still owned his mother. He had been sold at one of my sales and wound up in Dakota—and it was always the same tale that he was not for sale at any price, whatsoever. Absolutely."

"I made up my mind I'd just take his owner off his feet the first shot. I'd paralyze him with an offer he'd not refuse. I didn't want to take a long wild goose chase for nothing away up there in Dakota. If he wasn't for sale at any price I'd soon know it. So I wrote a short letter to his owner. I wrote, 'I know there is no use sending bird shot after big game. If I come up and look at Richard Fairfax and like him, and find him to be everything I've heard about him, will you take $25,000 cash for him?' I figured that would bring him to his milk."

"Very much to my surprise a prompt letter informed me that my offer did not interest his owner in the least. Richard Fairfax was not for sale at any price."

"So I looked elsewhere and forgot Richard. That was along, say in November. The following February, Johnny _____, from Minnesota, came down to see me. He was a young breeder who had great faith in me and my judgment of Herefords, and had bought quite a bit of my stuff. Johnny was to stay all night and go home next morning on the 7 o'clock train. I noticed Johnny was listless as he looked over my herd, and I knew something was wrong—he wasn't there to buy."

"After supper we went into the library and talked Herefords and everything else from the weather to politics. Finally I looked at my watch and said: 'Johnny, I'm getting sleepy. You leave in the morning at 7, and it's 1 o'clock now. Let's go to bed.' "

"Warren," he said. "I've got something pretty big on my mind. I want your advice. It's Richard Fairfax. I know all about your offer. I know the whole story. But I'm about to pay $50,000 cash for him, and what I want to know is if you think I am crazy trying to buy him at $50,000?"

"Well, Johnny! You're the greatest Hereford booster I ever heard of. You sure are! I don't want to discourage you, and God knows I don't want to throw cold water on the Hereford business, but now that you've asked me, all I can say is that I quit at $25,000. That's a terrible risk. Why, the bull might lie down and die tomorrow. $50,000 is a pile of money in Government Bonds, but it's an ocean full of money tied up in a Hereford bull."

"Well, don't throw up your hands until I get through, Warren. I've been thinking about this thing for a long time and been getting ready for it. I can get him insured for a maximum of $25,000—everybody says Richard is the best young bull in the country, and remember he's out of your grand old Perfection. I've been quietly buying up all his sons and daughters I can lay my hands on. I own 65 daughters and 20-odd sons, so I'd be pretty well fixed for a June sale of sons and daughters of a $50,000 bull. I figure that the advertising a $50,000 buy would give is a big thing. The more I think,the bigger it gets: the highest price the world has ever known for a bull. No other price has even approached that figure. Every big newspaper from New York on west will carry it on the front page, and a picture of Richard and me along with the story. I'll get more free advertising out of that than I would with 50 years of paid advertisements in all the Live Stock Journals published. And I'll see to it that 'Bred by Warren T. McCray, Kentland, Indiana' goes under Richard's picture. You are going to have a sale in May. You bred Richard Fairfax. About everything you own is close kin to him. How would a $50,000 bull that you calved help your May sale?"

"Well, Johnny, I see the enormous possibilities. Still, $50,000 is *some* bull money."

"I'm not through yet, my good friend in need," Johnny said. "And here is where I have to have your cooperation if the deal goes. I only have $20,000 cash to put in Richard now. I figure that in an ordinarily good sale of Richard's sons and daughters, they would probably average $500 apiece. If I pay $50,000 for their sire and get the advertising I think I'll get, the 80-odd head really ought to double that amount— I'm trying to be conservative—But I can't go to my bankers and say, 'Gentlemen, I'm paying $50,000 cash for a bull, I have $20,000 and want to borrow the balance from you.' They would say I was plumb crazy, try to get a guardian for me and collect all I owe them, right now. You know bankers. There is no place in the wide world I can borrow that sort of money, except from you. You know that."

"Johnny, let's go to bed. I'll let you have an answer before the train goes."

Mr. McCray said he thought until 6 o'clock, then got up and got a hurried breakfast into Johnny and took him to the station. When the train got within about two miles of town, he said, "Johnny, go to Dakota and look Richard over. Examine him as you never examined a bull before. Find all about him—whether he has been exposed to any diseases; have three vets go over him piece by piece—Then go off and think for 24 hours. If you decide to buy, send me a telegram saying, 'The Republicans will win easily next election.' Buy him, get the $25,000 insurance, render up a short prayer and draw on me for $30,000—and the draft will be honored."

Within a week or 10 days, McCray told me, he got the prearranged telegram, then advertised his May sale as he never had before. He played up the $50,000 Richard Fairfax sale to the limit. The free advertising the sale got was far beyond his wildest thoughts. Virtually all the big papers carried it both here and abroad. Miss Busch, his secretary when he was Governor, and who was in Paris at the time, sent him a front page of one of the large Paris papers carrying the picture of Richard and Johnny.

McCray sold 120 head in his May sale. They averaged $3,636—the world's record for sales. He sold a full brother of Richard for $23,000 and a half-brother for $7,500. He figured the brother and half-brother didn't stand him out over $500, so if Johnny never was able to pay a cent of the $30,000 loan, he was still even, to say nothing of the additional prices the remaining 118 head brought.

Let the old ex-Governor close:

"In June, I went to Johnny's sale. Instead of $1,000, they averaged $1,750. Next day I came back with a $30,000 draft, plus interest."

How is that for a bull story?

> Good luck to you,
> "Bull" Durham

The plain wooden chair

"Old Settlers Day" address delivered at an annual celebration, undated.

Mr. Chairman, Revered Old Settlers and Visitors:

. . . Primitive man lived in trees, where he rushed to safety at the approach of danger. Directly, he learned to use a club and climbed down from the trees and fought his way to caves for shelter. From these caves he would sally forth . . . Eventually, men began to congregate and to band together, first as a family, then a tribe or clan and later as a nation, and in so doing they put in practice that great fundamental truth on which is based all progress: "In Union there is strength," exemplified in modern times by the bundle of sticks, so well known to some of us. . .

Our early Pioneers in Putnam County followed the rules of conduct prescribed by their predecessors in frontier life in Kentucky, Virginia and Ohio, and followed the lines of least travel resistance, generally along watercourses—by way of Eel River, up Big Walnut and Deer Creeks—and thus throughout the County. Once located, and having few and distant neighbors, and with communication more or less difficult, a barn-raising, log-rolling, quilting bee or spelling match was an event of some moment and not of such common experience as to be ignored.

As time wore on, roads were established; settlements became thicker; mercantile trade followed barter, and money began to circulate and to be offered and accepted in payment; wagons and buggies replaced saddles and saddle bags; railroads were built; newspapers and postal service became more numerous and easier; the telegraph and later the telephone annihilated distance; churches and school houses sprung up; the regular preacher took the place of the circuit rider; factory-made shoes drove out the "pair of fine boots"; power looms and hole-proof socks (in name only) routed knitting needles; and so on, until now Sears-Roebuck is trying to rout everybody and everything.

All these and many, many, more advances have been inaugurated within the memories of many of you here today. Those among the oldest of you have had the extreme good fortune of living within the period of the last 75 years or more, when greater progress along scientific lines has been made than was achieved in the 4,000 years preceding your time. Think of it my friends! . . . What great good fortune has been yours!

What progress the future has in store I cannot know. Time only can tell, and time goes on, while you and I dwell here for comparatively only a day. And yet, if I were required to hazard my judgment, I should be compelled to admit I firmly believe you have seen more beneficial progress than will fall to the lot of any individual to be born in the future. . .

To you Old Settlers this day has been set apart by the folks of this community for your enjoyment and retrospection, and for our education and benefit. . . And when those of us here on the programme have finished, we want to hear you, by word of mouth, recall those early experiences that will forever be lost unless you impart them, that we, in turn, may hand them down to the generations yet to come. They will soon be most valued traditions. Books, paper, diaries and records have a most useful place, but some of the things of greatest human interest are not set down in the books or records—those little touches of color and everyday heart interest, those daily privations and abstinences—they never break into chronicle, and yet furnish a large part of our romantic history.

I have at home a chair—a plain, hand-made wooden chair with a wooden seat, with rectangular and cross red stripes, and on one panel in the back is a hand-painted bouquet of flowers in colors—all showing the hand of a careful, neat and skilled workman. Underneath the seat is a faded and torn paper label on which is printed "Black and Sons, Chair Makers, Philadelphia, Pennsylvania."

Just a plain straightback wooden chair. A more elaborate one could probably be bought now for $2. And yet, my grandfather brought that chair to my grandmother for her parlor on horseback from Philadelphia to Russellville, in this County, some 80-odd years ago, piled high on top of a big horseback load of goods. Think of the effort it took! Think of the space it took away from profitable calico! Think of the many, many times on that thousand-mile horseback ride that grandfather looked back and felt to see if it were coming along with the balance of the load. Think of the many times it slipped to one side or the other and had to be retied. Think of the many nights it had to be unloaded, and the many mornings it had to be tied back on again. And lastly, my good folks, think of the joy it gave that little old woman up at Russellville—how she showed it to the neighbors; the care that was subsequently given it; the wonderful pleasure it gave her; and the proud feeling it secretly gave him. . . It was she who told their children the story of that little chair.

That, my friends, is the kind of heart throb we are gradually learning to ignore in these days of financial struggles. There are those among you, who by denying yourselves, have given your wives, sons and daughters saddle horses, pianos, automobiles and even farms—and at great sacrifice—and there are also those among you who have given your families their first iron stove, a candle mold, calico dresses, and perhaps a little straightback wooden chair.

Therefore, today let us go back. Let us forget the things to which we have applied ourselves too assiduously, the things that modern conditions have forced us to adopt and strive for. For the day, at least, let us turn back to the days when you were young and this community was young: To the days when you courted and were courted in the chinked log house before the stone fireplace; back to the time when catnip, tansy and peppers hung from the rafters; back to the days of the smoke-house with its pungent tang of hickory bark and corn cobs; when tomatoes were grown for ornament and thought to be poisonous. Let us again go down to the spring house and get a bucket of water to set under the gourd on the kitchen table. Let's stir up the fire in the fireplace, hang the pot on the crane or test the heat in the Dutch oven; carry the ashes out and put them in the hopper. Let's you and I and all of us go up and see how the dried apples are holding out, and then look the hams over to see if they have any worms in them. Let us hie back to the days when all debts fell due at Christmas time; when mortgages were useless and practically unknown, and when every man's word was his bond. Let's eat a dinner of bacon, corn bread, milk and honey, and other wholesome things of those days, on the back porch or in the summer kitchen, while the younger girls shoo the flies off the table and the chickens off the porch. And then tonight, after supper, let's gather around the candle on the table, with Mother in the little chair knitting and mending with her hands, and rocking the cradle with her foot, while Father takes down the family Bible and piously reads a verse. Then, on our knees, and with heads bowed, let us hear that hallowed voice of Father, from whose nerveless grasp have long since dropped the working tools of life, rise in fervent prayer to Almighty God to protect us and keep us all safe from harm.

Grandpap's Bourbon County Bill

By Everett A. Mahrug

Pap took a pen name—his own rearranged in a "sort-of backwards" fashion—to tell a story based on an ill-fated attempt by his grandfather, Jacob Durham, to form a new county, with Russellville as the county seat. According to family lore, Jacob intended to place the court house on a parcel of land he owned in the center of town, surrounded by other property he owned, including a store. Years later, Frank Durham gained sole title to the "courthouse" property and deeded it to the town.

Grandpap, Jacob Mahrug, had come from Kentucky in an "early day", and located his new domicile equidistant from four surrounding county-seat towns. He laid out a new town and named it "Mahrug."

In the center of his town plat he carelessly left a large "Square."

As a boy back in Kentucky, Grandpap learned the blacksmith's trade, and followed that vocation for a while. . . At his new place of residence he started a general store, the first store in Mahrug. Both he and it prospered. He sold lots in this coming town. The town grew. He bought and cleared, and sold and rebought farm lands roundabout. He became a "Squire," and administered justice without fear, but probably with some favor. He journeyed on horseback to Cincinnati and Philadelphia to buy goods, transporting them overland by wagon from the closest navigable point in the chain of rivers. His store came to be the trading point and social center for miles around. He extended "store credit" anywhere and everywhere, and it was universally understood that Christmas Day was pay day. . .

In this environment, Grandpap started his family of four boys and one girl. . . He had the first carriage and the first piano in the county, even though Darter was the county seat and center of culture and population.

His mother back in Kentucky signifying her desire to visit him in his new home, he sent the carriage, the two older boys and three "hands" back to bring her to Mahrug in State. The trip took over two months, and she had to wait until the next summer to find weather and roads suitable to make the return home. Back in Kentucky, she advertised him and the new country so extensively that two of her neighbors bought enough land of Grandpap that Fall to make back to him all the expenses of her pilgrimage, and then some.

In somewhat less than due time, considering his status as an immigrant from another State, Grandpap got elected as a Democratic member of the House, in the State Legislature. Early in the first Session, he introduced a bill to substantially increase the Governor's salary. . . By a mere coincidence, it was referred to the Fees and Salary Committee, of which Grandpap was a member. It was unanimously reported favorably to the House by the Committee at its first meeting after introduction. Passing the House and Senate intact, it was reluctantly signed by the Governor, and became law.

At the next roll call, Grandpap introduced another bill which came to be known as the "Bourbon County Bill." Its purpose was aimed to accommodate the people around Mahrug with a nearer court house and closer county seat. Without trace of partiality, it would simply carve a new county out of the four existing contiguous counties to Mahrug, make Mahrug the county seat thereof, and give the new county the name of "Bourbon", (a name most likely suggested by scenes from Grandpap's nativity). True, it did provide for the bonding of the territory comprising the new county to procure funds to acquire land for and construct the court house, jail and other county buildings, and "other necessary expenses," but these things were naturally incident to the formation of any new county.

Through another coincidence, the Bourbon County Bill was referred to the County and Township Business Committee, of which Grandpap was Chairman. It was promptly reported favorably to the House by the Committee. After some delay and a little explaining, it passed the House by a very substantial majority and went to the Senate for its action thereon. . . The Senate's County and Township Business Committee in turn named a subcommittee to "examine thoroughly into its merits" The subcommittee was composed of two experienced and dependable members of the Majority party and a Whig member who had a bill pending for a separate judicial court for one of his counties. . .

Within the next two or three days, Grandpap's Bourbon County Bill, in some mysterious way began to take on the ear marks of an "Administration measure." Therefore, it was not lightly to be cast aside. The subcommittee, in their earnest desire that justice and fairness be done, sought first hand and unbiased information and facts, wherever they could be found. . . and was soon ready to report. However to make assurance doubly sure, it was deemed advisable to finish its labors by interviewing the Governor. . .

The Executive Chamber's heavily-upholstered, plush furniture and cushions were done in deep red. The windows were heavily curtained in the same color. Prismatic glass pendants featured the oil-burning lamp chandelier, with three circles of 8, 16 and 24-lamp capacity, the whole suspended from a liberally-adorned ceiling ornament by a gilt rod of considerable tensile strength. The walls were patriotically hung with pictures of former Chief Executives in immense velvet-lined gilt frames of a uniform character, arranged chronologically. The majority portrayed a pioneer soul of stern and earnest demeanor. Some had struck a Daniel Webster pose, thus straining and disguising themselves. Others had cherubic countenances, and were men such as slept o'nights. All wore magnificent whiskers. . .

The Governor's Secretary announced the Senate County and Township Business Subcommittee, and discreetly retired from the Chamber.

His Excellency, that stalwart adherent to Jeffersonian principles, slowly arose from his desk and greeted the subcommittee with outstretched hands. Following the usual formalities, they got down to business, and the subcommittee chairman asked the Governor his opinion on the Bourbon County Bill.

"Uh-m! Well, first let us see what your investigation disclosed. What have you found out?"

"We find they're pretty much for it. I've talked to a good many, and so have these other gentlemen here, and about all we talk to, or see, want it. . ."

"Yes, I know! But is it geographically sound?" the Governor queried.

"Why-y, yes! They've never had an earthquake anywhere's around there that I . . . ."

"No. No!", interrupted His Excellency. "I mean do you find the country around there needing a court house at that particular place? Geographically speaking?"

"Oh-h, that way! Yes, I think it does. Mahrug is over 20 miles from the nearest court house. And as luck would have it, there's a 'Square' already laid out there in town, ready and waiting . . . ."

"And what do you learn, Senator?" The Governor turned to the other Majority member of the subcommittee.

"I find they're all for it down there. Mahrug is over 20 miles from

Darter, the county seat. Three big creeks separate them from it. You can't ford them in high water. And one or the other of them is nearly always high. They're all mud roads and hard enough to get over in dry weather, and when it's wet or raining you have to take to the sides. Nine months in the year you can't get over them, only on a horse."

He paused. The Governor was leaning forward in his chair, beaming at him.

"Go on, Senator!" the Governor urged. "You are stating some very salient and important facts. Those are what I want to hear if I am to be of any assistance. Facts that go to the very heart of the question! Go right ahead!"

The Senator was both pleased and encouraged. He wanted the Governor's good opinion. He desired to "stand in" with him. He had a little bill up himself that his County Chairman was interested in getting passed. And if it got past the Senate and House he wanted the Governor's signature without any quibbling. Governors sometimes vetoed bills. He had heard it said if you knew a Governor rather intimately, there wasn't so much danger of a veto. Governors were that way.

He cleared his throat and proceeded. "There is considerable litigation over around Mahrug, from what they say, from horse stealing on down. An apple jack still house down on Muskrat Creek causes considerable trouble. Most of it is only hand and club fighting amongst the boys and men there in the neighborhood, but there's coming to be more cutting and shooting lately. The authorities down at Darter are so far away they don't pay much attention to it, or just don't care."

"They are coming in from Kentucky and other places, and land trading is pretty brisk and on the boom, and every time they make a trade they've got to go to the county seat to get the deeds made. . . My investigation shows me the people down there want a court house, they need it, they ought to have it, and I say give it to them."

"That was a . . . most enlightening and instructive dissertation on the very meat of the question," said the Governor. "And you Senator?" He swung around a trifle to face the Minority member.

"Well," he began in a hesitating way, "Some say they need it and some say they don't. . . Some of the boys on our side say there's politics . . . ."

"We can't help what some of them say," interrupted the Governor with a slight frown of annoyance. "What do you say."

". . .As I started to say, our Floor Leader is dead set against it. The counties they're cutting this new county out of are kicking like bay steers," (He noticed the Governor learning forward) "but the people in the new county want it, no doubt about that a-tall . . . ."

"There you are!" triumphantly exclaimed the Governor. "That's it exactly! The people in the new county want it just like the people in one of your counties want a separate court. And the people in the counties it is being taken away from don't want it, just like the people of your other counties, from which this new court district would be carved, don't want your one county to have it. Don't you see these two bills are alike? One is about one thing and the other is about another, but the principle is the same in both?"

A dawning sense of the similarity of the two bills swept the otherwise expressionless face of the Minority member. The whole thing unrolled like a scroll. He resumed, "As I was saying, the people, down there want it. The community needs to be developed, and those people want a court house of their own. They need it. That's why I made up my mind so strong when we first started out to help them get it. We're not up here for politics. The people don't send us here for that. They sent us here to do the right thing by them. I'm for the bill! Don't forget that! I'm strong for the bill. I've done a lot of talking over on our side. They can't bring politics in this thing while I'm around . . . .."

His Excellency arose majestically. He fondled his beard, adjusted his waistcoat, cleared his throat and began, . . ."This conference has been a mental stimulus for me. Your unerring logic has been a revelation. Your arguments have convinced me beyond the shadow of a doubt of the absolute merits of the bill. . . I glory in your decision to push, er, I mean pass, this bill. It *must* pass. You and I shall see to it. . . I am particularly pleased with the fearless and unwavering stand on the bill your Minority member has taken. As he has so well said, we are here not as partisans, but solely as the representatives of the people. God forbid that politics should ever enter Legislative Halls, or the Executive Chambers during my Administration! . . ."

His Excellency excused himself momentarily, and returned with a decanter and four ample glasses. Filling them generously, he handed one to each of the conferees, raised his own and said, "Let us drink in the old bourbon to the success of the new Bourbon."

The toast was enthusiastically drunk without the aid of water or other pollutive non-essential. . .

Following the findings and advice of the subcommittee, a general Committee Report recommending passage soon followed, and was adopted by the full Senate, over a very scattered chorus of "No" votes from the Whigs.

The bill had successfully hurdled its first major Senate hazard. There still remained plenty of time for trouble. Second reading was in the offing. It was then that bills were open for amendments, which could, in one minute, absolutely undo almost a whole Session's hard thought and planning. Just such an amendment as the dour Minority Floor Leader had prepared. . .

The Bourbon County Bill was put in the direct and personal charge of Senator Winker. . . He was a "steering committee" of one. . . He thought and planned. He cogitated and mused. The Majority Whip was a promising young fellow, a good mixer, and the Minority Floor Leader had taken a liking to him for some reason. The two had a habit of disappearing somewhere about the Spencer Tavern at night.

Senator Winker was cognizant of his Whip's ability, and somewhat familiar with his habits and associates. He sought him out and had words with him. . . The Senator, having laid his plans and fortified himself accordingly, determined to hazard the Bourbon County Bill for second reading the next time that order of business came around.

According to rules, the members called various House Bills assigned to them during an alphabetical roll call of the membership. . .

With his ear to the roll call, then approaching the S's, the Majority Whip strolled casually past the Minority Floor Leader's desk, and with a knowing wink, whispered to him, "Come out in the corridor a minute. Four of your friends from over in the House want to see you."

The Minority Floor Leader knew instinctively who they were and what they wanted. He followed his young Judas into the long corridor to face the four gentlemen he had expected to see. The conference was merely to pledge a mutual presence at, and arrange the minor details incident to, a friendly poker game in Room 232 of the Spencer Tavern at 8 o'clock that evening.

The whole thing took less than ten minutes, but the timing, with reference to the specific thing to be accomplished, was perfect. When the two gamesters returned to the Senate Chamber, the Bourbon County Bill had passed second reading without amendment, or offer of amendment, and the Senate was on another order of business.

Thus, was the second major leg of the Bourbon County Bill's flight negotiated safely. . .

The bill had been posted for third reading for more than two weeks. The Session was nearing its close. Senator Winker had purposely passed several calls wherein he could have had the bill handed down for passage. The times had appeared inopportune. He wanted to give the Governor and Administration authorities ample time to work on the recalcitrants. The bill was known to have stubborn opposition, and the Democrats a bare working majority. Speaking generally, the Senate had shown itself in a surly mood lately. Several sharp clashes among the Majority members had accentuated that mood. They were not functioning smoothly. A wild idea to license the sale of intoxicants had just been fought out—and strange to relate, passed—leaving some serious political scars in its wake. There was no personal liberty left any more. The mere thought of a fool legislature trying to legislate what a Sovereign People could eat and drink was showing what the State was coming to. Many spoke of the "Oregon Country," where they still had a little liberty left. And as always happens under such circumstances, the Minority were all the closer knit and serene.

It was not their fight. They were not in the saddle. As a result of all this, several near-Administration measures had been killed summarily, and apparently for no particularly good reason. Just another quirk the legislature had about it.

Eventually there were signs of a change. The Legislative atmosphere cleared. The Solons became more tractable. . . The time was ripe.

The bill was called. The roll began. Something was wrong! Senators here and there, who had been counted on to vote affirmatively were voting "no." The Minority member with the separate court bill voted, "Aye." The rest of the Minority seemed to be voting "no" solidly. Senator Winker glanced at the Minority Floor Leader. He wore an inscrutable look. No, on second glance, it was—sinister. Why? The Senator looked roundabout for the answer. It slowly dawned there were several Democratic seats vacant.

He rushed the Whip out to find and bring in the absentee brethren. Some came. Others could not be found. They might be in hiding. A tally was showing a considerably greater number of "no" votes than "ayes". . .

A motion to "excuse the absentees" prevailed. . .

Grandpap's Bourbon County Bill was killed, by one vote. . . Senator Winker plumbed the depths. Back of it all, he could not forget the fact, he had nine good Majority votes unaccounted-for in the tabulation—somewhere in the Legislative wilderness. . .

Next day the separate court bill met a similar fate—only more directly. The Minority helped do that.

The death of the Bourbon County Bill was a crushing blow to Mahrug's future and Grandpap's dream. But it did one thing. It fixed, once and for all, his and our family politics, if by any chance our politics needed any stabilization. It is true that Uncle Ben turned to be a Republican during the Civil War. But that was to preserve the Union, and incidentally a considerable amount of U.S. Bonds he had acquired at most attractive discounts. Thereafter Pap and Uncle Ben studiously avoided all mention of politics until the first Cleveland campaign. By that time all of Uncle Ben's evidences of Federal indebtedness had been retired at par and accrued interest, and he was free to return to his first political love. . .

Stick with the articles

September 8, 1936

Curtis Publishing Company
Independence Square
Philadelphia, Penna.

Gentlemen:

Please let me congratulate you on this week's *Post*—what reading the Sharkey, the Harding and the Dizzy Dean stories made!

I realize love stories must always have the big pull, but speaking for one who has reasonably recovered from that phase of life, surely there must be hundreds of thousands of your other readers who sort of skip love stories for the ARTICLES.

As a staid country lawyer, I actually stayed at home Tuesday, September 1st, until after the *Post* had come to the house in order to finish the "The Way I Beat Joe Louis" story—and I've never seen, or expect to see, a prize fight either. I liked the unusual subject and the style of the telling of the tale.

Therefore: as a member of the probable great and unwashed minority, I trust you will increase the ARTICLES, although I'll be glad when the Election is over, and Mrs. Republican and Mrs. Democrat can stop, and political stuff generally, although the recent Allen (or White) story on Landon was a masterpiece of shrewd political propaganda—and I'm no Republican, or Progressive, or Coughlinite, or Landonite, or much of a New Deal Democrat, by a hell of a sight.

Very Respectfully,

In the wild west

May 1, 1937

Mr. Henry H. Miller, Atty.
Title & Trust Building
Phoenix, Arizona

My dear Mr. and Mrs. Miller:

Back home again in Indiana, after a considerable of a sojourn – for a Hoosier. The unsuspecting Public, viewing me as I flow up and down the main thoroughfare of Greencastle, little suspects that only lately have I reveled in orange blossoms, irrigated yards, camel-back mountains, Pima Indians, featherweight grapefruit, rattlesnake Pioneers and *over-stuffed* lemonades. Said Public is not cognizant I have dined (and wined) at the Arizona Club with the flower of Phoenix Society, made a complete and minute survey of the entire northeast section of Phoenix and contended with a western sirloin at the Sip and Bite grand piano table, semi-surrounded with nasal singers and aesthetic dancers who would find their acts uncomfortably chilly on an open air platform in the environs of, say, Duluth. And further, it does not know I have met the Great and Only S_____, and been permitted in his office, from whence emanates 80% of the Arizona corporations, about all of which have probably lost money for the gullible investors.

After leaving Phoenix, my first stop was Los Angeles. Thence to San Francisco via "The Daylight," a beautifully-appointed train but woefully short in the extreme speed. Thence to Grant's Pass, Oregon, and two days with my erstwhile Putnam County political advisor, Dr. W. A. Moser—his son, Dr. C. J. Moser and wife and three boys, about 7, 9 and 11, go to Tahiti for deep sea fishing in June; the young Doc showed me his fishing outfit, with reels about the size of the reel on my John Deere corn planter—Thence to Portland. Then Seattle, where my old "frater" at Indiana 32 years ago, Adam Beeler, has just gone off the Supreme bench of Washington (thanks to the Democratic uprising)—Adam drives a '37 Packard (which petered out on us about 30 miles from town), his wife sings all over the Northwest (exclusive of Democratic Conventions), his daughter is divorced, and none of them seems to be on relief—Thence to Spokane, to Wallace, Idaho, etcs., etcs, home. . .

Very Respectfully,

And she's good looking too

June 5, 1937

To Tri Kappa State Scholarship Committee
Subject: Betty Broadstreet

Members of the Committee:

Careless politicians and businessmen of easy integrity have tended to bring the present-day letter of recommendation into the class of questionable literature, but at rare intervals each of us has an opportunity to make a recommendation whole-heartedly, and without the slightest mental reservation. Such is the subject of this letter, and I am happy to recommend Betty Broadstreet of Greencastle, Indiana, for the Tri Kappa State Scholarship. I do this freely and with the knowledge that I can forever remain at peace with my own conscience.

Your Committee wants facts. Upon investigation, I find from authoritative sources that Betty led her Class all the time she was in High School. This school year she had sufficient credits for graduation at, or about, Christmas. Much to her credit she dropped out and got a job, to help continue her education in College. Last Friday night she graduated here.

I have known this splendid young woman since early childhood. She has about all the qualifications any young American girl can have – honesty, health, ambition, modesty, neatness, gentility, industry and a mind that absolutely qualifies her to take a College education. All these are pretty hard to find combined in one person, but Betty, in addition, is positively a stunningly beautiful girl.

And so, in my opinion, she is exactly the type and character any father would be proud to say of her, "She is my daughter, that red-headed one over there with the blue eyes."

I therefore recommend her most earnestly for your serious consideration.

Respectfully,

Mistaken for Dillinger

Greencastle, Indiana
August 27, 1937

Mr. George E. Pitts
United Paperboard Company
171 Madison Avenue
New York, NY

My dear Judge:

The writer is the fellow who was in your office about three weeks ago consulting you concerning the transfer of some Paperboard stock, and for whom you so kindly and generously prepared an affidavit for the surviving widow to execute.

I thought you might be interested in the trials and tribulations of a hill-billy clean out of his environment, trying to make his way about town with a minimum of errors.

After inquiring of about every policeman in New York where 171 Madison Avenue was, my trusty grip and I eventually came to your door. . . And say! You folks aren't wasting the stockholders' money on any elaborate waiting-room. There she was, 6 by 12, three chairs, one settee, one high-up electric fan doing a noble job stirring up that hot 7th floor atmosphere, three Sawmill Journals and a 2 x 2 peep-hole, like the ticket window of the B&O R.R. here at Russellville, my old home town. The grip and I both got in, but every place I tried to set it down it looked like it would take up the space for a second customer if he happened to come in just then.

A girl looked through the ticket window at us—especially the grip—and I realized my mistake. I had the knowledge that John Dillinger was raised about 30 miles southeast of here, and that he had sometimes carried grips, and that maybe she had gotten us confused. She asked what I wanted. I told her I wanted to transfer some stock and wanted to see the head of the Legal Department. She told me she could take care of the stock transfer. I started to explain, and she started to explain, so we both explained. Finally, either due to the altitude or the heat, or something, I was supplementing the fan with the new $7.50 panama I had just bought at Macy's in order to get a New York label to show my admiring friends when I got home, and I begged her to just let me see some official of the Company. She relented, and a first class fellow came forth, not to the peep-hole, but right to where the grip and I were. I started to explain, and he started to explain, so we both explained. By that time I had the hat synchronized with the fan. Eventually, he got my idea—but the President was out, the Vice-Presidents were on vacation, and the attorney might get in around 3:30 p.m. or he might not, and would I wait or go out and come back later. If so, he would do his best to get a conference for me. I told him if I got out, I'd never find my way back, and that I would wait.

By that time my curiosity was at a maximum and I was wild to get on the other side of that ticket window, because I knew the place had to be lousy with red leather chairs, air-conditioning, ice water bottles, Chinese rugs and baled-up currency.

All things must come to an end. In due course I passed the forbidding door and was ushered into your office—after first having my grip taken away from me and deposited at the peep-hole girl's desk. And that grip is an inoffensive grip. In fact, it was given me by the members of the Legislature one time when I was the alleged Floor-Leader of what was then God's Chosen Minority—the Senate Democrats. Since I left, they—the Democrats—have perked-up and now have a big majority themselves.

But, to be serious, I want to thank you for the way you handled my case. You certainly know how to size up a situation quickly. I realize big Corporations must use all reasonable precautions when it comes to transferring stock, etcs., but there's reason in all things. You have been almost more than fair in your demands. You are not our conception of what a New Yorker is, and especially a New York attorney. Why, my-God, man! We've always been taught to first come to a full stop before going up the ramp at Grand Central Station, and sew our modest currency rolls on the inside of our underwear.

I hereby extend you an invitation to come out and rabbit hunt with me this Fall, with the reservation that you furnish your own blister medicine and liniment. I'll furnish all board, bed, guns, dogs and ammunition.

Again, I thank you.
Very Respectfully

The hospital needs a check-up.

The following two letters relate to Pap's experience at losing more money than he had counted on during a visit to the hospital.

August 10, 1939

My dear Mr. & Mrs. Cunningham:

You are probably slightly interested in knowing how I came out in my run-in with the Methodist Hospital over my hospital bill and some money I lost. I am therefore enclosing Benson's letter to me and a copy of one I just mailed him.

George, I want to thank you for being willing to say just what you knew and saw about my having any money on me at the time of the accident, because by reason of what you saw and knew, I just had to have two $1 bills and *some* other money in a bill or bills. Those facts helped write the enclosed letter to Benson. Then too, you know how a jury goes in a hotel run-in with somebody who isn't worth much, or anything. You don't have a chance. Same way with a hospital or a railroad. It's too bad it is that way, but it is.

And now Mrs. Cunningham, . . . I don't know what was the matter with my mental processes last Tuesday noon when I was in the hotel and called you. I knew I was going straight in to eat with Ike – I'd much rather have eaten with you—but I never thought of asking you to come along and break bread with me. And now listen how I thereby missed an opportunity to advance my social standing. When I got in, there was our Labor-loving Democratic State Chairman feeding his brother and some other "loyal Democratic worker" off of our famous 2% Club money, over on one side, and John Frenzel over in the corner feeding himself off of usurious interest money he had wrangled out of some unfortunate borrower. We'll cut out the Organized Labor-loving State Chairman and get to Frenzel, who is somebody—as a man and every other way including a whale of a good Banker with a whale of a good Bank. Now just suppose I had been escorting you into the dining room—you and your stately and dignified walk and manner, and Frenzel had looked up through a cigarette smoke fog. He wouldn't have believed his eyes. He'd have said to himself: "My G—, that can't be *her* with Andy Durham from that little jerk water bank down in Russellville. Yes it is, sure as I'm of German extraction! W-e-l-l, next time he comes in my place I'll not have the police lead him out like I wanted to do last time he was in. I'll bring him right back behind the rail to my desk and get better acquainted with him. He just has to be somebody—although he sure doesn't look it, and I'd never have guessed it."

See what an opportunity I missed if I could have had you along? I'll never do it again, even if I have to pay for a rum sour or whatever it is you get to go with your meals.

As ever,

August 10, 1939

John C. Benson, Superintendent
Methodist Episcopal Hospital
Indianapolis, Indiana

My dear John:

. . . Your adjustment offer on my hospital bill, under the circumstances, would seem fair to any disinterested person. You offered to reduce the bill by $24.35, and I insisted my loss was either $27 or $32, not knowing which myself—which looks rather bad on its face, for me.

But John, as sure as Meharry Hall is in the middle campus, and the Democrats are God's chosen, some low fellow (I'd ordinarily use a four-word combination we use and thoroughly understand over at Russellville to characterize certain men folks) there at your hospital rifled my clothes—and got either $27 or $32 in bills. The last thing I did before leaving Mooresville the night of the accident was to pull out my modest roll and give Doc White a $5 bill, and he gave me back two $1 bills, that I folded with the others and then put in my little watch, or ticket pocket, in the upper front part of my britches. Mr. George Cunningham, manager of the Claypool Hotel, saw that, and so did Doc White of Mooresville, I think. Then Mr. Cunningham and his wife and I got in his car, Mr. Cunningham in the front seat driving, and Mrs. Cunningham and I in back, and went direct to your place. Mr. Cunningham couldn't have robbed me, and wouldn't have if he could (there's some wording for you); it would be heresy to think Mrs. C. would (if you know her); anybody would have to be a hell of a sight worse off than I was to go broadcasting $1 bills enroute to a place like yours, knowing full well if he had any sense at all that if he stayed there a week he'd have to mortgage the back 40 to get paid out. So that last theory is plumb out. And all that remains is the aforesaid "low fellow."

The weak spot in my whole story is expecting the other fellow to believe me, and me alone as to just how much I had in money. I don't like to be in that position. I wouldn't want the other fellow to expect me to take his word for what he had. That's something like our railroad troubles. I've been attorney here for the New York Central since about 1916. In all that time we've never killed any live stock that wasn't a thoroughbred. All railroad attorneys get used to that and expect it. So four or five years ago the Springfield, Ill., Division of the B & O that runs through my farm at Russellville (and whose trains on that particular division run more by the compass than on the rails) killed my registered Hereford bull with one of its passenger trains. I knew their General Attorney at Cincinnati quite well, so I wrote him the facts and ended by saying, "and as is usual in railroad cases, *he* was a thoroughbred." Right back came his answer: "Your thoroughbred bull has nothing on us. We want you to distinctly understand ours is a thoroughbred train". But he paid me on a thoroughbred basis.

As the man on the farm says when he starts to give me advice: "Now, I don't want to tell you how to run your business, but I'd do so and so", so now in like manner I want to urgently request that you check up on everybody who handled my clothes from the time they took them from me in the X-ray room, or whatever it was, until the clothes got back in my room, and keep a watch on him or them. . . Whoever did it to me will try it again.

And now, I *do* have a request to make, and it's for my own benefit. Please call Mr. Cunningham at the Claypool and see if my story about the money is in fact true insofar as he knows. Then question Doc White next time he comes in. . . Anybody who is anybody would want to furnish as much outside proof as he might be able to get. Now John, don't come back at me by saying you don't have to ask Mr. Cunningham and Doc White because you believe everything I say, like Mr. Hess did over the telephone. Somehow that sort of nettled me. Mr. Hess doesn't know me from Al Capone. I'm serious in what I ask, and I'm going to check-up on you, old timer . . .

> Respectfully,
> Andrew Durham

Asking help with money

September 25, 1939

Mr. Wilbur O. C_____,
Lebanon, Indiana

My Dear Wib:

I was in Lebanon the other day and called you, but your good wife said you were in Lafayette.

Wib, here is what I wanted to see you about. Frank is in Law School and needs new clothes. I am in need of some money badly, and want you to help me out all you can. I am enclosing a copy of your note, with all the credits on the back. I am also enclosing a blank note. I had Ward Mayhall, down at Central National Bank figure out the balance of principal and interest as of Sept. 21, 1939 – $157.55 on that date. So please send me a check for all you possibly can, and if you can't pay all, then please date the blank note, make it payable in thirty days like the old one, and for such sum as is the difference between what your check amounts to and the sum of $157.55; sign and send to me along with the check, and I will be greatly obliged. The old note is simply covered with Intangible Stamps, with no room to put on any more credits. . .

Cordially,

October 30, 1939

Mr. Wilbur O. C.
Rochester, Indiana
Care of Barrett Hotel

My Dear Wib:

I am enclosing the note dated October 1, 1939 which you sent me some weeks ago, for the reason it does not seem to be drawn properly. The figures show the amount to be $160, but the writing shows an even $100. The former seems to be right.

I have been getting ready for Joan's wedding in New York next month, and have not had time to make this explanation and get a letter off to you until now. And anyway, it has been a month now and perhaps you can send me a check for something at the same time you execute the enclosed new note and send it back to me. The Lord knows I am in need of cash at this time—in fact I have been needing cash about all my life it would appear. . .

When I get the new note back in the correct amount, I will cancel the old one that is all gummed-up with Intangibles.

Respectfully,

It's no picnic

November 15, 1939

My dear Miss Robbins:

About the time you are perusing this tender missive, we and our oversized family will be on the "Southwestern" en route New York City and Joan's wedding, which latter will occur at St. Bartholomew's at 4 p.m. on the afternoon of the eve of Lord's Day next.

Let me tell you about another trip on the same Southwestern that happened about 14 years ago. Joan was 13 and Sugar Foot still getting regular eye doses of boric acid, and Ann Drew just out of the boric acid period, and so on up the line, when the Fair Calantha, as was her custom from time immemorial, started on safari via New York to Milford, Penna. She had passes—but what passes! Not good on Number this, and not good on No. that. In desperation I went to the General Superintendent, good old B.C. Byers, told him my troubles, and asked if he would make them good on the Knickerbocker. He looked at the passes, then at me, and said: "Why, you've only got walking passes." He thought a minute, then: "A woman with six little children has no business getting into New York City at 3 or 4 p.m.—then across town and the ferry to Jersey City, then by Erie to Port Jervis, N.Y., and then by auto into the mountains. Give me those passes. I'll make them good on No. 12. I'll make your reservations, and I'll have No. 12 stop at Greencastle and pick them up." All the which he did.

The train stopped, and old man Keith happened to be the conductor. He was in a huff about having to stop his long heavy train at any town like Greencastle. He stood to one side and the patrons started climbing up the steps: Mother, nurse, kids, boxes, suit cases, bird cages, more kids, grips, violin cases, dolls, milk, kids, a kitten, lunch boxes and more kids. He turned to me and asked, "Is this a picnic or a family?"

I said: "It's a family—and they're no picnic by a d— sight."

Yours,

Aunt Margaret's splash in journalism

December 3, 1939

My dear Julia and Anna:

I saw a couple of "features" written by Joan and published in today's Indianapolis Sunday *Star*, so I clipped them, and here they are. One uses her own by-line, and the other "Betty Clarke." If I get the story right, some Betty Clarke wrote for the Associated Press on cosmetics, etc. Her successors have used that same name in turn. When Joan writes on foods, she uses a by-line of a "Mrs." somebody—I don't know the name – because a younger unmarried woman now-a-days knows practically nothing about foods and wouldn't be believed, or taken seriously. . .

Well, as you know, Joan was married in St. Bartholomew's Church (Episcopal) in New York City Nov. 18 last. She married a William H. (Taft) McGaughey, as you may already know if you read Walter Winchell's column of Nov. 5th, I think it was. "Bill" is a former DePauw boy, a Phi Gam., graduated here about 1932. Was a reporter for the

Indianapolis News after leaving school, then to the *New York Herald-Tribune*, I think it was; then on the *Wall Street Journal*, and now is Editor of the *American Automobile Manufacturers Association Magazine*, or some such name. Heretofore it has been edited in New York, but after January 1st next, they move him and the magazine, and Joan, etc., to Detroit, Mich., where the magazine will continue to be published. Therefore, if I understand it right, Joan will lose her job with A.P., and become a housewife—Good Gosh A'mighty!!—Giving up a job like that to become anybody's housewife – I don't care who, or where he comes from—and just when she had struck her stride. Understand I'm not kicking—he's a fine young fellow and alright in every particular, so far as I know and can learn. I'm just thinking out loud. . .

We were all at the wedding—the whole family, including Aunt Margaret, Sarah Jane and her husband. We stayed at the Waldorf-Astoria, just across the street from St. Bartholomew's . . . and otherwise disported ourselves as Russellville blue-bloods. And that reminds me of Aunt Margaret's splurge in the realm of journalism (Aunt Margaret lives at Russellville). Well, when Aunt M. learned Joan was to be married, she wrote Joan a real homey letter about it, including therein a recital of what she did in preparation for her own wedding years and years ago; that she began preparations a year ahead, made towels, spreads, dish cloths, muslin garments (I don't know what she meant by that) etc., saying she had some of them yet and about as good as new. You know the secret, if it was that—Aunt M. tried to "learn" the girls to be economical. . . She went on to say she hoped Joan and her husband would be well and happy, and would try to make home their chief object in life. And so on, in that sort of vein.

What do you suppose Joan did with that letter? She turned it over to another A.P. Feature writer, and he sent it out over the whole world about as follows: "A very charming young woman I know here in New York is about to be married. Her old-fashioned aunt out in Russellville, Indiana, wrote her a letter about marriage, which in view of the present day stress and strain and disregard of marriage vows, we think deserves a wider publicity. Here it is." Then he quoted the letter. The

Greencastle paper got hold of the release and printed it. Aunt Margaret got hold of the Greencastle paper and almost swooned. When she got to New York for the wedding, she found she was a famous writer and almost swooned again. Then she got sort of tickled and concluded it might make some of these young persons think, and eventually do some good. I have no copy, or I would send it. At the time, I was so busy rigging up my own treasseau, or however you spell it, I didn't take time to save any copy.

I think I should tell you about my wedding-clothes troubles. Joan's was my third wedding. When Sarah Jane married two years ago she wanted an evening wedding at Gobin Memorial Church here. That called for a dress suit for the old man. Mine was of the 1910 vintage. I thought that wasn't so terrible bad, but when I got it separated from the moth balls and camphor, I found that one or the other of them, or both, had tended to shrink it tremendously. Whatever it was seemed to have centered the attack on the waist band of the pants. Then too, some "low comedian" here at the house said the lapels looked like those of an "end man" in a Russellville home talent minstrel, and another said the tails were too short and seemed blunt and worn off, like an old feather duster. Now that couldn't be, because practically the last time I wore it was at my own wedding. I had put a telegram in an inside pocket—and there it was: "Veedersburg, Indiana, November 24, 1910. Sorry we can't be there but we're with you to a man. Congratulations. Fred S. Purnell." Well, we wound up in a one-sided compromise—a new dress suit from Bro. McMurray, 201 Board of Trade Bldg., Indpls, Ind.

Along came Joan wanting a 4 p.m. St. Bartholomew's wedding. That called for a "cut-away." So again I went to interview Bro. McMurray. He was delighted and thoroughly in favor. When I went up for a try-on, while Bro. McMurray was chalk-marking here and there, I took a hurried look in the glass, and Holy Nellie! What I saw took me back instantly to "Old Prince" at Russellville. Old Prince is a 26-year-old faded-out black work horse I own, spavined, two splints and stiff as Mrs. Stuyvesant Fish. In that cutaway, I looked like Old

Prince in a set of track harness.

I hope Margaret marries before the Japanese take the country, and that Ann doesn't decide on a grass dress.

Somehow, somewhere, sometime, this family will have to go into a huddle on these wedding signals, or I'm going to find myself with a lot of uniforms—and no clothes.

Yours for more clothes and fewer costumes,

Russellville has good credit at the Waldorf

March 17, 1940

Mr. B. C. Byers
1150 Oakwood Ave.
Dayton Ohio

My dear B.C.:

Well! Well! Well! I'm threatening to do a thing I've been threatening for about a year—write you a letter. . .

Joan was married Nov. 18th, 1939 in St. Bartholomew's Church (Episcopal), corner 51st and Park Avenue, New York City, across the street from the Waldorf-Astoria Hotel. Her parental father and his family retinue, large and small, married and unmarried, were hosteled on the 12th floor of the Waldorf. And you can imagine what a stir among the employees we simple country folks made. They had seen nothing like us in that place since its corner stone was laid, and they haven't since. . .

Dr. Oxnam's (now Bishop Oxnam, stationed at Boston) wife and daughter were to be our guests at the Hotel in our suite of rooms—count them, 8 of them. The Bishop was to have been present to give a prayer—Joan had graduated at De Pauw when he was President there —but old St. Bartholomew said: "No. No Methodist, or other cult, can pray at an Episcopal Church wedding. We run the Church, and incidentally the wedding, and what praying is done, we'll do." So the

Bishop got sort of miffed and went on to Arizona ahead of time.

The wedding was at 4 p.m., the reception immediately following. Joan was a feature writer on the Associated Press in New York City—a splendid job. Naturally her associates were newspaper folks and writers, mostly men, who knew Kentucky Tavern from Coca-Cola. The wedding reception was to be held in the New York Newspaper Women's Club in the Midston House (hotel near Rockefeller Center). It had a bar, and Joan somehow got the silly idea it was the duty of the bride's father, for this occasion, to stock that bar with tools having an alcoholic content. . . So we brought along the main feature of the reception refreshments: 8 quarts in my grips, 8 in Frank's, 4 in Munny's, 4 in Margaret's, and Sir Walter Scott Behmer brought 3.

Mrs. Oxnam was to know nothing about it. She didn't—until she stepped into the Club rooms. Then anyone would know it, unless he had spent a lifetime refereeing skunk-squirting contests.

Old man Thomas, I think his name is, formerly Editor of the *New York Times*, now a sort of newspaperman head of the Pulitzer School of Journalism, and who had Joan in his classes when she went to that school, got tight and went all around telling the guests his great grandpappy was half Indian. His good old wife stayed sober, and as a result sprained an ankle on the scuffed-up rug. The woman Editor of *Vogue*, or else one of its principal writers, kissed me because she said I looked like her cousin who had his leg shot off in the Spanish-American War. In the excitement I kissed Mary Beth Plummer—top woman writer on the Associated Press and incidentally about the best looking — just to show my good taste.

Early in the game, Munny saw what was coming. So she shepherded Mrs. Oxnam and daughter away early. They put the daughter to bed. Then went out on their own, and in some unaccountable manner got into the bar of the Hotel, saw what they had done —and ordered lemonade. All Munny needed to complete the picture was a basket of eggs on one arm and a fresh dressed chicken under the other.

My Gosh! But we had a time.

What with buying extra booze, taxi-cabbing everybody all over

Hell's Half Acre, eating in the "Cert Room," which was named for some famous Spanish painter, or paperhanger, and tipping hundreds (it seemed), I thought I might run low in cash. So I slipped quietly around to a room labeled "Credit Manager," walked in and saw this woman sitting in the big chair. She saw the surprise on my face, smiled and said: "I am the Credit Manager. Are you looking for me?"

"My name is Durham. I live in Indiana, and they're taking it away from me around here faster than they do back home on Thursdays at the main gate of our County Fair. I may run out of money, and I want to know how I'd go about getting a draft cashed, if I had to."

"May I see the draft?"

I pulled out the bill fold, fetched out a $50 draft, and sure enough there it was in big letters, RUSSELLVILLE BANK, payable to me.

She looked at it, then at me quizzically, and said: "Are you the father of Joan Durham, the Feature Writer who was married yesterday over at St. Bartholomew's. I read her AP features."

"Yes mam," I said proudly, "I'm her Pap."

"Have you any sort of identification card, letter, driver's license, or something to identify you?"

"Yes, mam. I have a bad note on Peter M_____ back at Russellville for $20 I wish somebody would collect, a membership card in the Putnam County Farm Bureau and a New York Central pass"— cautiously saving the best for the last.

"The pass will be sufficient." She looked at it and then at me and said: "We will cash the draft any time you want it cashed—now, if you want it."

"No," I said, "but if that won't run me, is there any way to cash checks?"

We talked quite a bit—about Russellville (which she never heard of), the wedding, the Hotel, farming, cattle and hogs, etc.

Eventually she said: "We'll cash checks for you up to $1,000, Mr. Durham."

Well. By that time she was far, far ahead of me, so I tried to catch up. "Miss", I said, how long have you been Credit Manager here?"

"About six years", she said. "Why?"

"Because you won't be Credit Manager very much longer, giving out credit that way."

Then she did throw the witty bombshell. She said:

"Well, Mr. Durham, no one from Russellville ever gave this hotel a bad check yet."

And after a little more talk, in which she bragged, for my benefit, how she could tell people who wouldn't give bad checks, I left and went upstairs and bragged to Munny how Morgan, Loeb and I could cash checks at the Waldorf – just like that. . .

Yours,

Haven't you ever heard a radio?

March 19, 1940

My dear Mrs. Cunningham:

After the very kind and considerate treatment received from you, Harlan and his wife during my rather short stay in Miami, you must be thinking I am an ingrate for not writing sooner, but the fact is, I've blamed near been sick all the time since leaving there. Coming home I was a trifle dizzy for a day or so, but I attribute all that to those two singers who broadcasted from your music room that Sunday night. Good old Walter sized up my trouble in his efficient way, and knowing my background, realized those girls coupled with Miami's metropolitan hours and night life would make any native of Russellville dizzy. And so, he drove practically all the way home. . .

Passing through Jonesville, a town about like Waverly, Walter saw a sign, "Home Cooking." Of course we stopped and went in. A hill billying radio in the kitchen made the dining room hideous with its squawking. The Old Brakeman asked for grits, fish and sea food. He got boiled side-pork, boiled cabbage, boiled beans and corn bread. And later he was to get what was advertised as pie, but looked like unto no pie I had seen in my 58 years of active pie viewing.

I asked the waitress: "Where is that terrible noise coming from?"

With a puzzled expression, she answered: "Why that's the radio." Then something dawned, her face lighted and she asked: "Haven't you ever heard a radio before?"

"Is it a bird or an animal," I asked.

"Neither one," said she. "It's a little box you turn on and the music comes out. Ain't you ever seen one? We turn it on of a mornin' and it plays all day."

"No. But if we came this way again and brought company, would you turn it off while we're eating?"

"I shore will," she said—and she meant it.

The foregoing was among the lesser highlights of our trip straight home. . .

Was in Detroit last week. Saw Joannie, husband and apartment. The husband is as big as the apartment is small. It's an up and down-stairs affair. Little stairway from living room upstairs. The whole thing is about the size of a smallish hen-house, the upper floor representing the roosts.

As ever,

An aerial view of the Durham Family Farm, one mile east of Russellville, Indiana, site of many of Pap's adventures.

Pap and Munny and the three oldest
girls at Greencastle's Big Four Station in
the late 1920s.

Pap in front of the U.S. Supreme Court
Building.

Pap in front of the U.S. Treasury Building
in Washington.

Pap preparing to enter the White House.

A later "political family portrait" with one addition, Aura May. (l-r) bk. Joan, Pap, J. Frank and Jane; seated, Munny; ft. Margaret, Aura May, Ann.

Chapter IV:

The War Years—1942-1945

Pap was way too old for active involvement in World War Two. He had to be content watching his children play their parts (Frank and Margaret both joined the Armed Service, although the latter had to be consoled after being initially turned down for a commission). Pap's sideline role did not deter him from making wry observations about professed patriotism on the part of the legislature ("political hooey") and the effects of war on the home front (shortages, black market activity, travel restrictions and inflation).

He also kept in touch through the mail with his scattered children and his wife. Despite the difficulties of wartime transportation, "Munny" insisted upon making her annual summer excursions to Milford, Pennsylvania, to attend to property inherited from her parents. This caused Pap a bit of anxiety, as he feared for her comfort but did not wish to take undue advantage of his railroad pass perquisites. He also felt lonely at home alone, as his youngest daughter, Aura May, left for college. In some of his strongest letters, he expressed concern, usually with humor but sometimes quite poignantly, that family members should not interfere with each other's pending marital plans.

Otherwise, Pap tended to the farm, his lobbyist duties, and wrote a newspaper ad celebrating the 50th anniversary of the Russellville Bank.

Not trying is worse

Advice to a daughter turned down for a naval commission.

Sept. 3, 1942

Dear Margaret:

I was sorry to hear you hadn't made the grade and didn't get what you want, but I would have been much sorrier if you hadn't tried. That's what gets me—this not trying. And while you may be quite a bit disappointed, you tried all the same, and that is the thing that counts much, much more.

Of all things, I never thought I would have a daughter in the Army or Navy, but now that things have happened as they have, and women are going into the War, why, I'm getting used to most anything. . .

I'm not saying that you should be in the Navy, not at all, but if I were you and I wanted in, I'd keep pecking away until I got in. . . You said something about them wanting you to try for something like a job as a "private" in the Army. I am rather inclined to think you did right in not accepting that offer. You have an education, and better still, you have an ability that should rate you better than that of a private. It is true all of us can't be "Generals," but with your ability, your common sense and a world of other good qualities, you, if you want to, and will stick with it, will be able to get in WAVE, or whatever it is, from some other State—Indiana, for instance. There is a lot of bologna in this War, like all others, and I am told on good authority that it takes a political set-up to get the best. . . Honestly, when I heard you were trying Pennsylvania, I rather thought you would not be in the running. It just don't make sense for an Indiana girl to get a job like you wanted in the face of women (natives) in the second most populous State in the Union. . . Now above all things, don't repeat what I have said, and by no means give such as an excuse for missing the boat at Philadelphia, Just keep mum, keep your own counsel, profit by your experience and keep on trying in every way you can. If I get a chance I'll get to Indianapolis and try to learn what WAVE is doing in Indiana, if anything. I have been so busy, I haven't had time to go any place or do anything except keep the farms going, which is a big job.

Let me hear from you.
Pap

Helping the war effort

Aug. 2, 1942

Dear Frank:

There is not much news to tell you. We are more than busy at the farm. . .

I should tell you about an experience I had yesterday. The rain stopped us combining oats on No. 43 shortly after dinner. I came home early in the afternoon. Stopped in the Post Office to see if there was any mail. Doc. Sigler the Veterinarian was in there. Maybe you know him. If not, then you should. He is windy, used to run a saloon here years and years ago, and therefore is an authority as he thinks on all things alcoholic. Doc was in a talkative mood. "Have you tried the new beer, Durm?" he asked. I said I had not, and what was it. Then he proceeded to tell me. It is really old time keg beer put up in bottles – half gallon bottles. It is unpasteurized, and it saves caps and thus helps win the War. He was insistent that I try just one bottle. It was to be had at Robert Hoffman's storage plant—this unpasteurized beer has to be kept cold.

Naturally I wanted to help win the War, so I went outside, got in the Mercury and headed for Hoffman's storage plant on North Indiana Street. There was Robert and his helper, Jim Allen. . . I asked their opinion, and they both agreed it was the Wonder of the Age.

If one bottle was good, then more would be better, so I bought three. Then, as a sort of hedge, and to be on the safe side, and being that I was already there, I bought a case of Cook pints, as I knew what they were, and came home, put the case on the kitchen radiator and the three half gallon bottles of Doc Sigler-recommended, unpasteurized Champagne-Velvet beer in the ice box and awaited developments.

Later I went to the Lincoln for supper, then tarried downtown a bit and started home. Pearl O'Hair was on her front porch and called to me. I went down and courted her until after dark, then thought of my Champagne-Velvet Doc. Sigler-recommended unpasteurized beer in half gallon bottles that help win the War, and came home. I reached in where we used to keep milk, pulled one out and it looked bigger than a block-busting bomb. I got the biggest glass in the house and poured it full. It tasted rather alright, so I took another sample. Then others. The bottle stood the drain unusually well. Then I found a rubber stopper, inserted it, put the bottle back in the ice box and came in the front room to read the *News*. Then back to the half gallon bottle of unpasteurized amber fluid. That bottle "gave down" like a six-year-old Holstein with a new calf. . . Another round or so and we called "recess" for me to go out on the front porch for air. But duty called me back to the bottle. By that time I could see I was gaining slightly, and would eventually win if I kept up my morale. But it was a horse race with bets about even. Then back to the front porch for more air, then back to the half gallon bottle of unpasteurized that helps win the War. On one of these trips to the front porch I noticed the Electric Light people had inserted a bigger light bulb while I had been gone. But my patriotic duty called me back to the pantry and the rubber stoppered half gallon bottle. In desperation I again went to the front porch to bring in help, any kind of help, but the streets were empty. Then back to the kitchen, and then to the front porch where I was seized with a desire to go calling, anywhere, and anybody who could talk, or rather listen, because at this time the gods were unfolding to me a quick and brilliant scheme in which I was to outshine MacArthur and tip the balance to win the war—just like that. The plan was simple and should have been thought of before now. It was to furnish all enemy soldiers with half gallon bottles of Doc Sigler-recommended unpasteurized Champagne-Velvet beer, make them drink it and thus cause internal drowning. Simple, isn't it? But suddenly it became unnecessary, because back at the bottle and just as I was draining the last drop, there came through the ether, the short wave fuzzy joint and unconditional surrender of Hitler, Sitting Bull and the Pennsylvania Whiskey Rebellion.

As Ever,

Avoiding a state of nature

Aug. 4, 1942

My dear Aura May: (*then visiting in Worcester, MA*)

. . . I took time off today to go to Reiner's at Indianapolis to test out fur coat prices. They are high, but nonetheless, my offer stands provided you want one at this time. Your letter rather indicated you would as soon wait a year or so. That is sensible and also thoughtful, and it might be a year in College and an opportunity to look around and sort of study fur coats might be better than to jump in and buy one hastily. . .

Sarah Jane has her sights raised too high, I think. She says $419, exclusive of fur coat, undergear, socks and I don't remember what else she excepted. . . You are fine looking, well made and therefore can wear grass dresses, sarongs and Russian Sable with equal grace. In other words, clothes don't have to make you. And thank God they don't have to pinch-hit for your scholarship. Still, you should have good clothes, and you are going to get them. Sarah Jane must have smuggled you into Worcester after dark, because, according to one of her letters, you were naked, or practically so, when she took you to Canada. I hope your ears were clean.

However and nevertheless, Sarah Jane is doing her level best to help us all out in these, your clothes troubles. She is taking her time and effort, and all for the good of the cause, so let's all be appreciative. She thinks we are losing time, back tracking and creating a state of confusion—which we are. . .

I am therefore enclosing a draft for $300 and telling you you are free to do as you please in the selection of your clothes. After all, you will have to wear them, you are 18, an exceptional scholar, and you should be pleased and satisfied. This is not all the money you are to get for clothes, etc., this year, but God knows I think it is enough for you to start out on this Fall and Winter. If not, then we'll sell some shoats . . . and rustle up some more.

Ann has to have a few duds, you know. Margaret is in a state of nature as to clothes, and . . . Munny surely needs a new bustle and pair of arch-supporter shoes by now. . . .What I'll be needing is a pair of new corrugated rubber-soled shoes and plenty of cinders. . . .

"Pap"

Crossing the railroads

March 17, 1943

Dear Chilluns:

Back from the Legislative Wars, pretty well battered but gradually recovering. We took one bad licking. Under present law, generally speaking, municipalities and county commissioners may . . . "order in" grade crossing warning devices or watchmen . . . whether the railroads think them necessary or not . . . all at the cost of the railroads. . . We tried to change the law so the unit so ordering them in would have to pay 50% of installation, repair and maintenance. . . But the Senate voted us down 26 to about 18. The mayors got in their work.

There was absolutely nothing unfair about the bill in my opinion. It just would have stopped a lot of grafting mayors and city councils. For instance, a councilman in Anderson last summer introduced an ordinance requiring 44 crossing lights in Anderson. The ordinance

was so worded . . . that only one manufacturer could fill the specifica-
tions. A brother-in-law of the introducing councilman was the agent
for that factory. It was so raw the ordinance failed to pass, but it took
a lot of lawyers and time and expense to run all that down. Just such
things as that happen all the time. Some "worthy party workers" start
a manufacturing plant up in Lake County on a shoe string. Maybe they
can't get a site on the right-of-way. But they start. Then come to the
railroads and want a switch put in to the factory. . . The railroad in-
vestigates—the set-up doesn't look permanent—and declines to extend a switch. Then, the "workers" go to the mayor and council with
the tale the railroad is stifling business in that town, and so on. A big
howl goes up. . . The railroad makes another check and refuses. Then
the mayor sends word they will be wanting some more crossing devices in that town, to "protect the children," and there you are again.
Those crossing devices cost an average of $2,500 per set. Maintenance
averages $50 per year. These are only two of a hundred rackets worked
on railroads. . .

Not in the FDIC and proud of it

*On the 50th anniversary of the Russellville Bank, in 1943, Pap, as
Chairman of the Board, took out a sizable advertisement in the July 30 edition
of* The Daily Banner *(motto: "It Waves For All") of Greencastle. The ad
proclaimed in large bold type that the venerable Russellville institution was
"A Private Bank, not a member of F.D.I.C." The "Old Bank", as it was
referred to, had been started in 1893 by some 30 citizens of Russellville,
including Pap's father, James, and older brother, J. Ernest Durham, and
had grown to have capital stock of $15,000 and a surplus of $50,000, according to the ad. Excerpts follow.*

Type of Bank

Russellville Bank is a Private Bank. It is UN-incorporated. Therefore the individual liability of its stockholders for its debts (and your deposits are its principal liability) is not limited merely to the extent of the value of the stock owned in the bank—whatever that value may be—as is the case in Banks incorporated under Indiana law. Incorporation, among other things, means limitation of liability for debts. . .

Deposit Guaranty

We are NOT a Member of Federal Deposit Insurance Corporation (F.D.I.C.). We were invited to join. We declined, and, being an "A" Bank, were not compelled to join. We have been asked why we declined. Here is the answer: Many of you have been told the Federal Government guarantees all deposits up to $5,000 made in Banks belonging to F.D.I.C. If that were the case, we would probably have our application in for membership in the morning. But nothing is farther from the truth. The Federal Government does NOT guarantee one cent of anybody's deposit in ANY bank—National, State or Private, anywhere, anytime—whether a member of F.D.I.C. or not. But it does require ALL Banks belonging to F.D.I.C. to guarantee one another's depositors' deposits up to $5,000 for each depositor—A SORT OF MUTUAL INSURANCE. We are a small Bank, but mighty for our inches in a financial way. And we want to put all the force of all of our resources solely back of the deposits of our own depositors. Therefore, we thought then, and still think, it would be unfair to our depositors for Russellville Bank, with its comparatively overwhelmingly superior resources, to join-up and guarantee the depositors of a bank in the Rockies, about which it knows nothing and over whose management it has no control. So, excluding all other Private Banks, we assert we have proportionately more resources for the payment of every dollar of our deposits and other liabilities than any F.D.I.C. Bank in the State of Indiana has in proportion to its deposits and other liabilities. This is no idle boast. We mean just what we say.

Conservatism

In our 50 years of banking we have bought millions of dollars worth of securities for ourselves and our customers without loss of a single penny of Principal or Interest. However, during and following the "Bank Holidays", in a few issues—three we think, "to keep the record straight"—some bonds and some coupons were not paid promptly at maturity, although eventually all were paid.

Our Customers

Our customers are the salt of the Earth. Some have been with us during all, or practically all, of our existence (In that time we have, to be sure, lost some good customers, and we sincerely regret those losses.) During the April, 1943, drive for the sale of 2nd War Loan Bonds, the patriotism of our customers was immediately evident. The amount of approximately $29,000 was sold in and credited to Russell Township (our township), and of this the amount of $23,218.75 was subscribed by our customers and paid for with funds in Russellville Bank. We are proud of our customers in their War efforts. If peace should be dictated by the Axis Powers, it might conceivably happen our 50 years of careful, conscientious banking would all go for naught and that Russellville Bank, in spite of its enormous resources considering its size, might not be worth the price of this advertisement. It pays to be patriotic.

Ordering stove parts

April 2, 1943

Cribben & Sexton Company
700 N. Sacramento Blvd.
Chicago, Illinois

Gentlemen,

I am herewith enclosing check for $2.75 for two oven door springs, two pastry door springs, three black door handles, two simmer buttons and ttmx (whatever the devil that is), all as per enclosed card.

Mrs. Durham has gone to Pennsylvania, and the children inform me she eventually was able to find the "number" of our gas stove so the above repairs could be identified by you. Where she found that number or identification on our stove is still a profound mystery to me. She had looked, I had peered, the children had searched, gas men and plumbers had examined and thumped, and outside the "Strand Universal" toward the lower right hand corner, the job was as smooth as an undertaker's conversation when showing caskets and gently murmuring prices therefor to the bereaved family. Incidentally, your modest demand for the above gadgets is as "chicken feed" to theirs. You must be an honest and upright firm, for Chicago. Congratulations.

In conclusion, let it be known no Nazi spy will ever be able to report back to whoever he reports to the elusive number on our trusty gas stove.

Very respectfully,

Land away from home

October 23, 1943

Mr. Eugene M. Anderson
20061 Hull
Detroit, Michigan

My dear Eugene:

Enclosed find Russellville Bank draft . . . for $550 . . . in full payment of the balance owed by Ared Shaw and wife to you for the 27 acres plus north of the N.Y. Central station here in Putnam County. I am also enclosing a receipt for $1 from Central National Bank, which . . . charged each of you the sum for holding the papers.

I tried to peddle your contract but the chiselers had this excuse and that for wanting you to discount it. This is no time for discounting, and everybody knows it. Banks are glad to get good loans at straight 6% —mighty glad. I took it up with Russellville Bank and they wanted it. So they got it. . .

I expect you are glad to get the matter off your hands. It is no fun to own land a long ways from home. I have tried it—in fact I am trying it all the time—have land in Kansas and Texas I can't get rid of, and it's a nuisance. The southwest Kansas land is 160 acres, flat as a pancake—you could make baseball diamonds all over it—and never had a plow in it. Father traded a horse and buggy for it in 1893 or 94. Never saw it. It is in dry country. We have just paid taxes (very small) all these years until about five years ago I leased it for oil to the Standard Co. at $1 per acre. They have never drilled a well, but keep it for speculation, and each year pay $160. So, if that keeps up, we'll have our money back come 20 years more, or more or less. . .

Very respectfully,

Let the bride call the tune

Advice to an only son who has become a prospective groom. Note: The future bride's name was Frances Haberkorn, but Pap, who nicknamed everyone, called her "Francisco." (Undated)

My dear Frank,

From your letter, matters matrimonial in our family seem on a most decided up-swing. I didn't realize you had gone so far, but right now, once and for always, you can rest assured the "old man" is with you 200%. Wife and husband choosing is for the individuals themselves. Outsiders should look on, keep out, keep mum—and worry to themselves all they want to. I did a mighty good job of picking, and I'm perfectly willing to accord the rest of you the same privilege.

Your letter said Francisco would be down to have a final say in the matter—or words to that effect. That's right. That is the way it should be. You'll find a groom is the most unnecessary necessity modern society ever inveigled an unsuspecting public into. He bears about the same relation to a first class wedding that a dust cap does to a 12-cylindered, leather upholstered Packard.

Perhaps by now you know more about when and where. Naturally, the balance of us would like to know something about that too—especially if any are expected to be "among those present". . . If I am expected to be present, I'll have to arrange for somebody to do the milking, and get my shirt to, and back from, the laundry—both of which take varying times. But whenever, wherever and however, you can count on Munny for an absolute certainty, even if you can't count positively on a bride. Munny would be there to forestall any substitutions. If it is to be in Alaska, you can count on Munny trying on parkas tomorrow, and practicing blubber her next meal.

As ever,

Pap summoned up the following allegory in advising family members not to interfere with the wishes of the prospective bride for her own wedding.

To All and Sundry of the Clan of Durham of Putnam County, Indiana,

Greetings:

Legend hath it when the daughter of Simonides of Iulis was about to wed, a controversy arose between her and the prospective groom's kinswomen and some of his kinsmen as to what wines were to be served at the wedding feast. She contended for a wine whose grapes were grown on the east side of a mountain and facing the morning sun. His kindred strove for a less palatable but more potent wine whose grapes were grown on the south side of a neighboring mountain.

The controversy arose to political and diplomatic importance. Forsooth, she, having all the best of it in comeliness, charm, personal interest and common justice, prevailed—as all brides-to-be should, concerning their nuptial arrangements.

At the wedding feast his people were served with hemlock—thus forever ending the "in-law" question for her, and thereby reaffirming an almost unbroken precedent that in the days of your Grandfather Durham was summed-up in these cryptic words: "He who pays the fiddler shall call the tune."

Moral. It were better a volunteer of bridal suggestions to a bride-to-be were buried in the sands of the sea at low water mark where the tide ebbs and flows twice in twenty-four hours, than intimate anything, anytime to HER, and thereby court a return of the Iulisian custom.

(The foregoing went by mail, postage prepaid, to all members of said Clan whose addresses were known this May 21, 1944)

Some similarity

Frances' father was Henry Haberkorn, a vice president and trust of-
ficer of the largest bank in Detroit. Pap was chairman of the board of one of
the smallest banks in Indiana. He made the following observations regard-
ing this "similarity."

(Undated)

My dear Frank,

I wrote one letter to Francisco, and one jointly to her father and
mother. This week I received replies. Frances wrote a nice, sensible,
fine letter. Your pappy Haberkorn did the honors for himself and wife.
The letterhead disclosed he is one of the Vice Presidents of the National Bank of Detroit. He facetiously referred to the fact we had another thing in common—we both were connected with the banking
business.

Which reminded me of Charlie Buchanan, who appeared before
the Railroad Committee of the House in 1917 with a bill to allow the
Louisville, New Albany & Corydon Railroad to charge more than 2¢
per mile on passenger trains on his Road. Charlie was President of said
R.R. and it was a separate railroad corporation in truth and in fact.
He was also Auditor, Treasurer, Gen. Freight and Passenger Agent—
and Conductor on their one and only train. His Road ran from
Corydon and connected with the Southern at Corydon Junction –
some 8 miles of main track. He told us the following tale:

As do all R.R. Presidents, he went to their convention in Chicago, and there struck up Pres. Williams of the New York Central for
an exchange of courtesies of passes – he to give Williams a pass on the
L. N.A. & C. Railroad, and in return, Williams to give him a pass on
the N.Y.C. Williams seemed to have not heard of Charlie's Road and
asked him where it was. Charlie told him. Williams still was puzzled

and asked how long the Road was. Charlie answered it was a little over 8 miles long.

Williams said, "Don't you think you have a hell of a lot of gall when you have an 8-mile Road and we have over 16,000 miles?"

Charlie answered, "I know that Mr. Williams, but yours ain't a damn bit wider."

He got the pass.

And also our Committee recommended his bill unanimously. . .

And so, as between the L. N.A. & C. and the N.Y.C., and the National Bank of Detroit and Russellville Bank, I can't just put my finger on it, but hazily, there is some similarity, of some kind or other.

As ever,

The constrained romance of Uncle Ernest

Pap's conviction that family members should not meddle in affairs of the heart was on his mind, and showed again in the following letter. It was written long after the death of his older brother, J. Ernest Durham, generally referred to as "Uncle Ernest," but the memory of a romance impeded by an overzealous family was still vivid.

April 25, 1944

Dear Frank:

. . .Long, long ago I wanted a diamond like you want a bride. And so, I bought and sold calves, colts and horses; hauled campers to and from Eel River Falls; graded the old ball park at DePauw; etc., etc., and worked in staid, dependable, conservative, old Russellville Bank at $2 per week & board and clothes (I'll say it was conservative – Uncle Ernest started it in 1893 and had his first note loss in 1907. . .). I spliced my money, went to Walk's (the old time jeweler at Indianapolis) and bought myself one. They said it would be a good investment. They were only half right. It was an investment . . . Then the ring and I went on to college, and time went on.

Uncle Ernest liked the looks of said diamond—but not the price—and from time to time would borrow it. He had smaller fingers and would wrap white grocer's twine around the base until the ring about fit; then go to the Bankers' State Convention at Indianapolis, where, in trying to be a good fellow, he would eat a lot of cheese, pickles, blind robins, drink maybe a couple bottles of beer, and come home with an upset stomach and a hell of a headache. Thence to Billy Gardner's drug store for a new box of acetanilide.

Eventually, Frank Kennedy's girl went to some woman's college in Illinois to take music. Her teacher was a spinster of questionable age, named Colgate, from New York, New York. It was claimed, either by her or Frank's wife, she was a kinswoman to the dental cream and dirt-removing family of that name who have the big clock in Jersey across from New York City. Mother and Aunt Margaret were inclined to doubt it. Anyway, the teacher came home with her pupil at the end of the year for a visit. Uncle Ernest was invited down for supper next night.

That took a good deal of preparation. He spent most of the day away from the Bank getting ready. Frank Kennedy, the pupil's father, and host of the evening, was our leading barber. He cut Uncle Ernest's hair and shaved him. Uncle Ernest filled the galvanized wash tub extra full and took a thorough bath behind the kitchen stove. That took off about everything except the ink stains on his fingers. Mrs. Forgey, who with her husband, Jim Forgey, kept house for Uncle Ernest, recommended lemon juice, or maybe it was green tomato juice, for finger ink stains, but said she couldn't do anything about the ink stains on his best suit which she was cleaning and pressing. Uncle Ernest had won a bottle of cologne or Florida Water in some sort of a shooting gallery attached to Buffalo Bill's Wild West Show at the Chicago World's Fair in '93. He hadn't used much of it, so he doused a little of that here and there. . . All told they did a pretty fair job of grooming. The evening was a success and much praise was given Mrs. Kennedy's salt-rising bread and culinary art.

Uncle Ernest had a Model T of several years back. He had used it hard, and one day, trying to head-off a calf in the barn lot out at the old home farm east of town, had run through the gate with the door open. The door hit the gate post and was torn off. He had to tie it shut with baling wire. That meant he had to keep it shut and get in from the other side all the time. Most of the fenders held their respective places by virtue of more baling wire. He had also misjudged the height of some limbs on a tree up in the north pasture, and torn a hole in the rubberized textile top that leaked when it rained anything above a heavy dew. The back end of the coupe was loaded with an assortment of axes, grubbing hoes, pitch forks, spades, post hole diggers and so forth. Besides that, it had the mud of three counties plastered inside and out, and the upholstery showed sizable patches of cotton wadding. The car in general looked bad enough, and entirely too tough for social usage, but the thing that disqualified it absolutely for his impending purpose was that he had parked it overnight under a blackbird roost, and anybody who had done that in mulberry and cherry time knows what I mean.

Uncle Ernest had anticipated the visit by swapping his Ford for my new chummy little Saxon roadster – 35 miles to the gallon – and wherein, a woman companion couldn't keep very far away from you.

Their first trip was decorous and above suspicion. They went to the Rockville Chautauqua to hear William Jennings Bryan, and Cole Younger the famous outlaw and bank robber, lecture on "Crime doesn't pay." They got in by 9 p.m.

Their next foray was a bit more questionable. I think they went to a box supper over toward Montezuma. In order that there be no confusion and Uncle Ernest bid-in the wrong box, she pasted a picture of that women's college on the outside of her box. Uncle Ernest bid-in the right box and got to eat supper with her. They got in just after midnight, according to Frank Kennedy's wife's timetable.

However, any necessary atonement was made next day, Lord's Day, when they went to Crawfordsville and heard Dr. McIntosh, President of Wabash College, read his "Shakespeare, the Apollo Belvidere of English Letters."

Things gradually went from late to later, until one night they didn't get in at all—not until after sun-up. They had succeeded in running my Saxon off the road, sprung an axle and busted a light and fender, in a suspiciously out-of-the-way place between Deer's Mill and the Shades of Death. They said they got lost, and confused going downhill. I agree on the latter. Anyway, they hadn't crossed the state line.

Russellville opinion of the accident differed. It would. Suffice to say, no run was attempted on the trusty old Private Institution; the next reconnaissance by State Examiners showed said Bank to be in its usual sound condition; and a scrutiny of Uncle Ernest's balance sheet showed no unusual strain on his normal account.

The scene shifts to Greencastle: Uncle Ernest was bringing his "fair Calantha" to call on Mother and Aunt Margaret in the parlor of the old brick, where a solid line of Paris Green fringed the red carpet, unsullied these many months by human feet. The horse-hair upholstered furniture stood where I last saw it five years before. Aunt Margaret's painting masterpiece of 1884 still hung on the west wall, showing castle, moat and drawbridge (and the fair lady in green riding habit riding the horse down from the castle to the drawbridge hadn't made any mileage since then). On the east wall hung Aunt Margaret's effort of 1885 in paint on red velvet. It was intended to delineate our National Bird – the American Eagle – however, something had happened to her measurements at the time, or the noble bird had developed a pronounced goiter meantime.

Aunt Jennie Black, she of the piercing black eyes, who looked with suspicion on any thing or happening outside the confines and regulations of the Presbyterian Church, had been called by Mother to sit in—a job she was never known to flee from when it was her duty, which it always was.

Uncle Ernest had asked me to be on hand, probably for moral support in the event our womenfolk got out of hand.

The inquest got off to a good start. Pleasantries were passed all around until I was hoping against my better judgment. But alas, in her enthusiasm and heightened conversation, our fair caller, in an unguarded moment, dropped the fact she was a Red Cross worker in World War I, and had passed out cigarettes to the soldiers in France. Great God! I saw Mother's bosom swell, Aunt Margaret's lip twitch like it does just before she evades an unpleasant question or is getting ready to give a lecture on morality and church attendance; and Aunt Jennie's spinster chest flatten out flatter than usual, and I knew from now on the meeting was to be an inquisition in the real medieval meaning of that word.

Eventually conversation lagged, good-byes were said, the guests departed. The trio went into a caucus before I could get out of the room, and I heard Mother pronounce sentence: "We don't need any female cigarette distributors in this family." How times have changed!

That Fall, our Red Cross worker taught in Buffalo. Uncle Ernest got off for a short trip to San Antonio, but caught the wrong train and landed in Buffalo. Next Spring she taught in Cleveland. Again, Uncle Ernest headed for San Antonio, got the wrong train, but this time found out his error in time to get off at Cleveland.

Last Chapter: Uncle Ernest died in 1931. As Executor, I went through all his effects. Away back behind everything, I found a dusty Indiana National Bank canvas sack once used to express silver dollars and fractional silver coins. It was full of envelopes about the size of a two-thirds grown postal card, all addressed in the same handwriting, and all tied up in packages with grocer's soft white twine. I didn't know the handwriting, but eventually caught the full signature. I hadn't tried to read the letters – just sifted through them to make sure the envelopes contained only letters. Shortly, I came to one, the opening sentence of which caught my eye: "I am terribly lonesome tonight, Dear."

I quit reading. They weren't intended for Executors. I took off my glasses and sifted all the remaining letters one by one into a handy banana hamper. Some had snapshots in them. I took everything out and burned it. Somehow, I felt pretty bad. . .

As ever,

"Pap"

The hay and feed racket

April 19, 1944

Dear Sarah Jane:

. . . While we're on the "racket" subject, I think I have partially solved the "hay and feed racket" at the Indianapolis Stock Yards. We trucked the heifers to Indpls. Sunday afternoon. The buyers (a commission firm) insisted they get there the evening before – "to rest, get a good fill and good weight next morning, and be ready to be re-loaded alive in stock cars to go to New York." I've been skeptical about ever coming out even on a feed and hay bill. . . I had too bad a cold to go up Sunday afternoon in one of the trucks and stay overnight, so I got up Monday morning at 4 a.m., and got to the Yards. I found the cattle and just about stayed with them until it was all over. Eventually the hay wagon came along. They threw out two bales for our cattle and then distributed them in the hay racks. I watched the cattle. They weren't eating any of the hay, just none at all. It was timothy. They were used to alfalfa. . . The bell rang and trading started. Buyers came and went. Our heifers were better than any I saw. Kingan's (Indpls. local packer) man bought them. He had been out to the farm to see them two weeks before. I got more than he offered me out there. I marched along to the scales, counted, and saw them weighed. My bill, among other things, read: "400 lb. Hay @ 1.45 = $5.80". The two bales they threw out for us would total not more than 120 to 130 lb. Timothy hay delivered in Indpls. would not run over $20 per ton. They figured ours at $29 per ton, as shown above. The heifers didn't eat a quarter's worth all told.

However, there are worlds of straight people. Witness Ira, for instance; the Hazlett Brothers, who started with a boot and shoe and now can get about any amount they want at staid, old, conservative, dependable Russellville Bank, the bank that only guarantees its own depositors; Mr. Whitaker at the filling station here; and thousands of others, who, like kitchen utensils at farms sales, are too numerous to mention. . .

"Pap"

Patriots debate—the ballot or the bottle?

April 19, 1944

My dear Margaret:

Munny is on one of her many pilgrimages to Milford under disguise of most urgent business. I had seen it coming on, and the final break was made when I was called to Indianapolis by the railroads for the Special Session. She left the day after I did. This time she thought she would go by coach, paying her own fare, because in this emergency I have refused to ask for passes. The day I left she told me her intentions, and knowing how trains are crowded, next day I went to the station at Indianapolis to see how she was faring. I found her standing, and she had been standing all the way to Indianapolis and was bedraggled already, and with only about one-twenty-fifth of her journey completed. . . We got back to the Pullman conductor, stated our troubles, and he made the usual reply: "I have just one lower to New York, and she can have that". . . The coaches and aisles were crowded with soldiers, sailors, baggage, dirty newspapers, pop bottles, paper cups, lunch boxes and kids . . . and the last I saw of that day's first section of No. 12, the conductor was shepherding her back through the Pullmans . . ..

The Special Session brought out a holocaust of patriotism – if I am using the right term. The purpose was to make it possible for the members of "our armed forces" to vote next Fall. Each member tried to out-do the others. The two chambers and the corridors rang with zealousness in the interest of "our armed forces" getting the ballot. Those not running this Fall and the hold-over Senators were less voluble, but in the House, where everybody had to run this Fall, or else stay out, the rafters went off center from 7 to 9 inches. I haven't seen such valiant patriotism in a legislative body since the last war, when I was in it and up for re-election. I don't remember my conduct, but I expect it was pretty patriotic. I do remember I introduced a resolution in the House commending Wilson and the Congress for breaking off relations with Germany, so I evidently had my lightning rod up pretty high. . .

People generally had a fear about this Special Session, and were afraid it would hang and hang on amidst fervent patriotic speeches and many, many glowing accounts of the heroism of "our armed forces," and not adjourn *sine die*, maybe for the full 40 days. . .

The Session was remarkably free of drunkenness and wild parties—some of course, but not the usual amount. . . Thursday evening we had a private dinner in the "English Room" of the Claypool for quite a number of railroad executives who were in the city, partly on account of the Session. It started a drab and serious affair. The war was on and restraint was in the air. Railroad executives are like all other people—busy, serious and worried. The railroads are carrying an enormous load. Equipment is over-used and the replacements are just not to be had under the circumstances. And so, the dinner lagged. The talk ran to the Special Session, and each speaker praised the Legislature for setting in motion the plan to allow "our armed forces" to vote, and there was gentle inquiry as to how long the Session would last. Naturally, their patriotism would want it to be short, with nothing done against the carriers. Eventually they got to me, and for my opinion.

I told them I had sensed the restraint of the dinner, but as I had no further political ambitions, and was standing no stud horses, and had no past due notes in the Bank, I was more or less of a free agent, and would try to speak the truth; that it was my honest opinion the average soldier didn't give a damn whether he voted or not out there wherever he was; that not one out of four of our armed forces out there in the trenches would try to vote unless it was more or less compulsory, amazingly easy and did not interfere with whatever he or she was interested in at the time; that not one out of four of the ballots of those who did vote outside the U.S. would get back in time to be counted in the proper precinct for State and County offices; that I'd bet 3 to 1 that three out of four of said "armed forces", if given the choice between a ballot and a bottle of beer, would select the beer; and that over 90% of all this tremendous anxiety about the soldiers getting to vote was political hooey pure and simple. Also that no adverse legislation against the railroads would be offered, much less passed; that the Session should close by the end of the week; that the Republicans were already starting to take credit for this early adjournment by attributing it to a strong new leadership and a united militant front – which also contained a good percentage of hooey – and that early adjournment, if it did come, could actually be credited to two big factors: a world of back Spring plowing and the acute whiskey shortage – especially the latter.

You could just see them softening up and relaxing in their chairs around the table. They all agreed and from then on the dinner party went along like a good dinner party should go. The Session adjourned Friday night.

Now Margaret, if I were you, I don't believe I would show this letter to anybody. She won't know Pap and she might get the impression I was making light of the soldiers and the War. The Lord knows that is not my intention. Far, far be it from me to want to deprive soldiers or any other qualified person from voting. What gets me is all this fan-fare about setting up the machinery to allow a person to do what he has always had the right to do. That doesn't take any patriotism. That is simple justice. . . Those of us at home can show our patriotism by staying at home and off trains and away from crowded cities and hotels unless it is necessary; by raising more livestock, grain, grub of all kinds and fewer orchids and "rackets" of all kinds; and above all else, by cracking down on these strikers and damnable labor racketeers and stopping this criticism of the powers that happen to be – Churchill, Stalin and Brother Roosevelt. . . I'd like to carry the rosin bag for those boys. They are the ones who have kept most of the Russellville Bank stock in my name, and old Fred and Nellie and the work harness in the old log barn. I'm fer 'em.

Keep a stiff upper lip, and your hat on straight.

"Pap"

A patriotic cancellation

(Undated)

. . . All our Indiana Railroad Lobby set-up except me are Republicans. The State is Republican. Most of the Indiana Public Service Commission are Republicans. They got the idea of a National Public Service Commission Convention at French Lick this August. So two of our set-up went to Washington D.C. to see Brother Johnson, who is the head of the War Transportation outfit, and arrange for cars . . . They had their story ready, and particularly "the importance of the meeting."

Brother Johnson listened attentively until they finished. Then he uncrossed his legs and spoke about as follows: "There will be no convention at French Lick this summer. I wouldn't allow you one seat in one bus for the whole damned convention. We are going to move an additional 1,000,000 men and equipment in August, and 1,500,000 in September. We don't know how we are going to do it with what equipment we have left, but I know one way we are going to help – we are going to set off every god damned railroad executive and near-railroad executive we can find wherever we find him. That will help considerably. You go back to Indiana and tell those Hoosiers there's a War on in case they don't know it, and the thing for them to do is to stay home where they belong and not be cluttering up these trains."

That combination, "near-railroad executive," is what cooked our crowd. None of us is as high as a section boss.

The National Public Service Commission Convention for this summer at French Lick has been called-off by unanimous consent. "After studying the matter carefully, we have decided it might possibly interfere with the War Effort in some unforeseen way, and the patriotic thing to do is to take no possible chance in that regard".

As Ever,

Pap

How to sell

March 27, 1945

A letter to all the children away from home.

. . .But let's get down to more important things. First and above all else is Ann Drew's impending venture into making matrimony. . . What Annabelle Lee wants in the way of a husband is what I most surely want her to have. Besides that, Ralph is a first class young fellow, if I am any judge. Under the circumstances, I'd like him if he wore spats and drank tea. . . I do hate to have her get married away from home, but that is all right under the circumstances, if she does decide to make the jump away out there by herself in California. They tell me a marriage license issued out there (maybe I should have said a wedding ceremony) is still good here in Indiana.

Frank's young calf, of course, is a more serious problem. I don't know how to answer his inquiry about feed for a stray young calf, except to say that cow's milk is the solution. . . Incidentally Frank, you can get original first hand information, together with some startling dialog relating thereto, if you will ask Jim Anderson's wife at Russellville how she raised "Old Nellie"—the old sorrel mare we now have at the farm—when her mother died when she was born. I can write the details but it takes Stella (Jim's wife) to give the matter the proper wording. (It is a story for men only. Women crimp Stella's style). . .Well, the facts are these: There was that tiny hungry little helpless colt. They got her dried off and away from her dead mother into a box stall with plenty of straw. Then the food question arose. Jim drove up one of the cows; they milked some milk into a small crock; Stella stuck two of her fingers into the colt's mouth and down into the milk crock, and eventually Nellie got the idea. And so, from day to day, they repeated the scene. The leggy ambling colt waxed sleek and gained flesh. She got so she could drink, but preferred to suck Stella's fingers. One evening Ernest was there, and the usual performances were had, and everybody admired the colt and thought it very cute . . . when all of a sudden and all unexpectedly, Nellie backed square behind Stella, got the exact range and let fly with both feet, hitting Stella squarely on the axis and knocking her about six feet flat on her stomach. The air took on a blue tinge as it does in Indian summer, and no stevedore ever out-stevedored Stella's utterances, which were both long and loud. . . They started feeling for broken bones. Everything appeared to be in perfect alignment, but to be sure they started raising and lowering various garments until the bare truth unfolded before their anxious eyes. There, 'neath the warm, shimmering rays of a setting sun, in high relief from a grass bordered background, were two sizable red lumps soon to turn a darker hue— one on either cheek.

. . . I deposited $5 to Frank's account at staid, dependable, old Russellville Bank, a Private Bank, with more back of every dollar of its deposits than any other Bank in Indiana. As of this date, its capital stock remains at $15,000; we upped the surplus to $55,000 and upped the undivided profits to about $15,000. The deposits now run considerably over half a million. This increase . . . is not all money we made last year by a whole lot. It represents recoveries on real estate the Banking Dept. ordered us to sell back there when land was low. We just charged that stuff off out of earnings and undivided profits as we went along, as the Dept. ordered it sold or charged off. One piece the Dept. recommended we sell for $1,500 and take our loss we sold last fall for $3,300. Another they thought should be sold for about $3,000 brought $6,750 this January, cash in hand. Couldn't loan the purchaser a cent. That was bad. We've made money on every piece we took over, and have sold to date. And every property paid more than its way as we went along. . .

I really should tell you about the oldest piece of real estate we had on hands—at the extreme northeast edge of Russellville, east of the Carter house. . . It consisted of five little lots, as lonesome a five lots as you would want to see. Away back there, 20 or 25 years ago, Uncle Ernest loaned a fellow $300, and as a precaution pure and simple took a mortgage on those five lots. The fellow paid the loan down to $150 in drabs, got sick, moved away, and eventually deeded the Bank the lots and called the loan square. Time went on. No one thought much about those lots. Uncle Ernest died. The panic came on, and every once in a while, Mr. Boyd, our President, would suggest we sell "those lots up in the east part of town." In the meantime he rented the grass here and there. . .

About two years ago, Bill C_____ got drunk one day and offered Mr. Boyd $75 cash for the five . . . to pile junk on. I said "no", as they were too near the Carter house for one thing, and not enough money for another. Time went on. Finally George joined Mr. Boyd in wanting them sold, and they pretty near had Mr. Fordice in the notion of selling too. . . We were just adjourning when Bob Whitted walked in the front part of the Bank. I said to my brother Directors, "Let's sell those lots to Bob Whitted. He lives up in the east part of town." They said, "Let's see you do it."

I tackled Bob. He asked, "What do you want for all five?" I said "$350," just like that, and he didn't wince. He asked, "How do you want me to pay for them?" I said, "How do you want to pay for them?" He said, "By the month, and not more than $10 a month, and I wouldn't want you to squeeze me if I run behind sometime." I said, "Well, we're selling them to you at half price, so let's make the payments at half price—$5 a month, you to pay the taxes next Fall and from then on, and get possession today, and the deed whenever you make full payment."

He said, "How much intrust are you goin' to charge me?" I said, "We've made everything else at half price, so to keep everything balanced up, we should make the interest at half price too—3%.

He jumped up, ran his hand down in his pocket, brought up a $5 bill, and said, "I'll take you up—here is your $5 for a starter." The others were up front, but heard a good part of the talk. I called George back and we solemnly gave him the data, Bob stating the terms, and asked him to draw up a real estate sales contract. Then followed the shortest, quickest real estate sales contract it has been my privilege to view. It would have been still shorter except that I insisted George describe the real estate as "those lots up in the east part of town," not even mentioning the town's name. Mr. Boyd signed in behalf of the Bank, and Bob signed in behalf of himself and wife, saying he wanted "Grace's name somewhere on it." Bob went out. We all, including the book-keeper, looked at one another. Mr. Boyd shook his head and said Bob would never finish paying. I said, "It's a mighty easy thing to sell when you have good stuff to sell AND KNOW HOW TO SELL". . .

Saturday, George told me to get ready with Bob's deed as he was about to get paid out, and was asking about his deed already. Bob had paid away ahead of himself. Coping on his ownself. Must have sold his fox pelts. . .

Joseph N. Fordice once was in a serious quandary preparing a deed to two lots in Russellville where livestock entered into the consideration. He decided it was best to tell the truth. This resulted: "That _____, for and in consideration of $300 cash money and two hogs mutually agreed on (etc.)". . .

As ever,

Coping on his own

May 2, 1945

Dear Familee:

I spent the day at home. Yesterday and the day before I went to the farm and spent the days, easy like, grubbing and sprouting the fence lines inside the field west of the old house at Russellville. I thought I was going along pretty easy, but yesterday I must have gone at it too much in earnest because last night and this morning I had a very sore right arm, and it made me think of the pickle I got into last summer when that spell of rheumatism hit me. It was raining today, so I didn't miss much. It is a hard thing to do to go up there and just sit and loaf around. . .

Tom Walden, the "dynamite king of Russellville" is retiring from the business after 40 years of active duty. He and old man Ferguson were out near Russellville dynamiting some stumps, or rather trees, last Friday. They had set two charges and gone away about as far as they thought necessary. One charge went off, and after a reasonable delay, they went back to see what had happened to the second charge – and got there just in time. When about 8 feet away, she let go. Both are here in the local hospital. I went to see them Sunday. Tom's eyes were bandaged and at that time they did not know whether he would be blind or not. Otherwise, his face looked unusually free from abrasions or swelling, or anything in fact. It must be the charge had spent itself getting through the wrinkles. Old man Ferguson was a total mess about the face. Terribly swollen, and blue, red and black. One of his eyes may be gone. He was so swollen you couldn't see one eye a-tall. . .

May 6, 1945,

I got interrupted the other day while writing this letter.

In the meantime a fine package of cigarettes and chocolate bars came from Margaret. I hid them in the left door of the sideboard – the one that is hard to get open, and every once in a while I open the door, take a look and a good sniff, then gently close the door after a hasty glance around to see there are no eavesdroppers thereabouts. With one exception, it has been a long time since I saw chocolate bars. On the train going to Chicago to see about selling the cattle up there some time ago, I ran into a young couple (Army folks) on their way west from Norfolk. In the conversation I said something about not having seen a Hershey bar for a long time. I noticed she went down among their luggage and pretty soon he turned around and offered me a 5¢ Hershey with almonds. I didn't want to be mooching off them, but they wouldn't take no for an answer, so I took it, all the time feeling like a sheep-killing dog. The company has streamlined its product. When I got the wrapping off the two almonds stuck out like knobs on some of those red oaks up in the east pasture.

I have also had a letter from Joan. I had sent her the green hide of Seminole IV, or whatever number he bears, in an open lard can with part of the hide sticking out the top, and green hide effluvium oozing out at the bottom. Joan's description of the pimply-faced delivery boy was vivid. He asked: "What is this thing anyway?" She replied: "A cow hide, my boy. I make rugs out of 'em." The carcass of Seminole IV is safely ensconced out in the lockers awaiting the day when some dentist comes home with a formula for non-skid false teeth – the ones I have are roller-bearing – or until some of you pass this way with containers of a modest cubicle content. . .

I and my two bed sheets were well on the way to some sort of a record when Footser stepped in. Munny has been gone to Milford something like approaching two months. The weather has been cool, and I haven't been working very hard physically, and then too, have been taking baths quite regularly, so all in all my sheets were holding out splendidly. Naturally, they would wrinkle some, but any discoloration, if such there was, was gradual and uniform, except in one place – about shoulder high and between me and the radio were some streaks of chocolate running toward the radio. That happened at the time, or just after, Munny left. Each night when I crawled in, those streaks would give me a feeling of insecurity until I remembered what they were. Than I could nestle in amongst them and go to sleep – but every night I had that small shock. About two weeks ago I noticed I had a big ridge in my back each morning when I got up. Then one morning it was raining and I made an investigation. The pad under the sheet had gotten out of focus. That was remedied quickly, and while I was doing that, I smoothed out the biggest wrinkles, and felt pretty well set until the really hot weather of August would set in.

My wool socks give me the most serious tremors. If it doesn't turn warm pretty soon, I don't know what I will do. I have four pairs. They can't be sent to the laundry. I have rotated them as scientifically as my ability permits. I have rigged up a chart on the marble top of the table whereon the radio sets, and I figure a day spent at the farm sprouting and grubbing bushes, etc., is equal to from two to two and a half days at the Bank. But I find that won't do. I have to make it either two or three days, one or the other. It would be silly to sit at the Bank until noon of the second day, come home and change socks, and then go back for the remainder of that second day. . . .

"Little" Ernest's 80 acres is sold and gone and I have the money to send him, perhaps tomorrow. He got a rather good price for the land —$6,000 cash. That is not to be sneezed at. . .

Both Tom Walden and Mr. Ferguson are going to be able to see, although both are still in the Hospital of course. I shall try to go out tonight to see what they look like now.

I eat my suppers at Mrs. Bridges'. If it weren't for those meals, I don't believe I could make it. These restaurants are terrible, and my teeth are worse than that. . .

Footser's last year's room mate – the Pulliam girl – is going to get married some time this month. Her father, who is principal or sole owner of the *Indianapolis Star*, gave her some sort of shower yesterday at Indianapolis. Footser evidently went, as did about all the girls down at the Theta House. . .

Time to quit, except to say that, with the European War about over, in my judgment Japan won't be hard or very long to clean out, once the Allies get started, so Ralph should be heading this way in the more or less near future.

"Pap"

Note: The "Pulliam girl", referred to above, later became an aunt of Dan Quayle, U.S. Senator from Indiana and Vice President under President George Bush.

Meat scarce, everything up but farm income

June 6, 1945

My dear Sarah Jane:

　. . . Of late, Ira has had me on the seed wagon, filling up the drill for him with seed and commercial fertilizer, while he rides the tractor and does the sowing. Between fills I try my hand on thorn and other sapling stuff, and Tuesday night I came home almost a physical wreck. Each year it gets harder and harder climbing up and down on wagons. I used to climb the fences but now I take to the gates. Ira says I should work in "gopher hole coal mines" if I really want to know what work is. In one of those things is where Ira got his hip busted—the darned thing caved-in on him. As a result he is crippled in one leg and can't run very fast.

　But you should see him running to get between young ground hogs and their holes. Monday we drilled soy beans on what Ira calls the "wind mill field." This field has a big tile ditch running through it, and along that ditch is a clump of willows. Ira was driving the tractor pulling the drill behind, when all of a sudden he flew off his tractor and ran to the willows. He had caught three young ground hogs up a bush. He ran to the holes and kicked them full of dirt—and here the young hogs came. Having no club he used his feet. His foot batting average was .666, meaning he got two of the three. That noon he "butchered", and that took half an hour. Skinning ground hogs isn't quite like skinning rabbits. Ira eats them and says they are fine. I say nothing because long years ago, Lum Alspaugh and I went to Eel River Falls to run his grandfather's farm while the family attended Methodist Conference at Greencastle, and we tried eating everything about in wild life that wears hair or feathers— rabbits, squirrels, quail, crows, chicken hawks, buzzards, ground hogs, skunk, domestic chickens, etc. Both did the hunting but Lum was head cook—in fact he was sole cook.

I did the dish washing, if it could be called that. . . I ate enough of whatever it was to be able to say I had partaken. . . Young ground hogs are not bad, but they aren't very good either – too greasy. Ira relishes them. I prefer corn fed beef. . .

And that brings me to your questions about beef. . . The hotels and restaurants hereabouts have very little meat. Sugar Foot tells me they have red meat at the Theta House one meal each week, so that may be an indication of the general situation. . . I killed a beef in April. He has been a Godsend for Aunt Margaret and me. What we haven't eaten and the attendants out at the Locker Plant haven't stolen is still there. If you or Bob could hunt around and find a box of the right sort that would hold, say, 50 pounds of meat together with 50 pounds of dry ice, and if shipping meat to children is not contrary to law, I think something could be done to relieve you and the rest of the children in this part of the country. . . I am too busy on all this land we have to be finding out all the details and hunting up all the containers. I get up from 3 to 4 a.m. and get to bed from 9 to 10 p.m.

Now about your so-called black market. A lot of that is "old wives" and political talk. There are black markets, especially in the big centers of population, but Worcester is no big center, and if the people there are the right sort, then there is no opening for much of a black market – unless the people themselves make it. Whenever you hear of a black market you can rest assured the inhabitants themselves are to blame, because if there is no patronage then there will be no market. I am sorry to hear you say you will patronize such a market if you can find it. That is exactly what causes black markets. Blaming it all on the government or anything else is not the remedy – it is only a flimsy excuse. . . We had an embyro black market at Russellville even. Two men went down to the Hazlett boys and tried to buy a steer they were fattening for the Indpls. market. They offered a good price – more than the steer would have brought on the legitimate market. They said they would butcher it there on the farm, then in the evening they would come down and truck it home. The Hazlett boys got a bit suspicious and came to me. I told them nobody could buy a steer and butcher it then and there, farmer or no farmer. The owner would have to feed it for not less than 30 days. They refused this sale. I told them to report the prospective buyers. Don't think they did. If they come to me—which they won't—I'll report them. We don't need that sort of people in and around Russellville, or anywhere else. . .

Footser goes to Mexico City, leaving St. Louis June 20 on the Missouri Pacific Lines. She has a lower to San Antonio, then another lower to Mexico City. . . So she is set for what she thinks is a nice time in Mexico in school at that University, taking Spanish. Just the fare there and back will take a sizable steer, at the price we get for our steers, so there is where I can put in a howl, good and loud. . . George Spencer told me that before the War he paid $1.39 for shirts at Montgomery Ward's. Today the same shirt costs him over $5.50 per shirt. And George doesn't lie or resort to his imagination. Just the cold fact. At the price we pay for shirts, we should be getting $50 for cattle on the hoof. We get $16 to $18. . . Yesterday I bought 5 bananas at A&P for 23¢. I think they were the first for two or three years. Based on that price, cattle should be bringing between $30 and $35. So if anyone has a kick coming it is the farmer—just like it always has been. . . Now the thing for me to do is quit howling and get out of the cattle business and into the banana or textile business—for both of which I am too old and inexperienced. But better still, is to wait until this War is over and go into politics for the farmer, teeth and toe nail—for which I am also too old to do the very best job.

"Pap"

Controlling squirrels is tough on the roof

June 28, 1945

Dear Frank:

. . . We had a lot of corn in the crib at Ernest's place over in Montgomery County. The squirrels were eating it at a fearful rate. I expect they ate about 50 bushels of corn. The whole top of the corn in the cribs were solid cobs. I didn't know squirrels could do so much eating. Ira had been telling me about it . . . Anyway, we went over one day to bring a couple of loads back to the home farm. When we got there, there were four squirrels in the crib that we counted. They went out the back end like flying squirrels. I had the gun along. The crib had a galvanized roof. One squirrel got right up in the apex of the roof . . . I let him have it. The shot splattered more than I had thought it would, so the roof is like a sieve. Another squirrel was on the "plate" just below the tin roof, outside the crib proper. So I let him have it, and that punched about 50 holes in the tin roof outside the crib. That was darned poor judgment, but the sight of those cobs had made me see red. They came to the crib by way of the walnut trees and other trees along the west line fence. As Ira loaded, I watched that string of trees. Didn't take long for them to start a procession toward the crib. When they got on the last walnut tree, closest to the crib, I let go at them. In all, we got eight. . .

The second day, Ira was discing and I was at the crib alone loading the wagon we had brought along. . . and throwing out cobs. During one of my rests, I heard one on the roof. Soon he appears inside the crib going toward the corn . . . and he jumped on a plate under the board floor right in front of me. I had one of your skeet loads in the right barrel for just such an occasion. I thought the wooden floor would protect the roof. So I let him have it, and the sky appeared through the tin roof as if by magic. . .

"Pap"

Oldest daughter Joan's wedding party held Nov. 18, 1939, at St. Bartholomew's Chapel in New York City. (Frt r, l-r) Mary Jane McGaughey (sister of the bridegroom), Marjorie Magill, Joan (bride), Jane Durham Anderson (sister of bride and Matron of Honor), Margaret Durham (another sister of bride), Ruth Lampland Rose (writer and editor of several women's magazines), bk rw, W. Leslie Douglas (of Washington, D.C.), J. Frank Durham (brother of the bride), William H. T. McGaughey (groom), Davis Snow, Wilmer Huff , Perry L. Tewalt .

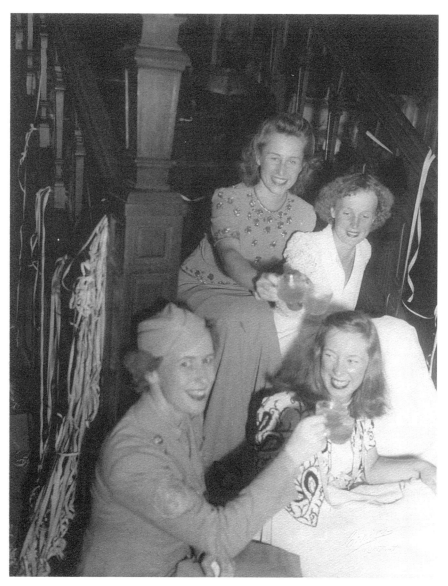

Durham sisters (minus Joan) present at brother Frank's wedding to Frances M. Haberkorn in Detroit, Michigan, on June 24, 1944.

Munny and Pap and others in the garden at Haberkorn residence during brother Frank's wdding. (l-r)
Dan Taylor (life long family friend), Munny, Pap, Jane Durham Anderson, Aura May Durham, Ann
Drew Weinrichter, Margaret Durham.

Army Private First
Class Margaret
Durham and Navy
Ensign J. Frank salute
each other.

Munny's pass on the New
York Central Railroad.

Complimentary pass on
the Panama Railrod.

Chapter V: Last Things
1946-1954

Pap was pleased when his son returned from the war to settle in Greencastle and join the law practice. In fact, as time went on, he turned over most of the cases to Frank, quit his lobbying position for the railroads, ceased attending legislative sessions and devoted more and more of his attention to the farm and his investments.

Pap being Pap, however, he could not resist using this newfound luxury of time to write scores of letters about numerous subjects to various parties. It was probably his most productive literary period. With tongue nestled securely in cheek, he wrote:

– manufacturers, suggesting new inventions (such as a carving knife made from razor blades);

– corporations, complaining about directors who had less confidence (or at least less stock) in their companies than Pap did;

– family and old friends, offering investment advice (don't speculate);

– Congressmen, opposing pork-barrel spending and advocating a balanced budget.

On at least one occasion, he even left a note attached to a package of dry-iced beef being shipped to a daughter in New England, beseeching the cooperation of railroad cargo handlers in facilitating the endeavor.

Pap took some trips with Munny or his grown children, to check up on his property in Kansas or to visit with old friends, and went on one extended journey through Latin America.

And always, he wrote.

These were Pap's "Golden Years," and he felt entitled to let his mind wander back a bit, reflecting on his youth and past glories. He was not shy about relating these memories, even to total strangers, sometimes in an allegorical manner to make a point, and sometimes just for fun.

A double-edged carving knife?

December 1, 1946

Gillette Safety Razor Company
Boston Mass.

Gentlemen:

Did I see it, hear or read about it—or did I just dream it? Somehow, somewhere or someway I have the notion a contraption was, or is on the market, consisting of a thin metal holder in which, say, three or four used double-edged razor blades can be inserted in a line, and thus make a carving knife. . . Is there such a tool, is it practical, where can it be bought and what does it cost?

Gentlemen, strange as it may seem to you, I am in dead earnest about this seemingly frivolous matter. I don't have the knack for sharpening carving knives. Scissors grinders are few and far between in a town our size. Since the advent of chain-stores, butcher shops are passé, and chain-store managers look on you as a sort of moocher when you ask them to sharpen your knives . . . Then too, a dulling carving knife slips up on you like a heavy wine. Sooner or later you come home and there is a fowl to be carved, the stores are closed and the knives are dull. Only last Thursday I rassled a turkey all over the dining room. Hence, all this is fresh in my mind and I am writing this inquiry before I again forget about it – temporarily.

I am enclosing stamped and addressed envelope for your convenience. Please do me the favor. After a fashion . . . you sort of owe it to me. I bought my first Gillette when in college sometime between 1900 and 1904. I still have it. I have used no other kind except trying an electric affair the folks gave me one time for Christmas, but I couldn't get the hang of it somehow. One of the children commandeered it long ago. So, in truth and in fact I am a 40-odd -year customer of yours. . .

Yours, for sharper carving knives,

Never on a Sunday

July 27, 1947

My dear Ann Drew:

The new Buick came a week ago last Thursday. It is some sort of supersonic model and the hind end sticks out of Ben Curtis' garage. . . Right off the bat Aunt Margaret wanted to drive the following Saturday to North Manchester to "see Ida." She telephoned Ida, who got us reservations at the local hotel for Saturday night, and up we went. . . to see Ida at the Peabody Home —an elegant place for a place of that character. Ida now is one of the oldest inhabitants and has a front room. . .After supper we drove all over town and a short way into the country and Ida liked that very, very much. Then back to the home where the evening's conversation ran to bad eyesight, constipation and poor circulation, and Ida was worried about contracting some drug habit. Aunt M. suggested whiskey to my utter surprise, and Ida countered she would be afraid she would contract the whiskey habit. The field narrowed down to fruits and fruit juices. . .

Next morning, we took Ida for a good long ride in the country. Then started for home. Things went fine until we got past Wabash on our way to Peru, and Aunt Margaret's conscience began to catch up with her, and she started quoting: "The Lord made Heaven and Earth in six days and on the 7th He rested . . . Six days shall thou work and . . . remember the Sabbath to keep it holy (etc.)" – Really, sometime she had taken a good deal of trouble to learn all her quotations – they lasted most all the way into the edge of Peru. Finally, I said: "If I felt that way about it, I wouldn't take any more Sunday trips—and she agreed heartily. . .

Somewhere between Kokomo and Crawfordsville, Aunt Margaret suggested that we "come by Frank's orchard south of Morton and get some Early Transparents," as she wanted to make a little jelly. To do that we would have to go out of our way and over a lot of loose gravel and through a lot of dust with the new shiny car, so, after a proper interval, I said: "Well, I don't know whether you would want to do that on Sunday or not"—just like a first class undertaker would say it. She thought a moment and then said: "That is right. I forgot. We can let that wait until some week day."

Between Crawfordsville and home she suggested that "we go out to Arcola next Sunday and see Aunt Laura and George." I let that one go and it was agreed she would write Aunt Laura that night and tell her we were coming. . . She wrote, but along about Wednesday she asked me if I still wanted to go out to Arcola. I said: "That is up to you". . . Friday evening she called me over and wanted me to send a telegram to Arcola saying we would not be there Sunday—her conscience had caught up again. I sent the telegram, and that was that.

That morning bright and early, Frank came over and, after the proper preliminaries and maneuvering, told me several of the VFW were going to Lebanon, about 40 miles from here, Saturday to a District Meeting; that he was to be installed District Provost, or some such thing; that the back seat of his new Ford was not very comfortable; that he was to take five of them along with him; that five would make it very crowded and uncomfortable in that small a car; that on LONG trips a Ford didn't ride as easily as a larger car; and that he was just wondering if he might take the Buick for a long hard drive like that, etc., etc. Lord! How my sympathy for those old veterans—two of whom were over 30 years of age—welled up in my throat and almost stifled me. Of course they couldn't be asked or expected to submit to the jolting and short wheel base of a brand new Ford on a trip of that character. I suggested soft pillows and plenty of wool blankets, and offered to ask Mrs. Pierce or George McHaffie, who drive cars (both octogenarians) to do the driving and see after the parking and care of the car on arrival so those foot-sore and war-wracked shells of their former selves should be put to a minimum of pain and inconvenience.

Result: They went in the Buick. It rained like hell. Frank took the Buick home and washed it, then came past Aunt Margaret's and told her what a nice ride they had had. Then home to put the car part of the way in Ben's garage.

Further result: Aunt Margaret called me at 1 p.m. today and asked if I wanted to drive down to Shakamak State Park, about 30 miles south of Terre Haute. I told her it looked like more rain—and it did—and then asked if she wanted to drive that far on Sunday. She actually laughed out loud, said she had forgotten, and to just let it go.

Time to quit,
Pap

For clarity's sake

August 13, 1947

Dear Footser:

I am trying to make this a round robin letter because since my last missive of that character I have heard from all of you except Ann Drew at least once. You will have to show this copy to Margaret and Munny, and that way everybody will have equal access to my words of wisdom.

As seems to be my custom, according to most of you, I will start out in a more or less critical vein. Your letters are hard to read, and you are to be some sort of bilingual secretary to someone having a decidedly foreign name. . . Now, down to business. You start at $35 per week, which in these days isn't much probably, but at that you have a start of $33 on me—$2 is the munificent sum I received as Head Janitor and Assistant Bookkeeper at staid, dependable, conservative, old Russellville Bank. . . Anyway and however, don't let the starting salary get you down. Everybody has to start, and those who start on a small scale sometimes get to be those who end with a big auger, boring a big hole. If the job is what you want, then the thing to do is to accept, and try it out. As long as you try and apply yourself, and work at it for the interests of your employers, you can rest assured I will help you out financially–that seems to be what us old fellers are here for.

I have written a pass for you, New York to Greencastle and return. I don't know whether it will come or not – the Roads are tightening up, especially on children who have reached maturity. . . The big roads now have a rule of issuing only so many passes to each family every year, and they evidently base the number on a normal family, as normal families go these times—so we are handicapped right at the start. . .

Sarah Jane asked about beef, and the chance to get some in some way. That is much easier said than done. it involves a whole lot of things. I will not be fattening—that is, corn feeding—any cattle this Winter. I do not have the corn, and the present crop looks mighty bad. It is quite probable I could buy a whole carcass or half a carcass for her here, but there is no easy way getting it to her. It would be very expensive, because it would have to be processed here, then shipped to her in dry ice, and dry ice is hard to get. It has to come from Indpls. and is a problem to go get and then pack around the beef back here. Then too, freight handling is questionable and it would be a mighty easy thing to get side-tracked and thus spoil. Beef out here is also very high. . .

Find out where the roller towels are. The one you and Margaret left was a bit dirty when you got away, and now it looks like the one at the old high school building that hung at the side of the printing press . . ..

Pap

Thanks for the compliment anyway

February 3, 1948

The Honorable Frank M. Martin
Spencer, Indiana

My dear Frank:
    . . . You have made it hard to refuse your kind and thoughtful offer to make the after-dinner talk in March. There are many, many reasons why I should not, among them being I am totally out of practice, and my experience with false teeth has been fearful—and unexpected.
    Frank, I want you to realize I am sincerely obliged for your thoughtfulness in asking me down. Invitations of that character are coming fewer and farther between. As a matter of cold fact, however, I am oratorically about where old Anthony Battle, an ex-slave, was financially a long time ago when Uncle Bob Black operated a horse and mule sale barn here. Needing some change, he turned to Anthony and asked him if he had change for a $10 bill. "No suh", said Uncle Anthony, "but ah thanks you fo' th' compl'ment jes th' same."
                                                    As Ever,

Tickets to the Indy 500

March 17, 1948

Mr. B. Ryall Chant
Care: Chant & Co.
Port Jervis, New York
My dear Ryall:
    I have your letter of March 10th, concerning tickets for the 500 Mile Race and hotel reservations for May 28-31, 1948.

I have had reservations made for you at the Claypool Hotel. . . Due to the tremendous demand for rooms all hotels hike their prices for the Race and all require advance deposits. . . Your entire room bill will be $53—$45 of which must be paid in advance. . . The Claypool is the Royal Baking Powder of Indianapolis hotels, but the Lincoln is beginning to cut-in. All Race activities, however, will be centered in and around the Claypool.

Tickets for the Race are something else again. They begin going in the Fall prior to the Race. Being a Democrat and therefore in disrepute in Indiana these past three years, I had to work through Railroad connections to the Governor's No. 1 man, who is a R.R. associate and who assures me he will get the best tickets available, due to the fact the Race people always retain desirable seats—just in case. I tried to get you in a box within hailing distance, at least, of His Honor, but in my judgment, if you ever see him there at all, he will appear about the size of a blue-bottle fly. Remember the track is two and a half miles per lap and all the grandstand, paddock and other seating is outside the track. . . Naturally, I am getting you as near the starting (and finishing) wire as is humanly possible this late date. . . . I do not know the cost of the tickets, but my guess is $15 to $18 each. . .

You will probably see a half-mile of 100 and more massed bands coming down the stretch, as one of the preliminaries. All the Fords, Firestones, Chryslers, Buicks, Packards, Goodyears, Nashes, Goodrichs and Perfect Circle Rings will be among those present, and you will look over a square mile and better of solid parked cars. Castor oil fumes will make you think of Ma and Pa long years ago. . .

Yours, for more paddock seats,

Some genuine Indiana maple 'molasses'

March 24, 1948

Hon. S.C. Murray, General Counsel
New York Central System
La Salle Station
Chicago, Illinois

My dear Mr. Murray:

I am sending you some maple molasses almost hot from the evaporator. These molasses are the product of the President of our small Bank at Russellville, Mr. Harold A. Fordice, who is a Presbyterian, a Wabash College graduate, a Phi Beta Kappa, a Republican—and a bachelor. He is also a most ethical gentleman, and therefore far, far from adulterating his molasses with anything whatsoever, as is now pretty much the custom by reason of the fact maple molasses prices have soared about like I did the time I first took the oath as a Member of the General Assembly at Indianapolis in 1913 . . . adulterated flavor is almost forgotten. Children, generally speaking, do not like it. They prefer sugar syrups. What you will be receiving is the pure article. . . Maple molasses hereabouts are almost a thing of the past—like wild pigeons and Democratic landslides. The old trees are dying out, and no new ones coming on. Lately, the new President of Wabash College sent down to Russellville a general order for 100 gallons. . .

Respectfully,

P.S. A real old time genuine Hoosier never speaks of the Indiana brand as being a "maple syrup."

A.E.D.

Where's the beef ?

Undated note attached to a package of frozen beef shipped by rail.

To whomsoever reads this:

This baggage contains some frozen beef an old Hoosier pappy is taking his daughter and grandchildren in Worcester, Mass. It left Greencastle, Ind., at 12:50 p.m. (?) 3-29-49 on N.Y.C. No. 12 (Southwestern). The old pappy and his meat will probably part company at Buffalo, where his car will be transferred to N.Y.C. No. 28 (New England States) that evidently does not carry baggage. So, where and how his meat will go from Buffalo on, only you will know—the old pappy hopes the quickest and most direct way, and therefore respectfully asks your help, if you can give any.

The meat you are sitting on just didn't happen—like paw paws and wild black berries. It is out of an 1,800-pound, nearly three-year-old Hereford steer, dry-lot and corn-fed for over a year. In case you don't know . . . the 1947-48 and 1948-49 winters in Indiana weren't exactly like Miami Beach of a sunny Sunday afternoon. . . Rain, snow and sleet. Cold rubber boots in February mud. Sockless shoes in July dust. All the clothes you can pile on in winter, and about all the law allows you to take off in hot summer. . . The cement water tank has to be kept full of clean drinking water in summer, and the tank warmer going on below freezing days.

"Seminole IV," as we called him, to finish out well, had to have a clean place in the barn to eat, to stand in, and to sleep in. That called for a pitch fork, a strong back, and a conveniently placed manure spreader. Fresh bedding, feed grinder going every other day, a handy block of salt, a little ground alfalfa hay, the gates and corn crib doors kept shut. . . We'll say nothing about the 150 odd bushels of ground corn it took to put Seminole to 1,800 pounds, but it didn't just sift itself into his feed trough automatically—from nowhere.

No. There was more to Seminole than the well-trimmed sirloin steak you see on the kitchen table all ready for the broiler.

And so it may happen after grandpappy is gone and the grand-children are grown-up and in well-worn harness themselves, they will say, "Well, the old fellow was a pretty good sort after all, but, on the other hand, it does seem that with the War prices they had in his day, he could have left a little more if he had tried a little harder."

Just in the event you want to make some comments and have the time and inclination to tell of Seminole's progress and last whereabouts, I am enclosing some addressed post cards for your convenience. Nothing compulsory—wholly voluntary.

> I thank you.
> Prayerfully,

Cuban divorce, not horse disease

June 17, 1949

U.S. Senator Homer E. Capehart
Washington, D.C.

My dear Senator

I am in rather urgent need of learning all the grounds for Divorce in Cuba. Is that information easily available to you there in Washington? If so, I would greatly appreciate such information. The information I am seeking is of considerable value to some interested clients here.

In your experience as Senator you have doubtless had some rare requests from the "folks back home." This inquiry of mine should rank rather high. A year ago . . . I could not then visualize my divorce practice getting much beyond the confines of the State of Indiana.

This letter reminds me of an experience I had long years ago. . . I wrote my Congressman, Ralph Moss, asking if he would send me a copy of Jefferson's Manual. In due course of mail here came a rather well-bound copy of "The Diseases of Horses," and a note saying he had had considerable difficulty complying with my request as the edition was exhausted. How it happened that way, I will never know—nor did Mr. Moss. . .

A better use for 'removable seats'?

June 24, 1949

Case & Sons
Robinson, Illinois

Gentlemen:

I'm having a devil of a time with a Case lavatory in the second floor bathroom here at home, and to me it seems far rougher than it should be. The cold water faucet sprung a drip—a most persistent drip. My friend and plumber, Mr. Lee Reeves, came up from time to time and eventually diagnosed the case (no intended pun on your name) as the water in the cold faucet having cut or worn a groove across the top of the removable seat for that faucet. He had none to fit, so he sort of filed the groove out, said the repair would probably be temporary, and in the meantime we'd both begin a quest for Case removable seats that would fit. I went to Indianapolis to the Central supply Co. They said they had none, but if they did they'd have to know the number or size of the lavatory, as different-sized lavatories had different-sized removable seats. I came home but could find no number. . .

I bought that lavatory from you in person, direct, about 1942— or just about the time the Government stopped your selling to the proletariat. I was frantic for some bathroom fixtures. The family had taken a fancy to yours on account of its alleged quietness. The girls were in the University here. It was brooded among my womenfolk that every time they had company the "old man" started the water going in the bathrooms and it sounded like Coulee Dam after a hard rain. I got in the car and drove to Robinson. You folks finally fixed me up with two lavatories. I brought them home in the car. It must have been that at that same time you ordered me a bath tub from Louisville or Cincinnati. . .

In due time the old you-know-what started her drip, drip, drip, getting worse. . . Yesterday Mr. Reeves came up with an assortment of removable seats he had collected. He took out the offending removable seat, and sure enough, the water or pixies or gremlins had again cut a channel across the top of said removable seat. He thought he had a removable seat that would fit—it seemed the same size as the original—but it didn't. In desperation he gave up the job. We turned off the cold water intake at the valve underneath. He took the old offending removable seat for further efforts to get a duplicate. We heartily damned removable seats of all and every kind and character and wheresoever situated, together with the companies who made 'em.

Woe is me. Evil days have come. The half has not been told herein. In my troubled sleep I am beset with removable seats. In my waking hours I am confounded by removable seats. Time was only yesteryear when I didn't know, or care, what a removable seat was. Within a fortnight or so removable seats have become deadly—like unto a cobra or black widow. The neighbors are clandestinely talking about a Guardian . . .

Can't you do something for us? Can't you find the original invoice (somewhere near 1942) or can't you decide from this enclosed masterpiece of a drawing of mine what kind and size of removable seats we are needing, and send me four (two for each lavatory, just in case)? I need removable seats. I long for removable seats. Send them with the compliments of the Company, or else enclose a bill and I'll gladly pay it—I suppose. I'm not so sure about the "gladly" part. . .

And yet, withal, removable seats of a sort could be a boon. I am thinking now if they could be available to our womenfolk who have reached or passed the age of 40 years, say. We live here in the older, more conservative part of town—what you might call the Eastern Star and DAR section. I have mentally canvassed our one block. If you can devise a practical feminine removable seat, I can give you every reasonable assurance you will get from one to two orders in every house and apartment in our block. I personally guarantee one order. This being true, then visualize all the States (particularly the corn belt), and then the entire known world, with special stress on Holland, parts of Germany and all of Italy—to say nothing about the Eskimos and Africans. It will stagger you, as your faucet removable seat has staggered, yea, paralyzed me.

And thus I leave it. Do something, I beseech you.

> Prayerfully,
> Andrew E. Durham

In subsequent correspondence to daughter Margaret, Pap related that the above letter had the desired effect, because by return mail the company sent him four removable seats, at no charge. However, the world is still awaiting action on his suggestion for a broader application of removable seat technology.

Of questionable repute

November 5, 1949

Hon. Claud Bowers
U.S. Minister to Chile
Santiago, Chile

My dear Ambassador:

This is a voice from the long, long ago. It must have been about 1904 you were a candidate for Congress against old man Holiday. I was just out of college. During the campaign you made some very force-ful and logical speeches backed by excellent oratory. I attended and was fascinated—got the political bug. I am not quite sure I got in on what we called the "Week's County Drive" of your campaign, where the "small fry" in the last cars of the cavalcade ate miles and miles of gravel and road dust kicked up by the cars on ahead. If not, then I sure got in on them later.

My daughter, Aura May Durham, and I hope to arrive in Santiago, December 20, 1949, during a rather extended trip into South America. I am enclosing a copy of our alleged itinerary. We are having consid-erable—very considerable —trouble arranging for some six visas, or their equivalents. But we expect to arrive on schedule if humanly possible, provided I retain my heretofore good health and reasonably fair mental facilities. I have been vaccinated and "shot" for about ev-erything except treason, but my lack of a criminal record is univer-sally questioned south of the Equator. Our local Chief of Police has, for the past four weeks, valiantly signed varying documents denying varying insinuations I have a criminal record and . . . our local banker has spent long nights compiling "letters of commendations and respon-sibility" that would tend to meet the requirements. . .

All this and much more has gotten me to where I am. It is too much for a small-town Hoosier lawyer to stand—and a Democrat to boot. And so, if on or about December 20th, you see a rather sprightly young woman leading a doddering old man in his upper 60's into the lobby of the Carrera Hotel, then charitably reflect, "it was not always so with him."

Naturally, I would be immensely pleased to see you.

Yours, for more respect and credibility South of the Border for small-town Hoosier Democrats,

Andrew E. Durham

Speculation no, boarders maybe

July 17, 1950

Dear Footser,

Your AT&T dividend check just came this morning. The Quaker
came the latter part of last week. I waited until both were in before
mailing same to you. You evidently have 32 shares of the former and
10 of the latter—not a bad showing for one of your age—far more
investment than I had at your age. Looks like, with a little more investment, you will be getting something like $1 per day from invest-
ments alone. That will be something not exactly to be sneezed at. . .

Annabelle Lee wrote me that someone had advised her to sell
her Quaker and take her profit, lay the money aside and then invest
in something else at a low price. That, to my way of looking, is bad
advice. The money might lay and lay, and then when she did invest,
she might buy something that would not be so good. Then too she
would have to pay income taxes on the profit. . . Good stocks do not
rise or fall rapidly. It's the "cats and dogs" that do that. And there is
where the speculators come in. They are *supposed* to know a good deal
about "cats and dogs" . . . Two or three or four years ago, I bought 100
shares of General Motors for about $4,000. It sells for more than double
that now. All of which is quite fine, but you bet your boots I am not
selling mine for the profit. I bought that 100 shares to keep. It is nice
to see your stocks on the uprise – fine and dandy – but if I sold it now,
what would I put the money in, with my limited knowledge of stocks
and stock prices, advances and declines? No, the thing for me to do is
to keep it and hope that the company gets stronger and stronger, and
better and better. . .

Tommy Rivers, of Russellville, has finished installing the dish-
washer, two sinks, dispos-all, and cabinets. Together, they take the
whole south side of the kitchen—a formidable array. Munny was bent
on having two big sinks, and now, by golly, she has them. The kitchen

looks like a city hotel kitchen, so now, I've been casting about for boarders. . . We've just got to make that outlay back somehow. . .

P.S. The dandelion count is now 20,130.

Pap

A specialist in fashion reform

April 2, 1951

Beymer & Beymer
Lakin, Kansas
Attention: Mr. Clyde Beymer Jr.

My dear Mr. Beymer:

On March 23, 1951, I wrote my nephew in California by Air Mail concerning the proposed sale of our quarter section in Kearny County.

I look back. When I was about the right age for such things, my father's $12 to $15 suits and 10¢ socks, especially the latter, looked pretty common to me. Also a lot of other things about him and the family generally. I expressed as much. At first he paid no attention. I persisted. He wakened one day with this:

"I've been thinking about your case a good deal. You seem to have the making of a fine merchant tailor and big city haberdasher. I've accordingly made arrangements. Next September you are going to a Military School (in those days considered more or less of a high class reform school) where they all dress alike, and where you can do them a lot of good in dress reform. So get ready."

And you know, after graduation there in 1899, on coming home, and thereafter, Pap's 10¢ black socks and unvarying gray suits got to looking better and better as the few remaining years went by. . .

Respectfully,

Skip the 'hearts and hands'

October 22, 1951

Hemphill, Noyes, Graham, Parsons & Co.
15 Broad Street
New York 5, N.Y.

Gentlemen:

I am just in receipt of a faded and washed-out 8x12" sheet of paper . . . that at first glance would seem to indicate I am now the proud owner of 100 shares of the common stock of Dun & Bradstreet, Inc., but subject to enough whereases, to-wits, here inserts, and/ors, etc., as to make me wonder just what it is I do have. . .I say "faded and washed-out." That is a true Churchillian understatement. I feel rather sure some of the Dun or Bradstreet children must have thrown my whatever-it-is in the creek back of their house where it has laid immersed since Oct. 2, 1951, the date I was supposed to have bought 100 shares of D&B.

Said certificate bears this hopeful imprint near the top—"TEMPORARY CERTIFICATE: Exchangeable for Engraved Certificate when ready for delivery." That is more or less encouraging but a bit vague. Who or what is referred to in that statement of readiness—the Company, or me, or the Engraved Certificates after they get dried-out from being in the creek too?

The above reminds me of the marriage license situation in Indiana. Here, prospective brides and grooms appear together before the Clerks of the various Circuit Courts to make out preliminary papers and then buy their licenses. The State furnishes a plain, printed 8x12 license for $1.50. That one is authoritative and originally intended to end the fee then and there. But our Clerks of today are away ahead on Court House psychology. And anybody who has ever been a groom knows grooms are totally *non compes mentis* on such occasions. So here is what happens to them. . . The affable Clerk says nothing about the $1.50 license, but with solemn and measured tread goes to the safe, which is always in plain view, fumbles with the combination and, after a bit more fumbling in the dark recesses of the safe, as solemnly returns with three shiny, crackling parchment rolls of different lengths – a 10x14 lithographed Sheaf of Wheat with the usual recitals in scroll, price $5; a 12x18 Gates-Ajar beauty with even more scrollwork, price $10; and a magnificent 16x24 Heart and Hand master License, with a beautiful red heart just over the clasped hands, and endlessly scrolled, price $15—"something I knew you fine young citizens of our County would want the moment I first saw you come in the door," etc. . . .

But to get back. Would you please enlighten me as to just what I do have, and what, if anything, I can expect in the future, and when? If you are on speaking terms with any of the Messrs. Dun & Bradstreet, tell 'em your corn-fed Hoosier customer, while considerably puzzled with what he has, is onto the County Clerk's racket in Indiana, and he doesn't want any Heart and Hand permanent D&B Certificate, but just an uninundated one the Company furnishes, and he wants it free, including postage both for the new Certificate and the return of the water-soaked variety – although he doesn't think the latter is worth return postage. . .

Yours, for readable Certificates—for free,

Fast thinking in a revolving door

February 5, 1952

Mrs. Cecil Harden
Member, House of Representatives
Washington, D.C.

My dear Mrs. Harden:
Having been a Member of the Indiana Legislature years ago, I

know what it is to receive letters, memorials, petitions and remonstrances from "the best constituency in the World," as your remote predecessor, "Red" Purnell, used to say. I wanted to know who they were and what sort of axes they had to grind. Hence, here is a short pedigree of your correspondent. I live in Greencastle; am a farmer, small town banker (Russellville Bank), married, 6 children—5 of them girls, Presbyterian, Notary Public, Democrat, can balance diced potatoes on my knife with the best of them, and encountered my first revolving door at Tiffany's in New York City in the year 1905.

This last was due to the fact "Red" and I had gone to New York to show the effete East just what sort of young manhood the Mid-west was producing, and hoped to impress them accordingly. Vain hope. "Red" was engaged to Elizabeth (his wife). I was to be "best man." On the train enroute, "Red" decided he had to get Elizabeth a silver spoon with the name "Tiffany" on it. After riding up 5th Avenue on one of those busses that had a spiral stairway at the back leading up to the open air top (it was January and we were up there alone of course), the better to get the panoramic view, we alighted. . . "Red," being the prospective purchaser, led the way to said door and into it—and came around and right back again. At Indiana University I had taken a course in Public Speaking with the ultimate object of supplanting Senator Beveridge and William J. Bryan on the speaker's platform. In this course, Prof. Clapp had stressed "learning to think with lightning speed on your feet." There I was on my feet and eager to demonstrate that father had not sold shoat after shoat in vain, for my educational expenses. With lightning rapidity I diagnosed the error and went in and stayed in. "Red" made it his next try.

The above was intended to be short but something led me to think about "Red", and away I went.

I want to call your attention to a matter . . .

Why don't you come to Greencastle one of these days and come to see us? I don't believe we've had a Congressman regularly in the house since "Red" Purnell used to infest us. It would advance our social position.

Yours, for social advancement, and a change in the top brackets there in Washington next Fall,

A pass

June 23, 1952

Honorable George W. Henley
Citizens Trust Building
Bloomington, Indiana

My dear George:

A Monon Railroad pass? Manna from Bloomington! . . . I am tremendously pleased and thankful for your kindness and thoughtfulness in this matter. I don't want to sound egotistical but I think I am known as the "Railroad man" of these parts, and as such, I have been asked if I carried passes, among them of course, if I had a Monon pass. Naturally it was none of the asker's business, but when in telling I had none, it was a trifle embarrassing and caused a sort of wonderment on the part of the inquirer, because, among other things, I never failed during the years when talking at the University or the various Service Clubs to get in a thought as to how the Railroads were being imposed upon and receiving very unfair treatment at the hands of the Legislature and Public generally. I think it has paid off, because after these long years, our and bordering Senators and Representatives in the Legislature have been inclined very generally to protect the Railroads. Not always, but quite generally.

Please be assured I do not want any paying employment at the hands of the Monon. I have virtually retired and turned things over to my son, who is Prosecutor here. I just handle a bit of probate work —old clients. . .

Cordially,

A modest family art showing

July 30, 1952

American Telephone and Telegraph Company
195 Broadway
New York 7, N.Y.

Gentlemen:

Under date of July 21, 1952, three of my family and I subscribed for a total of $5,900 of your 3 % debentures... On July 26, I received a telephone call from your New York office saying you had received the subscription. The woman to whom I talked answered in detail all the information I had asked for, clearly, distinctly, concisely and to the exact point. She was a whiz.

A short time ago I found myself a trifle out of place in the midst of an enthusiastic discussion of Art, art galleries, beautiful paintings, elusive smiles, precious lights and shadows, inconceivable imagination and some superlatives far, far beyond my ken. Suffice to say, in my corn-fed Hoosier simplicity an engraved Certificate for 100 shares of American Telephone and Telegraph is about the prettiest picture I have seen.

Therefore, patiently anticipating a very modest October private family showing of Art at its best, as I see it, I remain

Respectfully,

Judging by the dampness

September 16, 1952

The First National Bank of Chicago
Chicago, Illinois
Dear Sirs,

I am herewith enclosing 3 certificates of the Capital Stock of Standard Oil Company (New Jersey) as follows . . . It is my request that the above certificates be combined into one . . .

It may be I should have sent these certificates to the Transfer Agent rather than you, but . . . I feel more at home with your Bank, for, let it be known, I am still a part of Russellville Bank in this County. As head Janitor of that Institution in the mid-90's, we opened an account with your good Bank, and it is still open. Later I rose to such responsibility therein I was permitted to write with pen and ink (Arnold's Ink in earthenware bottles or jugs) Russellville Bank's Letters of Transmittal to your Bank. That done, I would carry said letter back behind the safe to the "letter press," open the thin sheeted copy book and . . . lay my letter face up below a clean sheet. I would then pick up the 3 gallon bucket and go to the town pump down the street toward the railroad and get a fresh bucket of water. Next I would put a rectangular piece of cloth made for the purpose into the bucket of water and then squeeze it to a proper stage of dampness. Then spread it over the clean sheet . . . Then close the copy book and put it in the press and start revolving the wheel of said press much like the old time brakeman would "set" the brake on a box car before the advent of air brakes. The process would give us a copy of said letter of transmittal and at the same time a questionable policy of insurance against you big city Banker slickers claiming you never received a check of correction from Butler Brothers to our local general store, Inge, Ross & Co.

It is true that success of operation in all of this did depend in a minor way on getting the component parts in proper order—a boy had to be alert at all times, as was becoming a future teller and money changer, but the real artistry and measure of responsibility lay in getting the proper dampness in the cloth. If too wet, the ink of the letter spread to hell and gone. If too dry, the sturdy dependable Arnold's Ink made no impression on the clean sheet.

You who read this may have become disgusted with all this old time stuff long before now and said to yourselves, "Why all this junk when the main idea is to get a new Certificate?" The answer is I got a bit retrospective as I was writing. I got back to the $2 a week days when father insisted I save at least 10¢ a week out of that.

But bear with me just a little longer. The copy book cloth technique I acquired at Russellville Bank was to become a boon later, when, as the six children came along, seemingly with too much regularity, I could slip an educated hand under the bottom of a sleeping infant and measure the dampness thereof to a nicety and judge to a fraction just when the cloth *HAD* to be changed. Maybe those Russellville Bank experiences were later to save me the possibility of facing the notoriety incident to an indictment for infanticide by drowning.

Yours, for bigger and better posting machines, et. als., and sharper carbon paper,

Hitler's favorite picture is safe

Sept. 27, 1952

Dear Sugar Foot:

Munny and I returned last evening from a short visit with Mr. and Mrs. Walter J. Behmer at Culver, Indiana, on Lake Maxinkuckee or however it is spelled. Had a fine time. . .

Yesterday, we got an early start home. I wanted to see a little private bank at San Pierre, Ind., away up north of Lafayette on old No. 43. It used to be a private bank, but I found out they had changed to a state bank just this last January. Didn't stay there long.

Munny wanted to see Elizabeth Shoaf Purnell (Red's widow) who lives at Attica, Ind. . . . (She)was giving a party tonight for another old woman friend of ours, and who is her cousin, the former Miss Sina Booe; then became Sina B. Songer; then Sina B. Ross; and now has a new husband, some Frenchman whose name I do not remember and am too hurried to look up. They were married about the first of this year. She met him at Hot Springs, Arkansas—and is he a honey? He is. (After seeing Elizabeth we came home by way of Veedersburg, where Sina and said husband now live. Sina's parents struck oil years and years ago, and built a rather pretentious house in Veedersburg. At the time of the striking of oil, Red Purnell said to me that the "oil would agree with Sina," and it has). If ever I saw an adventurer for a rich widow, he is it. She is about 75 and he is 12 years younger than she. Therefore he will outlast her, in all probability. I doubt if he has ANY business, but says he is a sort of artist; sells pictures or something like that. Says he will be having an exhibit soon in New Orleans and southern cities. For a wedding present he gave her two pictures—God knows what they are. I think I probably saw them but am confused with the multitude of objects he showed hanging all over HER house. She takes all that stuff in like a real soldier. I have seen four flushers in my time —but he is tops in my opinion.

This new husband talks a blue streak and he fails utterly to speak illy of himself. To be truthful, I was amazed the way he talked. Maybe the highlight—if there could be a highlight in his conversation—went something like this. On the grand piano (Sina's) was a small picture in a sort of glass rope frame. We think the picture was named "Blowing Bubbles." Anyway, it was one of Hitler's favorites and Bro. Hitler kept it on his desk. In some miraculous way, this new husband of Sina's got hold of it. I think he said he stole it, maybe meaning he gave so little for it that same was next to stealing, but however he got it, it is now valued at $250,000, which I would say was a dam sight too high, but sitting there in Veedersburg on Sina's piano, right out in the open, I should venture the guess it will soon disappear once the Public finds out its value. There is one thing sure—I will never break into Sina's house to steal that picture. It is absolutely safe so far as I am concerned, much safer than the weather-beaten tomatoes on Ben's back porch right here next door.

Eventually he asked my business. I told him I was a farmer, and then the fireworks did start. Above all things on this Earth he wanted to be a farmer. That was his life's ambition, and on and on he went. I told him there was much more about farming than meets the naked eye.

Sooner or later Munny will give you the address up on 5th Ave. near Tiffany's where he is very prominent in some way or other.

This will do for today
Pap

Methodist pioneers think of Peru

November 16, 1952

Dear Footser:

. . . I have, in a rather small way, suggested to Munny and Margaret that we try to spend from mid-January to about mid-April in Lima, Peru. . . There was an article in the Nov., 1952, *Holiday* telling about Peru and how cheap it was to live there. . . I realize how much of a handicap we would be under. As time goes on, I get a little deafer, and God knows I am too old to try to learn any Spanish. . . If we could rent a modern furnished house and get reliable servant(s), then I don't know but what I'd try it. I just don't like cold weather. At the same time, I don't want to get into any particularly tight place. The article in *Holiday* was very favorable, as you know it would be. But the real facts might be far, far different. If I were 30 years younger, and without any wife or family, I think now, I'd sure try it just for the hell of it, if for nothing else. I wouldn't under those circumstances stand back, or even be fearful. But as it is, it is different. What do you think about it?

Frank and I had a whale of a time last month going to Kansas, Okla., Texas, Miss. and Kentucky. You just don't know how high in Methodist circles us Durhams are. I'll tell you. I found it all out on this trip Frank and I took. Grandpappy, my grandpappy, Jacob Durham, came to Russellville from Perryville, Ky., in about 1828. About three miles east of Perryville, on the way to Danville, is what is known even now as the old Durham Farm. A man named Godbey now owns it. Old man. He was there when Munny and I went camping on that farm about 35 years ago. His mother was a Durham. Well, since we were there, the Pioneer Mothers or DAR or Methodists or somebody have erected a granite monument to my great, great grandpappy, one John Durham. He owned the farm, and in 1783 he organized the first Methodist Church—then called "Methodist Society"—west of the Allegheny Mountains. He built a log church on his farm about 300 feet from where the monument now stands. The marker says that, and the records in the First Methodist Church of Danville back it up. My great Uncle Milton Durham in the 1890's, put a stained glass window in said church, with a full size picture in colored glass of what they must have imagined John Durham looked like. But there it is, brass marker and all. Uncle Milton graduated from Old Asbury in 1844, I think it was. Grandpa Durham put him through college. I have seen him. He carried the cane for a few years prior to his death. He was tall, and the cane didn't reach the ground. He was the first Comptroller of the Currency the U.S. ever had. Grover Cleveland appointed him in the '80s.

Now what do you think of all that? And to think this Methodist DePauw University some 50 odd years ago broke relations with me, and the faculty gave me 24 hours to leave—23 of which I still have coming to me.

Pappy

Pap's final reference above was to the university's intention to suspend him for organizing a fraternity dance during his student days. He beat them to the punch by switching to Indiana University to finish out his college years.

The indomitable Bettie Locke

Pap wrote this speech for his daughter Ann to deliver at a convention of sorority Kappa Alpha Theta.

Bettie Locke Hamilton—the fabulous Bettie Locke of Greek letter sorority lore and literature was no hand for dalliance, amorously or otherwise, in 1868 or any other time thereafter up to her death in 1939.

Indiana Asbury University (now DePauw University) located at my hometown, Greencastle, Indiana, decided to admit female students, beginning in the Fall of 1868, after a debate that started on a high level after much prayerful thought and meditation and ended in a knock-down and drag-out verbal fight that divided the dignitaries, bisected the Methodist Church temporarily, split the faculty into two hostile camps and put the town into a dither—from railroad depot to barber shop and livery barn.

Rumor hath it that promptly at 8 o'clock on the morning of opening day, Bettie Locke presented herself for admission—the first female registrant of Asbury. Later, four other young ladies of a more timid disposition presented themselves and begged registration... Two years later, Kappa Alpha Theta—co-founded by Bettie Locke Hamilton, Alice Allen Brant, Bettie Tipton Lindsay and Hannah Fitch Shaw—became the first "Greek letter fraternity known among women." And that too was as Bettie Locke would have it.

In her girlhood days, Bettie Locke showed a disposition that was to develop into a Will of Iron . . . Her vocabulary was enormous, her diction virtually perfect, her stage presence commanding. The Theta Convention at Estes Park, Colorado, was in the summer of 1930 or '31. My oldest sister, Joan, was a delegate from Alpha Chapter. Bettie Locke Hamilton went along. It was near the last convention she attended. Mind you that was within eight or nine years of her death, and she must have been well in the 80s at the time of her decease. She spoke extemporaneously, and "brought down the house". . .

Bettie Locke was free in giving both unsolicited advice and criticism, as witness the following true story. My father started practicing law early in this century. Clients were few and far between . . . He was standing in front of the stairs leading to his modest office when along came Bettie Locke. She saw both him and his head piece, a cap he had acquired in college days. She strode straight up and said, "Andrew, a cap is unbecoming a young man starting the practice of law. Take it off and never let me see it again." He did—and she never. . .

Bettie Locke had a positive opinion about almost everything. She loathed lipstick. She abhorred bobbysox, and her opinion of short hair and short dresses was virtually unprintable. But don't get me wrong in the inference of those last words. No one, no where, at no time ever heard Bettie Locke utter one profane, vile or smutty word. She was too cultured and had too good a command of the English language for that. She used sarcasm couched in such classical language that the targets of her shafts only wished she would wax profane and vulgar. . .

Our family home is just off the DePauw campus, and a great many students pass to and fro. Many has been the time Bettie Locke would come and sit and talk with my Mother on our front porch. And sooner or later the conversation would turn to the Thetas, and college girls in general and how they were doing, or drift back to her days—the 1860s and '70s. But just let a female in slacks—or shorts—I must mention shorts a second time—heave in sight and Bettie Locke was off and gone in a blistering monologue. And how she could blister.

Bettie Locke staunchly stood up for her rights. She never lost her voice. . . In her late years her teeth caused considerable trouble. She would not hear to having them all pulled and plates substituted, but allowed them to go one by one whenever the pain became unbearable. Among the last was a big molar, that by the time she had to come to her dentist had become so infected and ulcerated nothing could be done about it except extract it. The good Dr. Overstreet explained all this and then proceeded to extract it without further ado.

On the way home she thought it all over, and the nearer home she came the madder she got. . . Neighbors added fuel, and with it some "chimney-corner law," as Hoosier lawyers call it. Next morning she stormed into the office and went straight to the point, as was her custom. "Doc, I'm going to sue you. Indeed I am. And you needn't try to talk me out of it. You had no right to pull that tooth without my consent. You had it out before I knew what you were doing. I was not consulted." . . . Nothing ever happened, but the time never came when Bettie Locke ceased threatening him with that suit. . .

It was not to be for me to know Bettie Locke in her peaches and cream days. I was to know her in her poi and soft food days. We children were rather afraid of her. She lived alone. The house was dark and rather forbidding. Some . . . who had felt her verbal barbs sometimes referred to her as the "witch of Walnut and Locust Streets." In later life she harbored a kitchen and cellar full of cats. None were aristocrats. They were the alley variety and had a pedigree about as long as my Spanish vocabulary. . .

I can't afford to lose this chance for getting a little matter before you, because after this forensic effort I may never get the chance to talk again in public. It has to do with my Theta pedigree. . . I virtually stem back to one of the Founding Mothers herself. . . Bettie Tipton, the one and only Bettie Tipton so far as we are concerned, and my Grandmother Durham were cousins—their mothers were Blacks and they all lived on farms near Mt. Sterling, Kentucky. Bettie Tipton was opposite of Bettie Locke. She came from the blue grass and was as feminine as baby breath. . . She too had a hectic experience at Indiana Asbury, compared with the sheltered home in the blue grass from whence she had come. Maybe I'll tell you that story some time.

Another early feminist

December 16, 1952

Mr. and Mrs. Garnett Reed Chenault
Mt. Sterling, Kentucky

My dear Mr. and Mrs. Chenault,

I have just received your very kind and thoughtful letter, together with the newspaper enclosure concerning the Tipton family in Montgomery County, Kentucky. You are a most considerate couple. On behalf of my sister, Mrs. Margaret D. Bridges, now about 90 and almost blind and quite deaf, and myself, I thank you. Mrs. Bridges, in the early 1880s, and as a sprightly young Miss, visited her cousin, Amanda Black Tipton and husband Burwell . . .

You possibly might be interested to know that Burwell's daughter Bettie (who married a Lindsay and after marriage lived in Winchester, Ky.), through a combination of ability, aggressiveness, chance and fate, came to be a famous woman nationally. Asbury College (now DePauw University) a staid Methodist school here in Greencastle, opened its doors to women students in 1870—an unheard-of thing. And here came Bettie, bringing along her charming southern ways. Females were frowned-on by the young college men as interlopers and undesirables, and were subjected to some indignities. Bettie et. als. persisted. Bettie, along with three other young women students, founded the first Greek Letter Sorority in the world, Kappa Alpha Theta. That brought another blast. Today Kappa Alpha Theta is the oldest, largest and wealthiest of the 35 to 50 others that have followed. Its assets run into the millions. And Bettie's name is known throughout the civilized world wherever a "Theta," as they call themselves, lives, because all Thetas are required to memorize the names of the founders as a prerequisite to initiation. I know. My five daughters are Thetas.

Another thing about the fabulous Bettie. When it came time to graduate, Bettie and some young man were nip and tuck as to leadership in scholarship, but Bettie's grades were a shade higher. What to do about Class Valedictorian? The College authorities approached the formidable Bettie on behalf of the young man. He was to become a famous Methodist minister and would go out into the world preaching the Gospel. It would add greatly to his prestige to go out as having been Valedictorian of his graduating class. As for her, she would probably marry, and by inference, thereby be relegated to the kitchen, nursery—and oblivion.

Our indomitable Bettie . . . told the good, kindly, God-fearing faculty members that her father had sent her all the way from Mt. Sterling, Kentucky, to Greencastle for her education and at considerable expense, and with much trepidation and prayerful contemplation. She also told them in no uncertain words that if she were entitled to be Valedictorian, then she wanted to be Valedictorian, and that was that.

She got it, and the theretofore man-dominated Methodist Asbury got an unexpected social shock to its sturdy limestone foundations. Rumor hath it even that one of the old buildings took a decided list to the south and had to be shored-up. More shoring was to be had as the years passed. . . .

Cordially,

Finding 'the best place to eat' on the road

March 15, 1953

Mrs. Lacy Stoner
Holly Bluff, Mississippi

My dear Mrs. Stoner,
    A week ago, just about this time, Frank and I were arriving at

the Stoner homestead in far-off Holly Bluff—home of pecky cypress at its best, and Frank was getting a second look at his beloved paneling. . . Frank is well-pleased with his lumber purchases, and with the trip generally. But coming up from your home . . . he was like an old mare headed for the barn. . .

We made Cairo, Ill., just before dark. As we started into town, I said, "Let's stop and eat at some good place." Frank said, "All right. I'll look for a good place as we go through." Pretty soon we were out of town. It had been raining off and on, and now it began in rather good earnest. In fact, come to think of it, it rained about all the way.

When we reached Marion, Ill. I said, "There is a time and place for everything. Drive up to that Standard station on the left. I want to ask him the best place in town to eat." He did, and I did. The fellow cited us to "The Hut." Enroute, I said, "Frank, I'll bet three to one The Hut is a dump. Whenever they recommend Huts or Mike's Place or Pat's Place or Joan's and Joe's or any Dinty Moore's, you can just about bet your wad they're dumps. I looked while he parked. It had eight revolving stools. I said, "Let's walk to that filling station yonder. I know this town has a better place. I saw an intelligent first class looking trucker just outside and asked him, telling him I hadn't eaten anything except segments of big Hershey bars all day long and I wanted good food and a table to sit at. He directed us "around the Court House following the traffic, then north to the place next-door to the Adam Shoe Store with the big electric shoe hanging out in front—you can't miss it." The place looked rather shoddy but it had three pine booths and nine revolving stools. A trifle desperate, we sat down. A fuzzy fat girl came from behind nowhere with one menu. I asked her for a big tall glass, two or three cubes of ice and an open bottle of Coca Cola. She said they had no ice. I looked at the menu but it was hard to read on account of the samples of soup thereon. I said to Frank, "Let's go." And we did.

Outside, I met an old codger. . . I asked the old question. He sent us up the street—"thataway, the best place in town, anything from soup to nuts." I asked, "Does it have tables?" He said, "Why hell, yes—and pepper and salt too." I felt we were on the right track. And indeed, compared with the others it was the "Empire Room" in the Waldorf-Astoria. Quite nice waitress, and I got my tall glass, etc. . .

Arrived home at 12:45 a.m. A trifle short of 650 miles. Thus endeth our pecky cypress safari. . .

Cordially,

Financial advice to a world traveler

March 16, 1953

Mrs. Ruth Ross Herrman
121 Devon Drive
Falls Church, Virginia

Dear Ruth:

Holy Nellie! You *ARE* going places, aren't you? I am told that many adventurous persons in New York are already engaging initial passage to the moon, so perhaps you should write for a reservation there before all the space is taken. I thought I had gone hog wild going to South America three years ago with Sugar Foot for the winter, even if we did have direct connection with, and were practically under the constant supervision and tutelage of General Motors, International Harvester, most all the U.S. Branch Banks down there, and others, but we were 4th rate pikers compared with you.

Your letter does not say how long you will be on safari . . . but rather indicates more than a year at the least. . .

Knowing more about U.S. finances than going around the world, I'll talk a little about that. You must own a house in Alabama and two in Virginia. That's too many houses by three to go off and leave—especially if you don't know when you are coming back. . . If you can make a little profit now, or break even, or even take a little loss, you'd better sell your houses. Rental properties are no investment for women at any time, especially now. Pay no attention to anyone who tells you to the contrary. The odds are overwhelming. I think you have considerable U.S. bonds. Bonds are rather poor property these days . . . because the buying power of money is now depreciating far more rapidly than the bond interest is bringing in—or more. Of course everybody should diversify—I mean everybody whose working days and money-making days are about over. Those out of business. . . Time was when careful investors had about 40 to 50% bonds, 10 to 20% in cash, and say 40% in high grade stocks, common and preferred. All that has changed. Bonds and cash on hand are losers from an investment point, but not so much so from the view of diversity and security. Careful investors now go as high as 80% or even higher in common stocks (good ones of high standing and long regular dividend experience, not cats and dogs and speculatives). . . The common stocks of AT&T, Standard of New Jersey or Indiana, International Business Machines, Eastman Kodak and dozens of others are safer and easier for you than probably any house rental on God's green earth. Now is not only the time for all good men to come to the aid, etc., but also the time for all good women to get out of the clutches of carpenters, electricians, repairmen, repairs and replacements. You may wonder how come all this free and voluntary advice. If I recall correctly, you and Helen used to consult with me about finances occasionally. And so, I just sort of got started and jumped the gun, so to speak. What I say is not compulsory, so take it or leave it. I'm not infallible or I long since would have taken the places of Morgan and Rockefeller. . .

When you get over there in Borneo and Java, and have the time and inclination, and the ink isn't at the boiling point, write and tell us what things are like.

And may your trains always be on time – which they will not.

As Ever,

Paying our own way

April 3, 1953

Mrs. Cecil Harden
Member, House of Representatives
Washington, D.C.

My dear Mrs. Harden:

I am home today with a slight cold. My wife and daughter are gone to Indianapolis shopping. Tomorrow the parcel post packages will begin rolling in. Our parcel post man is an understanding fellow. It has become a sort of standing joke when he stops his truck and starts in with various packages he smiles facetiously and says, "Well, I see the folks were in Indianapolis yesterday."

And so, tomorrow's delivery here at the house will add a tiny fraction to the already increasing postal deficit. Why? Parcel post rates are evidently too low. Mrs. Harden, that is wrong. Some helpless somebodys, somewhere, will have to make up that deficit. The postage on those packages should slightly overpay their way, not underpay them.

A year or so ago the Congress enacted Public Law 199, which cut down the weight of parcel post shipments and thereby helped considerably in reducing the parcel post deficit, which I think is still up around 100 millions. Now the boys who use parcel post at the partial expense of the general taxpayers want 199 repealed, and have introduced HR 2685 to that effect. It also raises the poundage to 70 pounds. . . I understand HR 2685 has been sent to a Committee of which you are a member. . . I should like to know your and the Committee's reactions thereto. . .

This week's *Newsweek* says to not be surprised if there's a postal-rate increase before long—perhaps a 4 cent rate for most first-class mail. Well, why not, if it takes that or 5 cents or whatever amount, to break slightly more than even? If my letters or packages aren't more than paying their way—and I mean just that —then let me pay more, or quit writing or sending, or else just deliver them myself. I don't want some fellow at Stonebluff paying any part of it. . .

Cordially,

AT&T Directors better stock up

April 4, 1953

To the Board of Directors of American Telephone and Telegraph Company:

Gentlemen:

Your April, 1953, Notice of the Annual Meeting would seem to indicate there are 19 of you Directors. . . To my utter amazement, I seem to find out that I own a few more shares of your excellent Capital Stock than a majority of your Directors individually own. A shocking revelation to me. Something must be wrong. Either I own too many or that majority owns too few. I think the latter is the case. So, what to do?

Therefore, in all Hoosier modesty, I suggest we adopt an Incentive Stock Option Plan for our Directors only, patterned after that proposed by Standard Oil (Indiana) for Key Executives. We must do something for our financially hard-pressed Directors, and I am one to help.

Please understand this communication is confidential between me and 18 of you Directors. I want to leave out that 30-share man because he is fairly well-up in an organization whose System pass I have proudly carried for lo, these many years. In righteous indignation he might rise up and take that pass away from me . . .

So let's centralize on our 25-share Director, Mr. W_____, as the example. He needs help—and badly. And who knows? If I should be the Good Samaritan to start him up the AT&T stock ladder, maybe he in gratitude would have me appointed Special Attorney for the Atlantic Coast Line and Louisville and Nashville Railroads (to avoid any Federal complications), and that way I could get to that American Shangri-La, Florida, for free. The possibilities of my strategy are intriguing.

But let it be clearly known to each of you (except the 30-share man) that if our 25-share man does not up his holdings to at least the low 30s between now and next year's Annual Meeting, and he is up again for re-election, and I am there which I won't be, and he is there which he should be, and is pointed out to me, I shall strike him for those two passes before all and sundry. He will refuse, and then I'll publicly expose his puny holdings in our most excellent Company. The Chairman of the Boards of two big Railroads has no business humiliating us by such niggardly holdings in our fine Company. And I am the angel with the temerity to say so. He can't get at me (The 30-share man can—that is why I am laying off him). As to the 25-share man, I carry none of his passes, I am not a candidate for office, and am standing no stud hosses. Other than being a Presbyterian, I am a free man.

This is no threat, but always remember that if matters come to the worst, I might come to some Annual Meeting, pull my Odd Fellows membership on Mr. Bell, my Farm Bureau card on Mr. Forbes, my Notarial Commission on Mr. Root, Jr., my Kiwanis standing on Mr. Craig, My Law School diploma on Mr. Taylor, my Masonic associations on one or more big stockholders who aren't Catholics, etc.; nominate myself for Director; conduct another whistle-stop campaign, and—·—·—·?. Then wouldn't our splendid Company be in a pickle, with a Hoosier farmer, and a Democrat at that, on the Board, and maybe a double-jointed Railroad Board Chairman or some other worthy individual thrown into the discard?

Something drastic must be done for our low bracket Directors. Let's do it—and soon.

I shall anxiously await your composite solution for the situation.

Fraternally, but apprehensively, Yours,

Beware doctors and watch the cows

To Heather Anderson, a granddaughter.

July 18, 1953

My dear Heather Bloom:

What is our Heather doing in a hospital? They are not places for young ladies. Hospitals are traps for old people with sore backs and failing minds and memories whom doctors inveigle into these medical spider's webs for reasons best known to themselves.

Some folks, mostly older women, glory in their hospital records. Each trip is carefully recorded and verified with unimpeachable evidence, and is to the owner the same as a home run is to Stan Musial.

There was a time when a young fellow, about your age now, cut his finger with a knife. What happened? Mother took a look. She washed the layers of dirt off with good old common cold well or cistern water, soused the finger in turpentine, then wrapped it in a clean, boiled white cotton rag, tied it round and round with Clark's white No. 70 thread, told him to keep it as clean as his conscience would permit—and in 48 hours it was well. Now what happens? The neighborhood is alerted, the ambulance called with orders to ring the gong vigorously enroute, doting grandparents are deluged with telegrams and telephone calls, the cigarette-finger stained family doctor is called and frantically urged to meet the ambulance at the back door of the hospital. He does. He inspects the knife gravely, sends it to the laboratory to check whether it has cut bread made from wheat infected with the dread wheat cholera or has come into contact with tuleremic pork plasma, etc. The case is too serious for him alone so he calls co-counsel. The poor little feller by this time is so bewildered he doesn't remember whether he cut his finger or wet his pants.

Grandpappy is grubbing and piling deadened thorn trees, piling brush, logs and dead limbs, spading-up locust, thorn, elm, osage orange and wild crabapple sprouts . . . and otherwise disporting himself in one of the big pastures north of town. . . Earlier in the year, a quail would perch on that big southeast corner post of the pasture. You would know he was there because he would whistle that shrill "Bob White, Bob White." If you weren't too anxious to work you would stop and try to figure him out. . . Once I was working diligently near the east fence line. All at once I realized a squirrel was barking at me. I kept still and located the sound, but I never got to see the squirrel. But I did see birds, woodpeckers, blue jays, rain crows and robins flying into a certain rather small tree, and I knew what that meant at this time of year—a mulberry tree. I tried to work toward it, easy like. When I got there the squirrel was gone but the mulberry tree and its ripening berries were right there where the sound came from. . . Where there is plenty of grass, cows never get hungry. They eat about all the time just to keep from getting hungry. If you see cows lying around in the shade, you know that all is well.

But you have to keep tab on your livestock wherever they may be. Inside the highway gate, but some distance away to the east, was an open tool shed. . . Day before yesterday, as I drove in the pasture and passed reasonably close to this tool shed, I saw a young calf in the shed on top of the hay. He'd weigh 100 to 125 pounds. I didn't stop. I thought he'd work his way out the same way he worked in. That evening as I went by, I forgot about any calf. Next morning as I went by, I was thinking about other things, so I didn't look in for the calf. About mid-afternoon, when I was working within hearing distance of the tool shed, I heard a cow bawling. It was the bawl of a cow that had lost her calf. When I came out, I stopped near the shed, walked over and looked in. There was the calf on the hay, and silent as your Uncle Frankfurter when he broke the stock of my shotgun. I went around to where he had gotten in and went in the same way, climbed up over the five or six feet of baled hay and then down toward him. He ran over the bales faster than I could climb. Back and forth, around and around we went. Finally I got him in the south part of the shed. He was tiring and I was already tired. He looked at me. I sort of fell toward him, giving out a big yell. He got a big scare and climbed those bales toward the hole he got in through like a mountain goat. When I got out the same way, he was half a quarter away and going strong. He must have been a hungry calf by the time he found his ma.

This will conclude the agricultural lecture for today.

The Grand Champion Ham

November 18, 1953

Honorable Frank J. McCarthy
Assistant Vice President of Pennsylvania Railroad
211 Southern Building
Washington, D.C.

My dear Frank,

Your Thanksgiving, or if you prefer, your Christmas ham deluxe is on its way, . . . part of an unbelievable success story to New Englanders and others east of the Alleghenys who feel that everybody or everything good must originate east of said Mountains. . .

Some six or eight years ago, a young fellow bought out a combination locker plant, meat market and grocery store in Waveland, Indiana, population about 500, and four miles from Russellville. He gradually went into processing pork products, particularly sugar-cured, hickory-smoked hams.

Last year the Meat Interests, or some such organization, of Omaha, Nebraska, held a contest open to all pork processors of the United States and Canada, from Swift, Armour and Wilson on down—or up—to Coleman, of Waveland, Ind.

All unheralded and unsung, our young friend picked himself out what he thought was the best of his modest stock of hams and had the temerity to betake himself and his ham to Omaha, where he entered said ham in its Class. It took first prize—represented by a big platter, on the bottom of which a ham was engraved. Not completely satisfied with taking first prize in its Class, our hero then entered it in the Grand Sweepstakes—the Grand Champion Ham of all Hams Class—of the United States and Canada. Know what? To the utter consternation of the contestants, that same ham again took first prize—represented by a washed-in-gold ball-topped contraption that looked more like a pilaster in a Masonic Lodge Hall than anything I can think of.

There remaining no more ham worlds to conquer, our Champion rewrapped his winner in cellophane and tin foil and brought it and the prizes home and placed them on exhibition for all to see. That is the story. . .

Now please understand I am not so naive as to be certain our man of the hour is a near-World's Champion ham producer or that chance and fate or pure gall did not, in some manner, enter into that decision. I just think the Champ is mighty good, and hope that you, after sampling his product, will agree he is in there pitching somewhere. . .

Happy Holidays and happy eating,

Thanks for the backing

February 25, 1954

Mr. Leslie A. Lyon
Lyon's Music Company
110-112 S. Green Street
Crawfordsville, Indiana

My dear Les:

. . . After my first, and in the opinion of the great majority, my most unexpected election in our Senatorial District (the first time a Democrat had ever been elected from Montgomery and Putnam Counties), I began to hear a lot about my so-called personal popularity. Personal popularity, the Devil! It was the wise and capable backing I got coupled with my willingness and hustle to follow advice. . .

But . . . Les, there must be at least more than a dozen excellent reasons why I cannot be a candidate. To recite them in detail on paper would take a sheet reaching from your store to the Court House. So, I shall not try to set them down on paper. But I do want to thank you wholeheartedly for the generous compliment you have paid me by even suggesting you would personally like for me to run. . .

Please remember me most kindly to all our good friends.

Sincerely,

For balance, let Canada go it alone

Response to a questionnaire from Congresswoman Cecil M. Harden, March 4, 1954

Memo—relating to Question No. 6.

I, a Democrat, along with thousands of others, not only voted for Gen. Eisenhower, but were glad to do so. . . No minor reason for doing so was that he promised to balance the budget – and soon. . . But the politicians have gotten in their work and he is wobbling just a trifle. . . At a very recent press conference, if he is quoted correctly, he said that if employment did not pick up in March, that fact would necessitate taking action, and tax reduction might be one of the first measures to be considered, and that the government wouldn't hesitate a second to do its utmost to stop any real recession. To me that is Roosevelt philosophy, pure and simple, which threw undue stress on consumer spending, and assumed the way to avert depression was to unbalance the budget, resort to pump priming, which can mean only one thing—more inflation.

There are three ways to balance the budget:

– Cut down spending and expenses, or
– Collect more revenue (increase taxes), or
– Do both

There are no other ways under the sun I know of.

The first of these is far and away the best. That is why my answer to your sixth question is an unqualified "No." The St. Lawrence Seaway would take eight or more years to build. The alleged Engineers estimated it would cost just short of one billion dollars to build it deep enough (26 to 28 feet) to carry 10% of the present ocean-going freighters. Which probably means it would end up nearer three billion in cost. And what would it cost to build it deep enough to carry the other 90%? To say nothing of the cost of dredging lake harbors, building docks, and dozens of other important expenses? For the most part it is to be located in Canada and subject to Canadian law. Canada says it will build it alone. In the name of the Great Jehovah and the Continental Congress, let Canada do it! Let some country, somewhere, sometime, some way or how, build something of its own—on its own.

It is now proposed that an immediate increase of $100 or more in personal exemptions for all income tax payers be made, and still more for next year. Will St. Lawrence and this increase in exemption help balance the budget? They will not. Neither should pass until that budget is balanced, if we are really going to try to balance it, and St. Lawrence should not pass at this time above everything I have as yet heard proposed.

Kansas can be cruel

March 29, 1954

Honorable I.C. Wiatt, Chairman
Board of County Commissioners
Lakin, Kansas

My dear Mr. Wiatt:

I have just read with deep concern your letter of March 25, 1954, to the effect your Board had received a signed complaint that our land is in a "blowing" condition, and that . . . "the former tenant" . . . would assume no responsibility for it. . .

Please bear with me, if you have the time and inclination, and allow me to recite a part of my experiences with that land. About the year 1895 my father bought the quarter section from the Entryman and his wife. . . During World War I, while returning home from California in a cold January, I stopped off at Lakin. As is the case everywhere, there is always someone who knows the location of land. In my case he was a man who owned about the only Ford in town. We struck west on the highway. Then by instinct, it seems to me, rather than by landmarks, he turned north over the unfenced land. In due time, he said, "There is about your southeast corner. . ." It was mighty lonesome-looking land.

Time went on. . . My next trip out was in summer. The land had a fair stand of buffalo grass. . . I found a young fellow who agreed to graze the land and pay the taxes. . . I never saw him again. He moved away before my next trip. I was also told he grazed the land, but I know he did not pay the taxes. They went delinquent. I got that straightened out, and incidentally learned a minor lesson about owning land so far from home.

You can imagine my reaction when, on the next trip out, I saw the land had been fenced and cattle were grazing on it. I went north perhaps a half-mile to a house near the east side of the road. A woman was there alone. Her husband was away working. They had come from Ohio. She was terribly discouraged. She cried as she talked. Two crop failures—possibly three. They were near desperate. . . I asked who owned the cattle. She said the Sheriff of the County owned them, and had also built the fence. She then told me how she wished she had that land for her two cows. They were almost starving, and she had little or nothing for them to eat.

And so I was up against the High Sheriff of Kearny County, and 1,000 miles from home. The Sheriff! If there is anything a non-resident needs to learn, it is to avoid a clash with high officials of a given section, if it can possibly be avoided. . . I was worried. Then I thought of William Allen White and of his famous editorial, and of other great and honorable men Kansas had produced, a good part of them farmers, like me. I decided to beard the lion in his den. . . He sort of braced himself, and I could see he was getting ready to get mad. . . I told him I wanted the fence left alone. I was arranging to turn this land over to the woman up the road for her two cows. . . "You can't expect me to give you that fence. . ."

Either he came to realize the probable justice of my stand, or else he concluded he might be a trespasser if he persisted. Anyway he did nothing to the fence. I wrote a contract in duplicate to the effect the woman was to have possession of the land for her cows until I gave her written notice to the contrary. No rent or charge of any kind was to be made. . . I never did see her husband. And I never saw her again. By the time of my next trip, I was told they had sort of given up the ghost and gone back to Ohio.

. . .Father was a bit proud of that "virgin soil", as he called it, although neither he nor mother ever got a penny out of it. Nor did the rest of us until lately, when it was leased for oil and gas. . . Kansas can, and has been cruel. In my early boyhood a few of those I knew went to Kansas to make their way in the world. Some came back footsore and broken-hearted. The droughts, hot winds and grasshoppers took them, as witness the Entryman and his wife who homesteaded this identical land in 1893. . .

. . .Two years ago I received a telephone call from a man in Lakin. . . He had about 50 head of starving cattle; was out of feed, with none available; he was desperate and could he turn-in his cattle on my land for not more than a month? . . . I have been short on feed a few times, but never out. I told him I would most certainly help in any way I could under those circumstances. Two months later I arrived on the land. Then came the big disillusionment. The cattle were not those of the man who called me. They were owned by one of the wealthiest men in the County. The telephone caller only worked for him.

At the time, I came in contact with three prospective tenants who wanted to farm the land. . . Mr. W_____ was most highly recommended. We talked terms. . .I told him I would think the matter over carefully going home, and if I decided I wanted to lease the land, would prepare a contract. . . I told him that if he did not hear from me rather promptly to just forget the land . . . You can imagine my utter amaze-ment when, last Fall, I went out and found a good part of the land broken up with perhaps 40 acres of it in a maize crop failure. . . Mr. W_____ said he understood the deal to be that if he did not hear from me to the contrary, then he was to proceed and crop the land. There you are. . .

Now today, after receiving your letter, I find myself in hot water. . . I know nothing whatever about wind erosion or how to deal with it. Whatever I have to do, I will have to do. . . I am a long way off. I do not drive a car as much as I used to. I am getting older. . . But I do know I do not expect to continue to farm it, if I can have my way, which I have not had in the immediate past. . .

Very Respectfully,

A first time for everything

May 7, 1954

The Milwaukee Chair Company
Milwaukee, Wisconsin

Attention: Mr. Block, I think is the name, President or Gen. Manager:

The 5 metal chairs . . . were promptly delivered to our office. They look and sit quite well and we feel sure we are going to like them for the reception room.

When in Milwaukee my son and I ordered some other and more expensive chairs—leather—at the same time we ordered the metal chairs spoken of above, and it is about the delivery of these leather chairs this letter is directed. We hope to have a sort of "opening" for our new offices and building about June 1, 1954. Naturally, we should like to have these leather chairs on hand . . . If we knew there would be a little delay in delivery we would try to delay our "opening." It is not my intention to try to rush you. I would just like to know for a certainty and plan accordingly.

I find myself in a dither like unto a situation that confronted me long, long years ago. I was a cadet a Western Military Academy, Alton, Illinois, 16 years old. . . In class, I sat next to a boy two years my senior and far, far more sophisticated. He was a member of a really rich family in St. Louis. He invited me to spend Easter vacation at his home. I was glad to go. Arrived in St. Louis I learned another St. Louis tycoon, a brewer and his wife, were giving a banquet and ball, and that I was scheduled to be among "those present."

My hostess looked me over carefully. In a casual way she asked, "Andrew, I'll bet you forgot to bring your dress suit along?"

The question amazed me. "Why Mrs. _____," I said, "I never owned a dress suit. Boys my age where I come from don't have dress suits."

What an understanding woman she was! I could see the smile come to her eyes. Without a moment's hesitation she said, "I know what we'll do. Both you boys will wear your uniforms. You are more used to them and you'll feel more at home in them. And the girls will just go wild about those uniforms. They are exactly the thing to wear."

Before the big event, she got me off to herself and after some preliminaries, asked, "Andrew, do your parents have liquor on the table or in the home?" I said they did not have any that I knew of.

She asked, "Did you ever taste whiskey or champagne?" I said I had never tasted either—that I had never seen any champagne.

The good woman fairly beamed. She was getting real enjoyment out of the interview. She then told me there would be worlds of champagne served at the banquet. Waiters would keep refilling the glasses. Older people might get a little tipsy. . . She told me many things. She said that at the first serving of the champagne we might all rise for a toast. My girl (for whom she had arranged) and I would sort of intertwine our wrists and glasses and she would take a sip out of my glass, but of course I would sip none of hers—that champagne was quite potent and might creep-up on one not used to it. . .

Before the interview was over, she had become my monitor and my excellent, trustworthy and good friend. One thing troubled me. I wanted her permission about something. I said, "I'll behave myself and you'll not have to be ashamed of me. All this is new. I have never been in a fine home before and have never been to a banquet. May I have your permission to taste that champagne out of my own glass? I have always wanted to taste champagne and I may never get the chance again."

That was too much for her. She had been aching to laugh out loud. She put her arm around me and let go, saying, "Andrew, you are just about the finest young man we ever had in our home. Of course you have my permission to taste the champagne. . . I just want you to tell me how it tastes."

The banquet and ball were howling successes so far as I was concerned. I made at least two big mistakes. . . I got the vast assortment of spoons and forks pretty well mixed, but soon corrected that by watching the middle-aged woman at my side. The awful and really devastating mistake was due to my appetite. Military School diet was rigid. I was young, healthy and hungry. I noticed my girl minced and toyed with the fish, soup and other preliminaries, but attributed that to some feminine quirk. I ate all mine in stride. When the canvas back, caviar and other unknown real delicacies came along it was too late for me. I was full.

On the ball room floor it was a much different story. I was young, lithe and limber—and absolutely sober. A great many of the deluxe elite were too heavy in the hock, too wide in the beam, and far, far too distended in front. One good woman couldn't see her plate and would have to pull her fork from under to see what its tine had speared. The guests graded from mild exhilaration to pretty dam tight. My hostess' son was pretty well left of center. I had sufficient presence of mind to ask my monitor for dances, far more than could reasonably be expected of a woman so old—probably almost pushing 40. . .

By this time you are asking, "Why all this boring life history from an almost utter stranger?" The answer is simple.

I have never seen, much less occupied, an office chair pushing $300. I must get acclimated to it gradually and by easy stages or else find myself in the same uneasy situation as that of a 16-year-old small town boy at his first metropolitan banquet and ball. . .

Respectfully,
Durham & Durham, Atty.'s.
By *Andrew E. Durham*

South in a box car, north in a Cadillac

Excerpts from an article written by Pap, in the Putnam County Graphic, *June 24, 1954.*

Some 35 years ago, a young man born and reared in Putnam County, near Greencastle, decided to seek his fortune elsewhere. Of uncompromising Republican political stock, he ignored Horace Greeley's admonition, "Young man go West," and took a different direction.

He had already arranged to buy on contract a modest acreage in the Mississippi Delta where the silt of countless overflows of the River had produced a soil more than 60 feet in depth—the deepest and richest soil on Earth other than the valley of the Nile. . .

And so, one typically bleak March day, he assembled his dog, a span or two of mules, his scanty farming tools and himself into a box car headed south.

In later years, when speaking of that momentous occasion, he said, "I think the most lonesome, homesick and desperate moment of all my ups and downs was the time I closed that box car door on familiar scenes I might never see again—and the wheels began to turn. It was so cold I made a sort of bunk, wrapped my dog and myself in the same blankets to help keep one another warm, and tried to go to sleep."

The trip took over a week. They all ate some days. Some days just the mules and the dog; and one day, just the mules.

Did you see a house float past?

So allow us to introduce the subject of this sketch, Mr. Lacy Simpson Stoner, and inform you Holly Bluff, Mississippi, was his destination.

Arrived, he had hardly become oriented when the rising Mississippi started his house toward New Orleans and the Gulf. Fortunately it lodged in some nearby trees, and as the river receded, he, aided by block and tackle, floated and pulled it back to its original or approximately original position, where it was made more secure.

In speaking of these floods, Mr. Stoner said, "It was nothing in those days to have some man from up the River come along and inquire, 'Did you see a three room, part-yaller house goin' by here in the last day or two?' "

Crops were good, with fair prices. He plowed back the profits into more and more land and better and better mechanical equipment.

And he took time to come back to Indiana and claim his bride, a Lafayette girl, the present Mrs. Stoner.

Again the rains came and the water flooded their first floor. They moved what they could to the second floor, where the water soon caught up with them. They tied some of the better and more useful articles up among the rafters, and had just selected the spot to chop out through the roof, to get to the boat which was moored to the house, when the crest of the flood was reached and the water slowly subsided.

Revolution in the Delta

Then followed more and bigger crops, bigger profits, more land, more mechanical equipment and less sharecropper help. Meanwhile, soy beans and other crops gradually supplanted cotton.

In time a new and modern home was built—on higher ground – nearer Holly Bluff and its modern school house. This home has a large and beautiful living room paneled and beamed in "pecky cypress", and it was there J. Frank Durham got his idea of paneling the new Durham Building here in the City.

Mr. Stoner now owns some 3,000 acres of that Mississippi Delta, virtually all of which is as level as a baseball park; a fleet of 12-foot combines, tractors, a vast amount of modern equipment and enough rubber-tired low grain wagons to fill a small-sized parking lot. He has a large interest in the community cotton gin, although cotton has almost disappeared from his land. He has many other and varied interests.

He revolutionized farming in the Mississippi Delta by introducing mechanized equipment and changing from cotton to other and better-paying crops that require less manual labor. These are a part of the secrets of his astounding success, coupled with ability, hard work and close careful attention and application to his business. . .

Week before last, Mr. Stoner and his comely wife came North — but not in a box car. Their mode of travel is a June, 1954-vintage, air-conditioned Cadillac, just off the assembly line.

Your editor met Mr. and Mrs. Stoner at a dinner party at Old Trails Inn being given by Mr. Andrew E. Durham in their honor. Messrs. Stoner and Durham were members of the 1917 State Scottish Rite Class at Indianapolis, and lived as neighbors west of the City. . .

The Farmer's Game

Mr. Stoner talked freely of his boyhood days in Greencastle. He and others of his age would gather evenings in the restaurants around town to eat hamburgers or some such food. They invented a pastime they called "the farmer's game". . . Slips of paper were shaken up in a hat and each member drew a slip. All but one were blank. The one who drew the slip labeled "treat" had to do just that.

In due time the boys improved the game to make it as sure for those "in the know" not to lose as the present day one-armed bandits. There would be, say, five in the game, one of whom was the "sucker". One of the conspirators would prepare the five slips. He did that by writing "treat" on all five slips. In the meantime each conspirator would have obtained a blank slip of the same shape and quality of paper. This he would have rolled-up in his *left* vest pocket—just in case.

The drawing would begin. The victim would have to draw a

"treat" slip because all five were labeled that way. Those in the know would draw, give a quick sort of look and put the slips in their *right* vest pockets, at the same time conjecturing aloud, "Mine was a blank. Wonder who got the treat slip," or some such remark.

One night, after being bilked three successive times, the victim became suspicious. Feeling he had served his apprenticeship long and faithfully, the others were ready and willing to admit him as a full blood brother. They told *him* to prepare the slips and conduct the drawing, which he of course did according to the "official" rules—four blanks and one with "treat". To the surprise of all, and rather contrary to the mathematical law of averages, he again drew the "treat" slip. This convinced him that the game was straight.

"And so," said Mr. Stoner laconically, "we saved him for another night, until he had learned his ritual better."

Mr. and Mrs. Stoner returned to Holly Bluff last week. Later they go to Hot Springs, Arkansas, for the baths, a semi-annual pilgrimage; then probably to Denver and the West Coast; then perhaps north to Oregon and Washington, where they may ship their car along and continue by steamship to Alaska.

Warning to Alaska

Last Saturday, during the open house for the Durham Building, J. Frank Durham received a congratulatory telephone call from his friend and schoolmate, V. Maurice Smith, at Alaska. He is the co-owner and Editor of *Jessen's Weekly* at Fairbanks, and also newscaster for a local radio station. Frank alerted his friend to the possible invasion of Alaska by Mr. Stoner and his "farmer's game," or improvements thereof. He advised his friend to keep his eyes "off that air-conditioned Cadillac and on the driver himself, as he is by far the more dangerous of the two."

Something on the carpet

July 20, 1954

Dear Footser:

... Which reminds me of your Uncle Charlie Bridges. He was a Deacon or whoever it is who gets to pass the plate at the Presbyterian Church for the collection.

The event happened during the First World War. The church needed a new carpet. Mr. Raphael, the Pastor, extended himself in the sermon about giving for the proposed new carpet. He extolled the brethren and sistern to "Give, give until it hurts. If you do not have the cash, just sign a piece of paper setting out the amount you will give toward the new carpet, put it in the collection box. The ushers will take care of it and you will be credited the amount on the new carpet". etc.

Charlie was passing the plate. He came to old Mrs. Cooper, a devout Presbyterian, who whispered something in his ear. Charlie straightened up and said, "Brother Raphael, Mrs. Cooper would like to do a little something on the new carpet, but she has no paper."

Pap

Pap on steps of Twin Lakes log cabin (referred to by Pap as "Loafer's Lodge") in 1944 just after first grandchild was born. (Baby is on his Aunt Jane's lap.) Munny had to go into the hospital while on vacation at Twin Lakes, Pennsylvania so Pap made a rare trip east to pose for this "non-political family portrait." Yes, there is another new face, but this time it is a grandson (daughter Joan's son). Those present were (l-r) back, Pap, Aura May, Joan, and Ann; front, Jane holding young Bill McGaughey, Margaret and Frank.

Three Andrews: Andrew Durham McGaughey, Grandfather Andrew and Andrew Henry Durham.

Pap with son J. Frank, and three grandchildren: Andrew H. Durham, Andrew D. McGaughey, and George B. Durham, about 1954.

Russellville Town Hall in 1997, formerly Russellville Bank

Russellville train depot still standing

Main Street, Russellville, 1997. The sign reads 'Sorry, No Right Turn on Red.'

No Richard Fairfax, but a modern registered Hereford Bull.

Last known photo of Pap taken in May, 1954, when he hosted a welcome dinner for his old friend, Lacy Stoner.

Chapter VI:

To South America and back

Accompanied by daughter Aura-May (alias Sugarfoot), Pap embarked on a two-month land, sea and air tour of Latin America in late November, 1949. This journey, extraordinary for the time, was recorded in a series of letters printed in successive editions of the weekly Putnam County Graphic, Greencastle, Indiana.

Each letter was hand-written, in pencil, on yellow, ruled tablet paper, and then mailed to the paper, where they would be set into the equivalent of two to five full columns of type. The touring was extensive, and the letters were inclusive, giving conjecture to just how Pap found the time to do all this writing? Aura May said that other than during the cruise down, he did it all at night after she had gone to bed. She remembered one time in particular when he awoke her at 2 a.m. to ask how to spell the name of the highest peak in the Andes—Aconcagua.

At first there was only a two-week delay between the writing and the publication, but these intervals grew longer as the tourists progressed from country to country, demonstrating the limits of postal departments and/or *carriers of the day. By the time the final letter was printed, Pap and Aura May had been home approximately three months.*

Embarking from New Orleans

At Sea, Nov. 27, 1949

To the *Graphic*:

We will start with Mattoon, Ill., where my daughter, Aura May Durham, and I went to catch the Illinois Central's "Panama Limited" for New Orleans.

This is a thoroughly-modern, diesel-powered all-pullman train. Among other things it has a folding removable ladder for all night access to each upper berth, which does away with the porter and his wooden stepladder and small washrooms at each end of the car, which permits the car to add two full sections. Time will tell whether this feature proves popular with the traveling public. The train is fast, the roadbed good. She was on-the-dot into Mattoon and about five minutes ahead at destination.

Our reservations were at the Roosevelt Hotel . . . centrally located a block and a half off Canal St., reputed to be the widest street in the world. The warm, soft dialect we generally attribute to the south is lacking. New Orleans has its own. I can't describe it. You have to hear it.

Well-suited to hospitality

Hospitality here, as well as in about all of New Orleans, is most cordial and unusual. Here is an example of what I mean: I thought it best to get another tropical suit—a rayon and cotton affair made by Haspel of New Orleans. I called the manufacturer's office to locate a retail store carrying the Haspel line. I was connected with the manager, A. Haspel himself. I stated my case.

He answered: "We are mighty proud you like our clothes. Tell you what you do. You go to such and such a store almost across the street from your hotel, call for Mr. A. or Mr. B. and tell him what you want. This is an off season for hot weather clothes. He may not have them. If not, tell him to measure you and call us and we will send down four or five to choose from."

"But," I said, "I want only one suit and in Indianapolis it would cost $25.50 and that is too much trouble for both of you for that money."

He said, "No amount of trouble is too much trouble for us to go to for a man who came all the way from Indianny to get one of our suits of clothes."

And that was what happened. The store was out, but I got the clothes.

The pilots union

That evening we went to the Roosevelt Blue Room for 8 o'clock dinner and floor show. I noticed a modestly, yet well-dressed bald headed, rather heavy-set man of about 60 eating alone at the next table. The waiters all knew him as did many of the customers who passed.

I said to him, "You are alone this evening. Why not come over and join us in dessert?"

He replied, "I shall be delighted, and consider it an hon'r to be asked to join you and this charmin' young lady, but you must excuse me from dessert." Turning to his waiter, he said, "Bring the bucket over here if you will, Pierre." The bucket was a bucket of Burgundy, fairly well gone. Naturally he asked us to share it, and showed no resentment at our refusal.

It took only a few minutes to discover that our new friend was a "trifle high," and gaining rather than losing altitude, as time went on. He was a river pilot of long standing, and simply superb at modest elevation.

Putnam County is a bit shy on pilots, but not New Orleans. If I

get the facts right, outbound and inbound ships have three pilots —
river, bar and the ship's regular pilot. The last takes charge only when
the ship is at sea. . . On leaving the wharf, the river pilot is in charge
until the bar of the Mississippi is reached – the narrows or jetties where
the river empties into the Gulf some 90 miles below New Orleans. . .
The "bar pilot" steers the ship through the narrows and out into the
Gulf. It is then that the ship's regular pilot takes charge.

It is these bar pilots who have a unique organization, virtually a
family affair. To become a bar pilot you must either be born into the
family or marry into it. Talk about your tight little corporations and
monopolies! Bricklayers and other trade unions are accused of limit-
ing memberships and daily numbers of bricks to be laid in order to hike
wages. This "union" does the same thing by means of a sort of birth
control feature. It's a honey of a trust. These bar pilots, I hear from
pretty reliable source, get from twelve to fifteen thousand per year and
work about six months of the year.

Last Tuesday morning, the Director of Commerce of the Board
of Commissioners of the Port of New Orleans called to invite us on a
tour of the harbor, along with some eight or 10 shippers. . . New Orleans shipping is tremendous, second only to New York. I casually
mentioned San Francisco and was told that New Orleans had more
shipping than the combined West Coast. Generally speaking, it draws
the territory drained by the Mississippi River. New Orleans has 10 to
12 miles of wharves. On the trip we surely saw more than 100 ships,
barges, ferries and other big water craft. Two ships were unloading
thousands of cases of pineapples, so our local A&P store should be
stocked with pineapple for you by now.

Time is a seasoning at Antoine's

That evening the director and his wife took a local Democratic
official and his wife and Aura May and me to Antoine's for dinner.
Antoine's is an institution. Established in 1840, it has served food

uninterruptedly, and is now owned and operated by a grandson of its founder.

The building, tableware and linen are severely plain. The waiters are noiseless and speak many languages. No bands, orchestras or entertainers—"You go to Antoine's to give your palate an undisturbed treat." No bar—"It is people who drink without eating who become paralyzed by alcohol." Yet it has a narrow wine cellar a block long, containing well over 5,000 bottles. The oldest wines date back to 1884, the oldest brandy to 1811.

Its gallery of celebrities contains over 2,000 autographs and pictures of distinguished visitors. Besides the main dining room, it has 15 others. One room's floor, the Mystery Room, is covered with sawdust. Guests have included Marshall Foch, Sarah Bernhardt, Will Rogers, Jenny Lind, Caruso, Edwin Booth, "Gentleman Jim" Corbett, General Pershing, down to enough U.S. Senators and Congressmen to ruin anybody's country.

The present head waiter has been there 40 years, his predecessor 50 years. Bus boys must serve an apprenticeship of 10 years. Time is a necessary element in the proper preparation of food at Antoine's. If you are in a hurry, Antoine's recommends you go to the corner drug store.

But let's get back to dinner before it gets cold. We started off with a cocktail of something. I think our host said it contained applejack, champagne and some other ingredient. It had a white collar like the beaten white of an egg. Then came "Oysters Rockefeller," so named because of the richness of the sauce . . . The recipe for this sauce is a closely guarded family secret. The dish consists of six oysters on the half shell. A much used pie tin is filled with rock salt to hold the heat indefinitely. The oysters covered with the sauce are imbedded in this salt and baked. The concoction, pie tin and all, is served on a plate.

Due to the salt, the oysters and sauce will remain hot for perhaps a half hour. Many a worthy brother's and sister's tongues have been blistered. Since 1899, the management has given with each order a post card showing the number of your order. Mine was 1301744. And so, figuring six oysters to each order, we find that the actual number of oysters used to date has been near eight million.

I had fish—*Pompano en papillote*—pompano served in paper bags (rumor hath it that the paper bag retains all the flavor), with *Pommes Soufflees*, or a glorified branch of fry or potato chips blown up like large flat pea pods with peas removed.

Dessert consisted mostly of Cherry Jubilee. Large, fat cherries are put in a metal bowl and covered with brandy. The lights are turned off over your table. The brandy is lighted with a match. The waiter stirs the cherries, flames and all, until thoroughly hot and the alcohol in the brandy is exhausted. Then he takes them to the kitchen, pours them over ice cream and something and brings back the portions, hot and cold. A Presbyterian deacon could eat Cherry Jubilee without a twinge of conscience.

All this took from 8 to 12 p.m., followed by a ride around the old French section, listening to the music of jazz bands as we passed the dance halls, winding up the evening's entertainment about 1 a.m. at the Morning Call—another New Orleans institution in a class of its own. Here rich and poor, young and old, meet on a common level and eat delicious doughnuts and drink cups of combined hot milk and hot coffee poured together simultaneously.

Nov. 24th, we sailed on the Del Mar. The ship's management distributed brightly assorted paper tape to the passengers gathered at the rails of the different decks and the farewells and bon voyages began. A Negro jazz band assembled on the wharf. One dancer was as nimble at catching coins tossed from the decks in an old plug hat as he was on his feet. The ship sailed at 4:20 p.m.

Shipboard and St. Thomas

To The Graphic,
Greencastle, Indiana

So we approached Charlotte Amalie, the only sizable town in the Virgin Islands, all white and gleaming in the sun and closely following the narrow shore lines. The high hills start almost abruptly from the shore. St. Thomas Island has a population of perhaps 12,000. Of these, Charlotte Amalie has well over half.

Taxis—good enough taxis—took those of us who wanted to go into town. . . When we met another taxi head-on at the top of a hill, he was on his left side, and so were we on ours. Woe is me, I thought. Here is where one of Russellville Bank's oldest directors gets directed to the nearest hospital, if any. . . During the time I rode taxis there in Charlotte Amalie I never got used to left-hand driving. What makes 'em do it? Even Aura May flinched. And I—I pushed the driver's seat forward some three inches or so.

Hotel 1829

One Walter J. Maguire owns and manages Hotel 1829. He and his wife "Pete" are natives of New Jersey, living in C.A. for some 10 to 12 years, since acquiring Hotel 1829. Yes, you have guessed it. The hotel was built in 1829, and it shows it. Stucco, brick and some frame. All doors and windows remain wide open. At least until a hurricane comes. The original tile floors remain, showing considerable wear. It has a mammoth combination kitchen, bar and dining room, with built-in ovens and walls hung with quart to five gallon shining copper cooking utensils. All cooking is done with charcoal and gasoline stoves. The second floor sills are closely spaced and exposed from the first floor. I don't know the dimensions of these sills, but if one loosened and fell on one, one would never know.

The hotel has a honey of a patio, like you see in travel bureau literature. All first floor doors are double and fasten from the inside with glorified gate-hooks that look like the twisted lightning rods on Mrs. Bridge's brick house west of Greencastle, only bigger and heavier. The one hanging on the inside of one of the front main double doors was about three feet long and the "staple" it hooked into was three-quarter inch solid iron. Hurricane insurance, probably.

Hotel 1829 has a maximum capacity of 24, although if remodeled for efficiency and waste spaces done away with, it could accommodate 124. Reservations are required and one hour notice for lunch and three hours for dinner. Rates: $10 per day per person, and up.

C.A. is a free port. Silverware, souvenirs, straw hats and sandals, cigarettes, wines and liquors and vegetable markets are predominant, but the greatest of these are wines and liquors. Old Gold cigarettes and the other three or four principal brands retail at 90¢ per carton, no tax. French champagnes like Moet and Somebody, $3.50 per bottle.

By the time we got there, the market was about closed. It is quite a place. It occupies a short block for length. The market has a roof; the sides and ends are open and the stalls are made of cement. A few stragglers remained with odds and ends of oranges, bananas, limes (4 for 5¢), lemons, potatoes, peppers and things of that sort.

Water shortage

Probably the biggest problem for Charlotte Amalie is that of good water, particularly drinking water. It is scarce and during the dry season, very scarce. Mr. Maguire told me drilling for wells is out of the question. They are either dry, or salt water. St. Thomas has no lakes, natural ponds, rivers or streams. It is even said that women sometimes wash their hair in the ever-present Coca-Cola. As a result of the water shortage, large patches of steep mountainside are cemented with water catches at the bottom for the rains when they do come.

All the police, the woman behind the window at the post office and the school children were Negroes, neatly dressed. No race problem here that I could see. A very few women carried loads balanced on their heads. When the ship docked about five or six rowboats of boys gathered on the bay side. The idea was to throw pennies, nickels, dimes and quarters down and they would dive for them. They rarely missed. . . They stayed from 10:30 a.m. to 3:40 p.m., when the ship sailed. One of the ship's officers told me the average take was three to four dollars.

Since leaving the island of St. Thomas we have moved steadily on. The ship averages something in the low 20's of our land miles-per-hour. . . Now we are far past the eastern hump of South America, have crossed the Equator, turned back southwest and are running along the coast of Brazil, and tomorrow we dock in Rio. The ship has a tiled swimming pool, well-patronized. The cabins, dining room, bar, latticed verandah, etc., are air conditioned, and well need be.

This is a fine way to rest and eat. Other than the ship's activities, all you see is a very few cargo ships, five miles to invisibility away, porpoises, flying fish, a gull or so, occasional low, dim landheads, the sky, the stars and moon – and water, reasonably calm but still as restless as a candidate on election night.

Sailing down the 'River of January'

To *The Graphic*
Greencastle, Ind.

We are southbound out of Rio de Janeiro (River of January, because I am told it was discovered in January). . . We docked early on the morning of Dec. 7th and sailed out at 6 p.m. next day.

I was standing at the rail when we docked. I have had feelings of helplessness many times, and more or less acute. But when I looked down some 30 feet and saw that crowd of coated, black haired and hatless men, and saw those upturned faces ranging from swarthy to ebony black, and heard that strange Portuguese as it came up in increasing volume along with its accompanying pantomime . . . I wondered and wondered what I was going to do and how.

By that time passengers were descending the accommodation ladder and strangers had come up. Shortly, the cabin boy came with a short, thin, wiry, coal black haired young fellow. He said, "You are Mr. Durham?"

"Yes," I said.

He handed me a card bearing the name of a well known American firm doing business in South America and said, "We received word you and your daughter were arriving and I am down to ask you to be our guests so we may have the pleasure of entertaining you while here. May we have that pleasure?"

"Son," said I, "you most certainly may—and before you have time to change your mind." And I meant it.

He looked a trifle puzzled. We went inside the Verandah Cafe and right there another less swarthy and older man accosted me in like manner, for a like purpose, and handed me a card of another well known American firm.

We sat down and ironed it out: the answer was most simple – and most satisfying to both hosts. We saddled ourselves on the young fellow the first day and on the older man the second day.

Come to think it all over carefully, that thing could have been rehearsed by said parties of the first part. Things fit in too well.

Unique traffic patterns

In Rio they drive cars mostly by horn. The balance of it is done by guess. The din and confusion is terrific. Added to this, pedestrians pay no attention to cars and drivers give no heed to pedestrians. The latter cross and re-cross the streets wherever and whenever they get the notion.

The first day in Rio we spent driving the downtown congestion along the beaches, and other sight-seeing. The big percent is one way traffic. To get a block or so away from where you are you execute some geometric figures they didn't have in the books when I took geometry.

This day we had an accident. Driving in the downtown congestion a car from the lane to our right pulled into us, tearing off the right hind fender of our almost brand new convertible. Traffic stopped momentarily only. You would think the two owners were exchanging pleasantries. They gathered up the pieces and pulled out what was left of the fender to keep the tires from scraping, and away we went. No cops, no report, no exchange of license numbers, no fight, no profanity, no nothing. It was a bit discouraging.

At noon we gathered at the head office, collected some more officials and our host took us to lunch at the Jockey's Club. . .With the aid of all present I ate those things for which Rio and Brazil are most noted. Some most excellent, some so-so. The famous coffee at the Jockey's Club, and elsewhere for that matter, must have bitter root and paint remover in it.

That afternoon, we drove to Petropolis, the summer capitol, about 40 odd miles up in the mountains over one of the few good highways. The paved highways of Brazil, a country larger than the U.S., have a total mileage of 450 miles. That wouldn't reach from Greencastle to Topeka, Kansas. Petropolis must be a half-mile above sea level. At places, where the highway ran near the cliff's edge, you could look down and see where you had been some 15 or 20 minutes before, but you'll never know how you got from there to where you are now.

Cavernous ex-casino

On the way is the Quintandinha (or some such spelling) Hotel— the biggest I ever saw. Here is where the Pan-American Conference was held. There it was on the mountain side, all quiet, no one about and just beginning to look a bit like our cattle barn east of Russellville, or "Happy" Cal's derby hat. The hotel is closed. The reason? It depended on its casino to keep it going. The new president of Brazil was instrumental in enacting a law making casinos illegal. So now the gambling element of Brazil is thinking of getting a new president. So you see, the world is pretty much the same all over.

We drove up under whatever it is that great big hotels have in front of them and there stood six or seven cars. Most of them held Del Mar sightseers. Nobody could get in. Our host disappeared somewhere and came back directly, saying we would get in. I asked, "How." He said, "Folding money." So you see, we are still pretty much the same, all the way around.

Did you ever see a whale of a big hay loft with all the hay left out? When we stepped through the front door into the dimness of that hotel, that was my thought. No lights and total silence. Everything on a tremendous scale and everywhere in semi-darkness. That conference room must be the size of our court house lawn, hitch rack and all. The flags of all the nations still hang. Hundreds of thousands of cruzeiros changed hands nightly under, and surrounded by those flags. Inside, I saw a swimming pool 25 feet deep at the deep end. The fellow who I think took the folding money told me in broken English the dome of the hotel was bigger than that of St. Peter's in Rome. I doubt that. I said to him, "It certainly would hold a pile of clover hay." That went clear past and beyond him. But who am I to tell a Brazilian how big his dome is?

Dom Pedro and his many fans

In Petropolis we went through the Palace of Dom Pedro. I'll not try to tell you just who Dom Pedro was, and how he came to be, because I don't know. I should, after all the Dom Pedroing I went through that afternoon, but I got confused. But Dom Pedro had to be some boy. Between him and his wife or wives and his sons and daughters and grandsons and granddaughters, and their activities, there wasn't much left to say about anybody else.

At the front door pious looking attendants slip felt slippers, open at the heel, over your shoes, and from there on through the palace you slide your way along the highly polished wooden floors (original). Dom Pedro, his wife (let's give him credit for only one) and their get were everywhere, in oil, bronze and marble, horseback and on foot. But Dom himself seemed to take pretty much to horses for the big pictures – the big scenes. We saw the throne room, bed rooms, dining hall, nursery and its cradles, uniforms, swords, state dresses, black-hair combs a foot high, old china and glassware and ladies fans.

Let me tell you about the fans. My Aunt Jennie Black was a fan fan—the kind that folded up—and the art was to fold and unfold them gracefully. Remember? In a way, cigarettes are to our coeds what fans were to Aunt Jennie and her era. Well, don't think Dom Pedro's queen and women folk weren't in there fanning hard with their fans, and long, long before Aunt Jennie and hers. A room the size of Crawley's pool room was full of them in glass cases. Hundreds, yes almost thousands of them: Wood, bone, ivory, tortoise shell, amber and whatever else that could be made into fans. Delicate filigree, gold, silver, mother of pearl, inlay of superb workmanship and so fine it should be magnified to show it is really hand work. Yes, they had fans in Dom's day, and just as many as Brooklyn has now.

And away back behind was a small cubby hole room where Dom and his Senators, or Cabinet, or advisers, or whatever it was he had, met and considered matters of state. Then Dom, after being duly advised, would go out and make his own laws. Up home you had Huey Long and some others I mustn't name out loud do about the same thing, so you see, we are pretty much . . .

Brightening prospects

Two full days in Rio is hardly enough to get much idea of a foreign city of a million and a half to two million in population. One man expressed it this way. "Rio has a limited number of rich to big rich, and a world of poor to very poor. We lack a middle class. We are very short on middle class. After the war people of Brazil flocked to Rio, and, far far oftener than not, left a position and life much higher than the one they attained, or could ever attain, in Rio."

Right now, they are slowed down almost critically by reason of a shortage of American dollars. They want and badly need to buy from us, but have no stable currency to pay with. Added to this, it would appear to the average outsider, they have some unfortunate and crippling legislation that doesn't help this situation.

We went to a cocktail party at the Copacabana Hotel. And there we met some 20 to 25 men from the States in various commercial and financial activities in Rio. It was the general opinion that the financial and industrial situation is rather bad. No impending panic seems evident, but a ripple of pessimism exists. As the evening advanced and the cocktails expanded, that pessimism dissipated. By the time some of us got to where a cock's tail blended into the rest of his feathers and where the cocktail party blended into the dinner party, it appeared a boom was about to start.

Labor and climate

Sailing out of Rio at 6 p.m. Dec. 8th, next morning early we docked at Santos. We loaded 400 tons of rather inferior bananas for Montevideo and Buenos Aires, all hand work except for the crane that lifted the sling of loaded bananas off the dock and lowered them into the hold. When they wanted to move a car up or down the track, about 50 men would surround it and push, and slowly she would begin to roll. At 11 a.m. the city siren blew and everybody quit work right then and there until 2 p.m. That gave us two full daylight days in Santos.

I had been told in Rio that another representative of one of the companies would meet and take care of us at Santos. The first day we drove to Sao Paulo, referred to by Brazilians as the "Chicago" of Brazil. To me, that is a Churchillian understatement. It is the manufacturing city of Brazil, some 50 odd miles up in the mountains from Santos. The two cities have rail and truck connections. I asked our host how come manufacturers would unload raw products or knockdown parts onto railroad cars or trucks, make the haul up to S.P., manufacture or assemble it there, then rail or truck it back down to Santos or Rio. Why not do it at Santos or Rio and cut out all that haul and extra handling?

The answer was "labor conditions and climate differences – mostly the former." After seeing those 50 men gingerly moving that banana car of half the capacity of one of Sir Herbert Martin's box cars, I began to catch the idea.

We had lunch in a super class French restaurant. For some unknown reason our host and his sprightly wife wanted to take us to The Jungle – a real, for sure Brazilian jungle some 140 kilometers on beyond Sao Paulo. We started, but long, long before The Jungle we practically ran out of road. They were improving and re-locating the highway. We held a caucus. Our host was as game as they come. . . Open revolt came when our host said he had inquired and was assured the road would get better farther on and that he would have us back aboard ship by midnight, perhaps before that time. A vote was taken. Three were for returning then and there, with one not voting. We turned around and headed back for Sao Paulo.

On the way out toward The Jungle we met truck after truck loaded high with sacked charcoal enroute to Sao Paulo where it sells as high as a doctor's bill back home. It is used in cooking. There seemed to be no coal. Gasoline is expensive and oil men tell me it is not as good as our "regular." No Ethyl.

Our host, knowing we had driven from Rio to Petropolis, at the day's end told us we had traveled almost half of the total good road mileage of Brazil.

No mink south of Key West?

At Rio and Santos we lost upward of a third of our original passengers. Newcomers filled all the vacated cabins, Portuguese or Spanish speaking peoples. Most of them were business men and not tourists out for a lark. Talk started about going through customs at Buenos Aires, and how many cigarettes and how much liquor we could take in. For some reason opinion on number and volume differed. . . As to liquor, the question centered around whether it was liters or number of bottles that counted, and if so what size bottles. All of which didn't help those who had it in jugs. I never will know how the jug crowd came out.

Sugar Foot's problem is something else. It has to do with a neck piece Mummy or someone else in the family besides me is sending to Ann Drew in California. Now you know why it is taking this roundabout way of getting to California, so why ask me that simple a question? But so far on the trip there has been no place for the display of furs, and the only way that comes to me now that we can achieve that air of affluence is for the hot water system of the flying machine to give out when we are 2,000 feet in the air going over the Andes to Santiago. But let's hope it doesn't. I don't want anything to happen to anybody that high up, much less Sugar Foot and me. I wouldn't want that to happen even to a Republican—provided there are any of them left up there by this time.

I see I started out telling you about Aura May's problem and wound up in politics. Her problem is this: she didn't declare said alleged mink neck piece on leaving the States. Now some low fellow tells us we will have trouble getting "back-in" with it. My hope is there are no mink south of Key West. And besides, the more I get the few glimpses of that neck piece the more I am convinced they're house cats made up to look like anything that has to pay a duty.

Interviewed by the Uruguay press

To The Graphic
Greencastle, Ind.

The evening of Dec. 10th we sailed out of Santos, redolent of coffee, and the next morning docked in Montevideo, to be met by another "angel" from one of those heaven sent Companies we've been blessed with so far. . . With the aid of an interpreter, we were to have our pictures taken and give an interview to a reporter for one of the newspapers.

They wanted to know how we liked Uruguay and Montevideo. Naturally, we didn't know, not having set foot on either yet.

Well, where were we going and what were we going to do – business, pleasure or diplomatic? And all this time I was repeatedly asked what advice I had to give to the people of Uruguay. You bet I had none—none whatever.

When this filtered to the reporter, he looked amazed and puzzled. He was thinking. The next perplexed question that came through the strainer was, "But you are a lawyer, aren't you?"

"Yes, I am a lawyer, but a lawyer is the last fellow you want to go to up home for advice—except politicians, veterinarians and undertakers."

They caught the "politician" part of it, but I don't think the reporter ever did unravel the rest of it.

He was a persistent pressman, however, and kept firing the advice question at me.

I finally said, "I have no advice whatsoever to whomsoever," etc. (using other big sounding words lawyers use when they don't know) "to give you splendid sovereign peoples of Uruguay. If I had to give something, it would be this: observe International Law and your Treaties to the letter, and then run your own country in your own way and without let or hindrance from anybody outside."

The interview was an unqualified success judged from the nods, gesticulations and shaking of hands. I got so I thought it was pretty good myself.

But alas. You should read what came out in the paper next morning. . . I was quoted to have said Uruguay had a most forward and socially stable government, or something like that.

Livestock—real and bronzed

Our friend, the manager of the company, proved to be most capable. . . We drove over the city after picking up his wife. . . Montevideo is much cleaner and more mechanized than is Rio or Santos, or so it seemed to me. The docks were less littered up. Perhaps people and business moved faster and more orderly. . . Saw a world of sheep. Sheep is a big industry in Uruguay—perhaps its biggest. There were also pen after pen of cattle. I never saw a steer there as good as Oscar Clodfelter's worst one.

If I have worked kilos into pounds and pesos into dollars correctly, prime steers are selling on the hoof there at the market at five to six cents per pound, our money. But always remember they're probably grassers and not the way the Hazlett boys or Jude Grimes corn feeds them.

Another thing in Montevideo. I've seen a real piece of art, a bronze piece of statuary "of heroic size." It sets in a park. It is called *La Carreta*, and depicts an early settler on a horse beside a two-wheeled pioneer cart with one big wheel sunk in the mud plumb down to the axle pulled by one bull and seven steers or oxen all yoked together, and with a spare ox tied on behind. I looked to see about that ox. He was an ox and the only possible criticism I have is that he should have been a cow tied on behind. Otherwise the thing is perfection to me. The cart slopes just right, the oxen look hard-worked, the bull like a bull, thick neck and all, the horse like a thin, tired horse ought to look, and the man like some men up on Raccoon I've seen in my time. Only he had on some local trappings my men never had. But there they are, the man yelling, the bull and oxen set and straining for every ounce, and all trying like hell to get out.

Maybe that cow was following behind a half quarter or so, and I failed to see her.

Cleared for Buenos Aires

We sailed out at 6 p.m. Dec. 13 for Buenos Aires. In the mean-time the Argentine doctors had come aboard to look us over and sort out the rots and specks. They, along with our ship's doctor and some of the officers were in the bar when Sugar Foot and I came back to ship. One man who had traveled before said they were being mellowed-up so they wouldn't be too technical with us. If they were, it took a long time. . . The Purser handed in Sugar Foot's passport. The doctor found the right page, took one look at her and stamped her "sound", remarked something about the beautiful senorita. They are good at that down here—mighty good. I don't know how many men have kissed her hand to date on introduction. . .They stamped me next and we were off.

A man from one of those blessed firms met us at B.A., and got us through customs in record time. Not only that, he got us and our lug-gage to a waiting car, and said, "This car and the chauffeur are at your disposal day and night during your stay in Buenos Aires, which we hope will be most pleasant. . . Don't hesitate to ask us for any information."

And here I had been worrying about two extra cartons of ciga-rettes all the way from St. Thomas.

We first got settled at the Plaza Hotel and then drove to see many of the sights. In B.A. they also drive pretty much by horn. I am told it is the second sized city in the Western Hemisphere—bigger than Chicago even. Anyway, it is big.

The sights of Buenos Aires are many and varied. About like any other S.A. city, only bigger. . . The shops are elaborate. . . Prices are reputedly relatively higher in B.A. than at home. I sincerely doubt this. I positively do. Especially if you get your money changed into pesos at what some are willing to give for American dollars. It may be a bit shady, but it is done rather openly. Never go to a bank. The banks are pegged. They can give you 9.3 pesos per dollar. Our blessed friend at the dock warned us. He told us to have our (get that possessive) chauffeur stop at one of the *cambios*, I think they call them, and go in—just like that. . .We got 15 for 1.

Due to the number of us arriving via S.S. Del Mar, we were not required to go to the police station to register. The authorities detailed a man to come to the Plaza Hotel and do the job. . . He had a big sign, "Silence," on his desk; also a typewriter. He assumed a very important look, much the same as the one I took on when the lobbyists began calling me "Senator." The job was soon over. We received our tourist cards with instructions to carry them at all times—or else.

Jockey's Club—where the beef is

Beef is the staple food, killed that morning. No self-respecting Argentine would touch ripened meat or chilled or deep freeze stuff. He wants it right off the hoof. And yet, I am inclined to think they want it fairly well-done. Sugar Foot has been having trouble getting hers rare enough.

The best meat I have had was at the Jockey's Club. Every town down here seems to have a Jockey's Club. . . All of them are owned and operated by the same people. Who started them? The farmers of the Argentine. Away back there these beef growers began to get rich. Then they got feudal. They were the Aristocracy of hereabouts. Big holdings and immense herds. Then they moved to town and took over. Now some of them have gone to Monte Carlo and Cannes and New York while the overseers and hired men run the place back home. That is the way I am told. . . To be a member you have to be one of those farmers. Or else a descendant of one of those farmers—you've got to have Hereford blood somewhere in you.

The Club has all the dignity it is possible to have. Marble floors, big well-spaced tables with large roomy chairs, heavy dark polished woodwork, immense wide stairways and steps with low risers, an enormous library with old men in dignified dress asleep here and there, kinda like English clubs, say.

On Sunday we went to the races at Palermo track. . . We had as our guests Captain Jones and Purser Stricker of the Del Mar and a Mrs. Somebody who operates a girls' school in Buenos Aires. The captain and Mrs. Somebody go to bet on the races, and bet they did, on every race. I said above that we were hosts. That's wrong. The good captain had the big thing—access to the Jockey's Club part of the track, the stand right at the wire. In my innocence I had asked them as guests. They had accepted as such. Having sat at table with the good captain for about three weeks, he had long since gotten my number and what I knew about Palermo and everything else south of the Putnam County line. He just bided his time and then let me down as easy as possible. He's that way.

Evaluating the women

I remember what Claud Smith (now a pious, sedate lawyer and ex-judge down at Princeton) said once when we had gathered in a room at Indiana U for the usual talk. In his blunt, matter-of-fact way, Claud spoke up first. He said, "Well, shall we begin talking about the girls right off the bat, or gradually lead up to them like we've been doing?"

So let's talk about these beautiful women down here. They know how to dress in a striking way. Black-eyed, black-haired with smooth swarthy complexions. Some are as sinuous and graceful as all get out. But my observation is that the majority are from trifling bulky to good and bulky. But you must bear in mind that I do not see much of the younger set. It is the older women I get to see most. . . I do not under-stand Spanish. That is a terrible handicap. But if they talk as intelli-gently as they do animatedly and rapidly, they're honeys.

Nevertheless and notwithstanding, I think I know where the prettiest women on earth are to be found in the greatest numbers, and I'll tell you where to see them. Go sit on the Boulder in East College campus when classes let out and you'll see them. You'll see more per square inch there than you'll see here per square rod. If you are too self-conscious or too dignified now to go sit on the Boulder, then I'll tell you, . . . if we had brought Miss Bess Robbins and Miss Sedelia Starr down here some time ago they would have won 99 out of 100 of all the beauty contests hereabouts. I'll add my sister, Mrs. Margaret D. Bridges. I thought she was the prettiest girl I ever saw.

Over the Andes by air

On a certain bright morning at 11:15 we started my biggest trial by fire or whatever the poets call it—going over the Andes in a flying machine. To me the plane didn't look any too new, or the paint any too fresh, or the pilot and crew any too much like I thought high-fly-ing Andes pilots ought to look. The passengers looked pretty heavy, and there was a world of baggage.

The takeoff was the usual one. We got higher and higher. The literature on the back of the seat just in front of me was none too as-suring. It said, "If you feel yourself getting sick just use the strong pa-per bags in the pocket on the back of the seat in front of you. Don't feel ashamed. Others before you have used them," or words to that effect.

We climbed and climbed. From time to time I thought I heard the engine sputter. We would hit bad going occasionally, the wings would dip up and down, and my seat would sort of try to get fully out from under me.

The best way I know to describe the scene is . . . rectangular straight sided patches of land of varying sizes and colors as far as one could see: green, purple, dirt color, straw color. Sometimes I thought there were streams of water. Houses or barns were mere ballot-sized squares, evidently surrounded with trees in full leaf. . . Inevitably each town had a plaza with spokes running out like those of a wagon wheel.

At the foot of the Andes the ground was closer and looked like the crinkled hide of an elephant. Then came the Andes. Soon there was plenty of snow. Eventually we passed to one side of Mt. Aconcagua, the highest peak in South America, 23,000 and some feet. We must have been 21,000 feet up. Then we saw its glacier, blue-green and cold. Up there we saw lots of blue-green ice.

In short order we circled over Santiago and landed. Gosh-a-mighty! Was I glad! We landed at 1:15 p.m., one hour change of time. It had been a three hour trip. And right there at the airport was a representative of one of those Heaven-sent U.S. corporations I've been talking about, ready and willing to take us and our one remaining jug of St. Thomas rum through the customs and to the Carrera Hotel.

And now we are going on our big adventure into and among the unknown. Daughter Joan and her husband, Bill, met a couple in Paris, France, last whenever it was who are from Nehuentue, in southern Chile, near the lakes and volcano region. Sight unseen they have asked us down over Christmas, and sight unseen we are going. They are of French extraction. Speak Spanish fluently, but no English. Sugar Foot speaks and understands considerable Spanish. But what am I to do? How am I to learn where the bathroom is even—if there is any.

In Chile: Rocky roads, big 'farm'

The train from Santiago to Temuco, where we were to meet our unknown host, is a three or four car diesel train. In English, it is "The Arrow." All seats are reserved and it is probably an extra fare train, all first class. The train left at 7:45 and arrived in Temuco, about 450 kilometers away, at 6:10 p.m.

Going south toward Temuco, we kept in the valley with fair sized mountains on each side, quite a distance away. Garden truck, fruit trees and wheat, cattle of European breeds, considerable dairy stuff, but nary a Hereford. *Huasos* (Chilean cowboys, corresponding to the Argentinean gauchos) in their *mantas* (cloth blankets with slits in the middle to put the head through) became common.

Temuco is the biggest city in south Chile, about 65,000. On the platform we met our host, a clean-cut, energetic young fellow about 32 years old, and another young fellow who turned out to be a schoolmate of our host in Paris. Our hostess was home with a slightly ailing four-month-old boy.

The two men were to take us southeast to Pucon in the lake and volcano country, 50 kilometers away. The road was a bit rough and we must hurry because we should see the scenery enroute and then spend the night in the fine resort hotel at Pucon. Then back next day to Temuco and thence due west another 80 kilometers or so to mine host's *fundo* (farm) near Nehuentue. It was all arranged.

We got in a 1947 Chevrolet that had taken a beating since it left the factory and started over the road described as "a bit rough" . . . Man of Samaria! Was that road rough! And did the loose round rock fly. . . Our car had a special network of steel bolted to the frame to keep flying rock from damaging the underside. And 7-ply tires – I never heard of them. And most of the time our speedometer ranged from 45 to 80 kilometers per hour, depending on how the road looked to our host. He mis-guessed many times.

We had three blowouts on that road to Pucon, and the first one tore the inner tube all to the devil. We never saw the valve stem. Our friends donned overalls, spread a piece of thick material and got under.

The blowouts caused us to change plans. We couldn't make Pucon and its splendid resort hotel that night, because we might run out of tires. We would have to stop short about 25 kilometers, at Villarrica, near a tremendous volcano of that name. Our host knew a French woman who ran a hotel there. Not much of a hotel for looks and all of the comforts, but the food would be exceptionally good. It was.

That late evening was the last time we were to see Villarrica. A mountain of a volcano, snowclad, it stood high above everything else, cold, white and still. It appeared shaped like one of the pyramids of Egypt, except that the top didn't come to so acute an apex. It erupted last year after a long period of dormancy. It awed me something like the Grand Canyon of Arizona does. Next day brought a big haze.

Quest for hot water

That hotel is something to write home about. The evenings and nights were cold. We wanted a room with twin beds and bath. By golly, they had it—such as it was. We wanted heat, but that they didn't have. The bed was too short for me, even sleeping crosswise.

Next morning I turned on the hot water faucet for shaving. No hot water. My interpreter, Sugar Foot, was asleep, so I thought I'd try to make myself understood. I asked the first girl I saw about hot water. She spoke and gesticulated rapidly, which opened the flood gates, and five or six more came running. Thus reinforced, we all ventured back to our room.

They must have forgotten all about any daughter being along. She was asleep and covered up, head and all. I called her. When she got unraveled and that head emerged, framed in all those aluminum and tinware bobby pins, the nearest girl gave a wild-eyed half shriek. When the baby of the family unwound some more, the girls, seeing no blood, finally consented to listen. With a something in Spanish or French that evidently meant, "Oh, that was what he wanted," the girls filed out. Aura May, in a tone they don't teach in finishing school, said, "They will bring some hot water as soon as they can make it."

She gave me a crab-apple look, turned over and wound up again.

In far longer than due time, a long-eared boy brought a pint container of water. It was just enough to take the chill off the bottom of the lavatory. And the rubber plug leaked, to boot.

The trip on to Pucon was uneventful, concerning tire trouble. We were never to have any more. The hotel looked all it was represented to be. There were few guests. The beach was as bare as our dry lots after a year of feeding. One motor "put-putted" out on the lake—30 miles long—but the occupants looked like they'd prefer being somewhere where steam heat was on. It is true that the season was just begun—hardly that.

We all four had had enough. We started back to Temuco over that same road. The day was cold with very poor visibility. Some of the volcanoes were no doubt smoking like they had for hundreds of years. We couldn't see them.

Something keeps telling me the weather south of Chile will have to change to make that hotel a good go. I want none of its stock. I'd rather have mine in Russellville Bank, and the Lord knows some of the stock holders think that is bad enough.

Tree fences and ox carts

But we did see sights I never knew existed. I'll tell you how they built fences 50 to 75 years ago. The country was full of big timber. They wanted less timber and more fences. They cut the trees into 9 to 10 foot lengths, split the timber into 9 inches to a foot for thickness, squared the sides, dug long trenches three to four feet deep, and set these timbers side by side, close and tight, and then filled in and there was your fence, horse high, bull strong and pig, yes, chicken-tight, unless they flew. There are thousands of miles of that kind of fence still down there, old and moss-covered but still pretty sound and serviceable. Think of the work and loss of timber that involved.

Another big sight is the oxen and their carts. On this trip most of them were hauling timber of one sort or another, logs or sawed stuff. We saw hundreds of oxcarts and oxen. Some carts had spokes, steel tires, steel axles and metal fellers, or whatever it is the axles fit into. Many of them had wheels made of round logs with no metal tires or other metal about them. The axles ran through holes in the bare wood. They were the primitive kind, but there were hundreds of them.

Worlds of caste

All the time we were passing huasos in their mantas astride their horses—hundreds of them. There were so many they almost got monotonous. Never was a "hello" said, or an arm lifted in salutation. We were in a car, and that was enough. Worlds of caste separated them from us.

The back track to Temuco was about the same. We missed a few of our original boulders but made up for it with new ones. To be sure, much of the little stuff, say from four inches down, we had shot from under the tires out into the wheat fields and pastures, so it was out of our way, but that was only a fraction of the available material.

We headed west from Temuco toward the Pacific. The road was to be about like it had been for some 55 kilometers and then get "rather bad at times from there on." The "bad roads" turned out to be dirt roads with big chuck holes.

We entered the Mapucha Indian country. They live in thatched shanties and lean-tos, some in sort of caves they had dug in steep banks along the roadside. There were plenty of dogs and children. Once, at some distance, I saw a lot of smoke coming out all over a roof. I thought the place was on fire, but our host, by way of our interpreter, Aura May, said roofs are made to let out smoke. An Indian builds his fire on the floor in the middle of the house. I suppose the rain comes in the same way the smoke goes out.

A whale of a *fundo*

The big moment came: We were at the home of our host and hostess. The big white house sits on a round natural knoll, the top of which is about 100 feet above the surrounding ground. Flower gardens practically surround the house and are about as well kept and beautiful as any you will see anywhere; some mighty tall eucalyptus trees; a fine cement tennis court with a judge's stand and seats all around for spectators; double garage; a long, turning, bowered walk leading from the base of the hill up to the front door, the bower made of trimmed and trained small sycamore trees.

A *fundo* in Chile corresponds to an Argentinean *estancia*—a big farm to a whale of a big farm. This *fundo* has some 3,000 acres. He has another down the road back toward Temuco. *Fundo No. 1* has a big Delco lighting system, so you know what that means—three or four all time men.

I shall not try to account for the army of men and women this "fundoist" (let's just coin another new word) employs, but I'll give you a rough idea. He pays off through a window of his office in the house. From about one or two p.m. to five o'clock that Saturday, when he and his overseer knocked off for tea, they had paid 62 men and women. After tea they went back at it and then again after dinner. I was never told the full count.

He always has a long list of potential employees. He is good pay. And yet I know a smallish man back home who gets exactly 10 times the money that this man pays his overseer per month. Now maybe you can begin to account for those beautiful gardens, those precision trimmed hedges, that spick and span house, those neat walks, weedless lawn, splendidly cooked meals faultlessly served, and so ad infinitum— a seeming inexhaustible supply of fabulously cheap man and woman power by our standards. Not so much down here by Chilean standards, in Chilean money, made in Chile.

Our room in the Carrera Hotel in Santiago with twin beds, tub and shower, service galore, large, airy and well-appointed in every way, on the 14th floor with French windows and magnificent view—a splendid room in probably the biggest and best hotel in town—cost us 606 pesos per day, sales tax and tips included. In our money, as we exchanged it, that means $6.06. Even a Durham wouldn't kick on that.

We will get back to the fundo and go out the front door, make a right angle and have a look. Below and directly in front are the barns, barn lots, drives, pens, slaughterhouse, enormous two story wheat granary, potato houses, stables, sheds, blacksmith shop, lumber room and sawmill pretty well equipped to make any wooden thing a farm needs, the Delco building, the flour mill, the cheese factory and probably a lot of other "small stuff" like that.

He had six riding horses in one stable when I looked in. Two of them were thoroughbred Chilean horses he seemed rather proud of, although he is extremely modest about what he owns. Aura May went riding to the nearby Indian town and back on the big hills, taking a look at the Pacific Ocean off there to the west about two miles.

Beyond the aforementioned barns and so forth is the highway, and beyond that is near 2,000 acres of about the finest bottom land in all Chile. It is supreme. It extends over a mile to the river and almost three miles up and down, to a very small town, Nehuentue, his post office. The river is rather narrow, but deep and navigable – salt water up past him, and with a small tide, say two feet. He has his own private dock on the river where he loads his wheat, potatoes, cattle, sheep and whatever else he may want to ship.

He appears to think his livestock is a small part of the fundo. And yet, when he got the idea I thought a good deal of cattle, he took Sugar Foot and me into a pasture of an excellent sort of strange grass where he had 50 or 60 grassers he expected to weigh 1,000 pounds by cold weather—next July or August. They were of all colors and duo colors, but good boned, uniform, and in good flesh—the best I had seen. I saw perhaps another 300 animals, 40 or 50 good-sized hogs and a good many sheep. And still, he isn't in the livestock business—much.

The missing purse

Early Christmas Day afternoon, we started to Temuco to catch the train back to Santiago. We had one of the four compartments on that long steam locomotived train, which arrived in Santiago the next morning at 10 a.m.

We stepped jauntily into a well worn taxi and started for the Carrera Hotel when Aura May jumped straight up. Where was her purse, her passport, over $300 in U.S. currency, about 3,000 pesos in Chilean money, the ship tickets to Panama, the flying machine tickets to Los Angeles, her hair tinware and other feminine goods and wares too numerous to mention? We got the driver turned around and back. The train was still standing in the shed. I had to watch the baggage to save what we had left. Aura May took off like a teal at Le Pas, Manitoba, five days after opening day. She flew past the gate man like he wasn't there. Gate men seem to know when women mean business. The last I saw, she was headed down the right platform.

To me a long time elapsed. . . Then here she came—with the purse, shoulder sling and all, intact except for a few hundred pesos she, in her gratitude, had scattered to whomsoever would take them.

The porter had promptly taken the purse to his superior. . . If you ever again hear me speak ill of Chilean porters, call my attention to this item of my experience.

Shipboard to Lima

The train ride to Valpariso, first down the valley, then over and through mountains took something over three hours. We arrived shortly after 11 a.m. Grace Line representatives at Santiago had assured us our ship, the Santa Cecilia, would not sail until 2 p.m. or later. On arrival . . . at the accommodation ladder, three coated officers said the ship sails at noon.

We sailed almost immediately, headed for Callao, port city of

Lima. We were first going south to San Antonio to pick up some copper, 44 tons (not gallons) of whiskey and 8 tons of brandy.

I knew we were to spend New Year's day on shipboard, but didn't think it would take that much.

This ship accommodates only 50 passengers approximately, and is more of a cargo ship than a passenger. Her length is just about 450 feet. The accommodations are excellent.

That evening at dinner found us again safely ensconced at the captain's table, only this time it is a table for four, whereas the Del Mar accommodates six. Capt. Tierney of San Francisco and New York presides.

We headed back north. Our first stop was Antofagasta, Chile, north of Valpariso. We arrived in the early morning. We were to take on 1,900 tons of Anaconda 99+ percent copper for New York. It would take all day. We were to sail at 6 p.m. New Year's eve. We were free for the day.

Too much money

By miscalculation of some sort we were hundreds of pesos too much. Here was our last chance to get rid of them. Sugar Foot and I footed it around to the main part of town to buy most anything worthwhile, small and light, and to mail some letters.

The mailing of letters, with reasonable assurance of their arrival at destination, is a real chore. You must go to the post office. So far as I know, post offices are always crowded down here. In the confusion of a foreign language you must first select the correct windows in the correct order, especially if you want to register and air mail your letters. If you send by regular mail, the addressees will be confined to wheel chairs ere the arrival of such mail.

We looked and looked to spend all those extra pesos. She saw nothing whatsoever. We did buy the Dec. 26th Latin-American edition of *Time* in English for 35 pesos, but that didn't make a dent in our sheaves of Chilean money.

Then she had a brilliant idea. "Tonight is New Year's Eve. Let's buy some Chilean champagne and burgundy for the table tonight. We still have three more nights on shipboard to use any surplus."

Two fairly heavy packages and two boys to carry them about solved our peso problem.

Well, about 9 p.m. it was announced—just like that—the captain was giving a dance and New Year's party.

New Year's Day, 1950, our first and only stop was Ilo, Peru, where we took on 47 tons of canned tuna fish. Some five miles out, going to Ilo, I saw drove after drove of . . . guano birds. I had seen the snow-like tops of the rocks on shore in the distance. Guano is a fertilizer and big business down here. If it hadn't been for the guano birds there would have been no Grace Lines, now 100 years old.

Most of the west coast of South America is a desolate place. Mountains of brown bare earth and rock rise and stretch inland, parallel to the coast. It just never rains. The cold Humboldt stream sees to that. The sun shines hot, but the air is cold, even in mid-day. The towns and cities look dusty and worn, like the dry sections of the U.S. Lots of adobe-looking buildings. The whole country is drier than a rambo apple.

Where Inquisition 'relieved' the rich

We docked at Callao about 6 a.m. Jan 2 for a week's stay in Lima.

The Tagle Torre must have been a sort of Foreign Ministry. It was built about 1735, as it had tile of that date in the walls. There is a lot of brown spindled wood in its make-up, both inside and outside. All about are tremendously large heavy gold leaf mirrors. A big oil painting of Pizarro, conqueror of Peru, hangs on the wall. Just inside the patio is a monster reared-up lion's head with a beam at the top. From this beam scales were suspended to weigh gold and silver they took from the Indians, or the subjects, or both, to send to Spain. Anyway, every thing of value that was loose or could be pried loose, went to Spain.

The next stop was the Palacio de la Inquisicion. Here is where they held the inquisitions. The idea was to "inquisite" rich men, the richer the better, and the more the "take" would be. They never let facts or the truth interfere in the least. Not in the slightest degree. And so they fabricated charges out of thin air and without element of truth whatsoever, against any man, provided he was rich. . . Cut off his head, confiscate his lands, sell off the Herefords and the old mule team, take their 10 percent "cut" and send the balance to Spain. They never fooled with poor people. They were like Robin Hood, only far more so.

A visit to the Inca ruins

The city has a museum of Inca civilization and it is a honey. Many original big long pointed stones with their carvings have been removed from in front of the temples, brought down and set up here. Big and little stones of very hard structure were worked into human heads, dogs, cats and so forth. Mummies, burial sacks, elaborate and fine fabrics of wearing apparel are everywhere. There are thousands of square feet of pottery of every shape, and still showing the original delicate colors. It would take weeks to even take a rather hurried look at the things that museum contains. Incas were a great and cultured people.

The closest ruins to Lima are the Pachacamac ruins, 32 kilometers away. We drove there one afternoon. High up was what was left of the Temple to the Sun. They are always on the highest ground as the sun cut more of a figure with the Incas than anything else. . .We drove through the narrow streets of the town, with the stone walls of the stores or houses rising high above us on either side as far as cars were permitted, or could go, almost to the walls. There was our temple in a pretty bad condition of decay. These ruins had long been sacked. Part of the findings was in the museum I told you about. The crumbling walls and stairways and moats(?) were of stone carefully and symmetrically made and laid.

The main stairway would allow five or six to go abreast. It had sharp angles every so often, and high walls, the better to protect and defend in case of attack, probably. Higher up it had no walls, just steps after steps and paths always leading higher. We got to the top—acres of it. Sand and ruins.

Over toward "town," and to one side and much lower were the ruins of the Temple to the Moon. It is being restored. . .You can see the original round wooden poles in perfect preservation. It never rains. But there is so much restoration there is little original left. Inside the temple is the original square bath(?) made good and tight of shaped stone. It holds muddy water with fish flopping now and then.

I suggested driving to the big Inca ruins—about like I'd suggest driving to Shawnee Mound near Wingate—but it is considerably over 1,000 kilometers from here, eight or nine thousand feet up in the mountains toward Bolivia. You either take a train, which is a very hard ride, or go by plane. In any event, it takes about a week if you want to see any considerable part of the ruins – there is something about plane schedules that interferes. And so, I shall never get to see the great big Inca ruins.

We were introduced to a young lady who was born right at the big Inca ruins. This young lady, who has lived here since she was seven, has a father who manufactures some kind of the finest of all fine wools, I think up there at the ruins. Anyway, he goes back and forth about every 15 days. Our young lady herself has found some minor pieces of Inca stuff. Her father has found many. And her grandpa got pretty well off finding and peddling Inca stuff, like Munny's Grandpa Wells did making and peddling wheat fans at black market prices.

Street noises and games

Our "fleet" of rooms is the noisiest place in town. And that is saying something. One night long after midnight I sat at one of these windows in my sleeping outfit looking at the crowd (yes, a crowd), thinking and trying to count the different noises. I was also thinking about my creditors, and how I was now getting closer and closer to them, and sooner or later, I'd have to face them. Well, what I have remaining in money value is getting pretty low. As to the noises, I got up to 14 but there are lots more than that. The honks, street cars and newsboys drown out the culls and low grade noises.

As Aura May has disappeared more and more from her father's side, he has ventured more and more in the marts of trade and commerce. About the first venture here was into the banana situation. I had seen push carts of fruit everywhere. Close observation, at a discreet distance, disclosed customers bought, peeled and ate the fruit and then dropped the peels in a receptacle on the cart. I could do that. I did.

Lightning calculation disclosed I was paying about two cents American each for the biggest ones. A young Indian had preceded me. I offered him one. He accepted. Word got over the grape vine. My clientele increased, and there we stood blithely peeling and eating and aiming at the waste basket. Aura May would have been ashamed for me. When a client missed, I cut him off the list. They caught onto that easily although no English was spoken except by me. The adventure cost me a full 90 cents. Try having fun buying 90 cents worth of bananas back home.

False crosses abound

The Grace Line decided to sail the *Santa Margarita* a day early (Jan. 9). That can be accounted for in that these ships are for cargo first, and secondarily for passengers. We sailed at 8 p.m. promptly. No, my friends. We are not at the captain's table, but we are doing our level best.

In my opinion to date, the Southern Cross is among the most overestimated sights down this way. Counting all three ships, I have been shown four or five Southern Crosses, all different, and at least a pair of False Crosses. From our patio outside the French doors of the hotel in Buenos Aires, I had picked out what I thought was the real thing, and was pretty well satisfied. Now I'm not so sure.

Last night, for instance, I was out alone and had selected my Southern Cross for the evening. . . Along came one of the seamen and I asked him to show me the Southern Cross. He said, "It is below the horizon now. It might be visible just before daylight."

Today the sea was calm and it is that way tonight. Today, by Act of Providence I won a shuffleboard game from the steward. That is about the first since the man with heart trouble who voted for Garfield defaulted to me off Brazil somewhere.

We arrived at Paita, Peru, Jan. 11, and anchored off shore about a half mile in 160 feet of water. We began loading from a sizable ship bearing the U.S. flag, named *Washington Star,* 40 tons of decapitated frozen tuna, weighing 20 to 60 pounds each, and cotton from the interior. Around us are row boats peddling bananas, mangos, alligator pears, wool blankets, silverware, leather boots, and "authentic Inca relics made down the coast," the owner of the Washington Star tells me. Some of the "art" figures are not to be found in D.A.R. collections. Two New Jersey doctors bought out the entire stock.

Ship's whistle marks crossing of Equator

At Sea
January 13, 1950

We are just now crossing the Equator northbound. One long blast announced our crossing. The temperature of the sea water is 78 degrees.

The 40-mile trip "up the river" to Guayaquil, principal port of Ecuador, was made in a Grace Line yacht, Santa Rosita, formerly a submarine chaser powered by a General Motors diesel capable of 27 knots. She is fast. She has to be. The Guayas River is not only fast but seems to cover about all outdoors hereabout. It takes power to buck the river's current. And when the tide is running out it takes still more power.

Guayaquil is a pretty rusty looking city to me. The population is about 250,000. The rain had stopped before our arrival. The day was cloudy, but it was very, very hot and humid nonetheless. The town was full of push-cart and sidewalk salesmen, all sorts of outdoor food sales and the ever-present Coca Cola. Our hats are off to the Coca-Cola people. Perhaps in only one or two places in far south Chile were we without the jurisdiction of a "refreshing pause."

Here were bananas and pineapples galore. A vendor would take an 18 to 20-inch pineapple by the stalk, pare off the outer shell quite deftly, slice it crosswise, and sell it by the slice at the end of a long sharp butcher knife. I don't know the price, probably two slices for a cent. Foreigners are told to lay off food here on the streets.

Practically all shops and stores are open air affairs. You just walk in and there you are among the dry goods. All have more or less useless trinkets. The small rooms are crowded to suffocation, with no room to turn around in. Panama hats are a staple. . . On the other hand, all shopkeepers and salesmen were courteous, attentive and tried to help. No high pressure salesmanship anywhere as you and I know it.

In one shop, a woman was carefully watching me. I thought it was to keep me from filching one or more articles. But no. She finally had the audacity to touch me lightly where the old wallet should be, and the proprietor spoke up, "My wife wants to know if the señor will tell us where he got his suit of clothes, and how much he paid for it.?" Seeing my chance to try to repay Haspel, the maker, who had gone to the trouble to send several different styles to the store across the street from the Roosevelt Hotel in New Orleans, I peeled off my coat and wrote down everything in the label except the number of the patent. And so, Messrs. Haspel up there in New Orleans, if a prepaid order comes from Guayaquil at the retail price of $22.50, please remember I am your "drummer" without portfolio and that I am not adverse to an unreasonable commission.

Coming back down the river to the ship, the passengers got into a general discussion of what they had seen and what they enjoyed. Some liked one thing and some another. But the consensus seemed to center on the beautiful, graceful and elaborate marble tombstones and mausoleums at the cemetery. So next time when in Guayaquil, go out and have a look at its No. 1 attraction.

Of the present passenger list, one of the most interesting to me is a piano playing timber buyer, or let us say, a timber buying piano player. I have seen a great many piano players and lots of timber buyers in my time, but this, I think, is the first combination of the two professions in any one man I have had the good fortune to encounter. The load he carries must be Herculean. At one time I was a piano player. That was after father and I decided the life of a pool expert was not the life for me. At the zenith of my interpretation and rending of the masters I was also enrolled in college, but even my best friends on the faculty were unanimous in agreeing I was not both a student and a piano player.

My new friend buys balsa by the ship load and sends it to the U.S. and England. We talked about walnut, oak, mahogany and then some Brazil and South American heavy woods. He got red oak mixed up with California redwood. We got that straightened out. Some enterprising Californians had inveigled him into buying some big red oak (redwood) wine casks and selling them to Chilean vintners. He got run out of Chile for that. "Baad taazt. No goot."

I finally worked out his pedigree. He was a Czech. A real pianist, he had played in Prague, Zurich, Vienna and all around. When World War II started, he started looking for a new home. He became a refugee and finally wound up in Guayaquil, where he expected to teach piano. That was optimism supreme.

Coffee by the ton, not cupful

Buenaventura, Colombia
Jan. 14, 15, 16, 1950

We have gone into the coffee business in a rather big way. We are to take on 43,000 bags, about 150 pounds to the bag. That makes over 3,200 tons, or more than enough to run Margaret and Frances over Labor Day.

This town has perhaps 30,000 population. Some tell me it has 65,000, some as low as 10,000. You guess. I went around into town. It is about like Guayaquil on a smaller scale. A native who is employed by Grace Line told me he was half Indian—his mother a full-blooded Indian—I don't know what the other half is. Colombia, according to him, is 60 percent Negro and 10 percent white. Spanish is the language.

It happened here in Buenaventura, of all places, and on shipboard. Something was said about Greencastle, Ind. A young Mrs. Burt and her husband were returning to the states after six years with the Kennicott Copper Co. in Chile. Mrs. Burt heard the remark and said her father and mother were both born in or near Greencastle. His name was Jack Reeves. He taught in the grade school in Greencastle. His mother was a Schafer. We knew her uncle, Frank Schafer.

We are tardy. We were to have sailed last evening (Sunday) at 6, then 9 p.m., then 6 a.m. today, then 9 a.m. The reason for the delay was too much coffee to load—and rain. I am told it rains here every day and that the annual rainfall is 360 odd inches.

We got away at 10 a.m. We are now on the high seas headed for where the Pacific discovered Balboa.

Hot times in the Canal Zone

Canal Zone
Jan. 18—21, 1950

To The Graphic,
Greencastle, Ind.

The ride to the Canal Zone was uneventful. Enroute, the question arose whether to stay with the ship and ride through the locks and canal to the east side to Cristobal, or to get off at Balboa and hunt our way to the Tivoli Hotel, as originally planned.

Two New Jersey doctors and their wives, the timber buying piano player and his wife and some of the ship's officers advised staying with the ship and then coming back here by train or bus, as suited best. Mr. and Mrs. Burt (nee Reeves) were also for sticking with the ship. All the women were going shopping on the Atlantic side for linens, ivory and oriental silks, etc. "at wonderful prices" (and they were—Tiffany prices). Then after dinner everybody was to go to a night club the two doctors' wives knew about. The ship's officers were ignored as to sailing time and matters of other unimportance to Grace Line stockholders.

We reversed ourselves and stayed with the ship.

To the Atlantic by ship

I shall not try to describe the feats of engineering the building of the Panama Canal involved: Ridding the place of mosquitoes and malaria; damming the outlet of a river so the mean level of the new, partly man-made lake would be about 87 feet above the Atlantic and Pacific Oceans; making cuts of 100 feet or more in solid rock; dredging the channel so our ship drawing almost 30 feet could steam through.

Three giant locks on the Pacific side lifted us almost 30 feet per lock, so at the third lock we could sail out into first a winding canal and then into that tremendous lake whose new level left thousands of islands of its former jungle hill tops in size all the way from a few square feet to hundreds and probably thousands of acres. Studded all along were thousands of dead bare tree trunks and forks still sticking up out of the water, and some of those trees went by us not any too far off.

Entering an approach to the first lock, six electric "mules" (three on each side) would take hold of us by heavy wire cables, get us midway from the sides of the giant cement walls. We would creep along into the lock proper. There we were, way down there below the surface of the lock, with a monster set of double steel doors ahead barring our further progress. Another pair of steel doors would close behind us. No way to get out. Then the water below started bubbling and we started rising.

The way that lock filled with water was a marvel. All the Baptists in the Southern Jurisdiction pumping simultaneously wouldn't have raised us the first foot in an hour. A young fellow standing at the rail with me said it took eight or 10 minutes and, after a rapid mental calculation, three million cubic feet of water. I made it 20 minutes and three billion cubic feet of water. The young man said he worked at the locks. Let's give him the benefit. So when I get home don't come bringing me a lot of authentic figures.

We got out into the canal and on into the lake and to the Atlantic locks, where the process was reversed and we were lowered about 87 feet. We docked after 7 p.m. We had started in about 9:30 a.m.

Now, for my advice. Go through it once by all means. Then never repeat. It becomes very monotonous and very hot. At times we only crept. The high temperature yesterday was 89. The low last night 77.

We went down the gang plank alone and unattended and into the early night and the arms of customs. He slapped on five blobs of glue, five stickers at the few remaining places for stickers and added five banker's initials and pronounced us pure and undefiled.

A Grace Line representative called and made a reservation for us at the Washington Hotel. An eager taxi cab driver loaded us and off we went.

All along I had been amazed at the size of the linen in South

American hotel rooms. Some bath towels were as long as I was. At the Washington Hotel we got out of the 5 x 6 foot bath towel area. The cotton manufacturers hereabouts must have lost control over the Legislature.

We hied ourselves to the shopping rendezvous, with Aura May in the lead. With true feminine instinct and bird dog accuracy she never faltered a step as we hotfooted it down to the "shopping district" of a strange town. She said, "They should be right along about here." And sure enough, there, three doors on down, they were—every one of them—the two doctors' wives buried under the two biggest table-cloths. . .

Trading slowed down. The ship's passengers went back to stow packages and get ready to night club. They were to come to the Washington and pick up A.M. Nothing was said about me. They never came. *The Santa Margarita*, faithful to the winds of commerce, sailed at midnight.

The night before we had been put to sleep by the gentle roll of the Pacific. That night we went to sleep with the Atlantic beating at the foundations of our hotel—almost.

To the Pacific by rail

I knew the general manager of the Panama Railway. Met him through a college friend. . . The railroad people gave us passes. They would send the railroad "jitney" to our hotel to pick up the baggage and us to catch the 12 o'clock train for Balboa. They would have a van at Balboa to take us to the Tivoli hotel.

The train ride of 30 miles took about one and a quarter hours—diesel power. We came first class. The right-of-way was bound by wild banana, reed and semi-jungle. The road had a good many bridges, cuts, curves, considerable grade and evidently cost a good deal of money. No featherbedding, I was told, like our roads unfortunately have.

We stepped off the train at Balboa and into a car chauffeured by a cap with three letters on it; drove four or five blocks and when we got out at the Hotel Tivoli we were in Ancon. And right down there a block at the foot of the hill is Panama City—the relatively new Panama.

Where oh where have our two-letter corporation guardians gone? Those alleged evaders of the anti-trust laws, who have so faithfully shepherded us these thousands of miles through the mazes of Portuguese and Spanish gyrations and possible malefactions?

We registered and A.M. asked for mail. There was none.

"Are you sure."

"Yes!"

"Haven't we had a reservation here for two months?"

"No."

"Sure?"

"Yes!"

Later I came down and went through the same procedure with another man, with the same results. Not satisfied, I tackled another clerk. He went through the books. Yes, we had had a reservation, but hadn't shown up the proper day. "Any mail?" He rummaged around and threw out a handful, all but one for A.M., . . . also a card noting we had not arrived as per schedule and if we should arrive later to call a certain number.

We did. He was the faithful manager of one of our two faithful conservators. He came around and took us sight-seeing: Through the slums, good residential sections, up and down narrow crowded one-way streets and the Broadway of Panama (Fifth Avenue) past the Oriental stores.

Ruins of old Panama

He took us out to the ruins of old Panama—the original Panama. It is on a bluff seven or eight miles up the Pacific to the left of present Panama. The monks who laid it out had an eye to safety. Up there the Pacific deepens very slowly from the shore. The bottom is mud and a sort of quicksand. You can drag one leg after another out nearly a half mile before you get over your head. Invasion ships would have to anchor a long way out, and that would give the town more time to get ready for the assault. On each side and in back was impenetrable jungle.

In about 1560 they built a wooden church. It burned down. They built another and it burned. Then they really built a church—of stone. The walls of one part of that church still stand, say 60 feet high. Then a convent. Things were really going good. The town prospered and everybody was safe.

In 100 years or so here comes Henry Morgan. He really knew how to set a fire. He pillaged, killed, sacked and burned things – completely. He did such a complete job the monks lost heart and came to the present Panama and set out building again.

Old Panama is a shambles. Pieces of stone wall stand out everywhere, as do crumbled stone pillars of foundations. All is desolation. The ruins, I am told, extend far back into the present jungle. Nobody seems to care to preserve what is left. We drove the car into the convent. There were the square holes where floor supports of wooden beams used to enter.

We don't particularly like this hotel. It is a mammoth sort of a wooden building. Big rooms, high ceiling, big doors, big windows, big halls, big slow elevator, big bathrooms, all of wood and everything could stand painting. Somehow I feel if the termites would let go hands, the place would crumble. We are on the third floor and I hope no Henry Morgan comes along.

Sightseeing, we passed government buildings, government tile-roofed homes for canal workers and PXs. Whenever you see government property you see order and paint. You fellers up there are paying for it.

We went to the San Jose Church, one of the oldest in Panama. it contains the gold altar the priests painted black on the occasion of an invasion. The invaders thought it had no value and left it alone. It looked to me like it had a lot of gold leaf somebody had overlooked intentionally.

We went to where "Congress" was in session. Senators in white suits had their heads stuck out windows and were conversing in low important tones. Inside, one Senator was gesticulating and yelling at the top of his voice how he had saved and now was again saving the glorious country of Panama from bankruptcy and ruin. Our host, who knew heated Spanish, said the oratory had something to do with another sizable raise in salary.

Hunting for shoe laces

Our last day, A.M. decided to do some shopping on foot and by herself. I made final preparations for our flight early in the morning to Mexico City. This done, I also went out on my own but not for the same purpose.

I had the National City Bank of New York branch bank in mind as one of my objectives; a bowl of Yardley's shaving soap as another; a shoe shine and a pair of shoe laces as two others. It is remarkable how many stores you can get into with good grace with that combination, if you are always careful to ask for the thing you feel sure they don't have. That opens the way gracefully for a pleasant conversation.

I gained friendly entrance to a world of places looking for the shaving soap, before I unexpectedly found it. That left the bank and the shoe laces to attain. The bank was a certainty, but in due time I actually became worried about brown shoe laces. I had asked in vain at too many places. Then all of a sudden my troubles were over—on ahead half a block was a sign, *Florsheim Shoes*.

I went to about where I thought shoe laces were located and asked the man for a pair of brown shoe laces. He answered he had none. He had black and white laces, but no browns. Brown shoes were outdated and always had been outdated. They were a thing a man of today was not using. The truth, so help me.

Shortly thereafter, still shoelaceless, I came to the National City branch, went in, introduced myself as a banker representing a bank that had had an account with the parent bank for over 50 years. The manager, a Mr. Cramer, was originally from Vermont, and therefore a hard man to crack, but the 50 years and the brown shoe lace trouble did the trick. He took me to lunch at the Union Club, a pretty nifty club quite near his bank and right against the Pacific Ocean. When we arrived the tide was out and the city's big cement sewer tiles were exposed for a quarter of a mile out. After lunch, which was delayed by three or four different kinds of rum, the rum or something had pulled the tide in and all the tiles were covered with water.

We got the brown shoe laces at a cobbler's shop, but they did have to dig under a big pile of old scrap leather and shoe shop saw dust to get them.

The Old Spanish Trail

In late mid-afternoon our big corporation host and his wife came to take us to one of the nearby jungles about 20 miles out. Not big like the Brazilian jungles, but thick as a new bride's potato peelings. The new highway now crosses the old Spanish Trail, which is in a part of that jungle. The Trail was laid out to cross the isthmus to get to the Atlantic. And there it was, round rocks and all. Not in good repair, of course, but a trace of what it once was.

The Trail was made for a purpose. The Spaniards would go down to Peru and rob the Incas. Then they would make slaves of some of them and bring them and the gold and other loot by ship to Panama. Then make the slaves carry the booty over that Trail to Puerto Bello on the Atlantic side, where the king's representatives would take their "cut". The balance went to Spain, as I have heretofore told you.

Our host wanted us to try some coconut water when we got back to town. The proprietor took two green coconuts out of the box, cut the ends off of each with a hatchet, reamed out a core into the hollow inside where the water is, set the nuts on the table and stuck soda water straws in the holes. The rest was up to us. . . It isn't particularly bad. There isn't much taste to it. Sort of insipid, like water in southwest Kansas in summer.

West Point connection

Our host took us to his home. I knew all along there was a good deal to this young fellow. His conversation was too bright and keen. His wit was too original, and to the point. . . But the house! Holy Nellie, what a house!! I presume it was his father's. However that may be, our host and his wife also lived there. Wrought iron grillwork, tile floors, furniture, rugs, silver and china tableware, oil paintings.

I shall try to describe just one item—a heavy, closely and beautifully woven wool rug that hung on one of the big walls. It had to be about 20 x 14 or 16 feet, and perhaps two inches thick. It was a reproduction of the Seal of West Point—eagle, arrows, colors and all. The names of the father and three boys were woven in the rug. It was made by Ecuador Indians who had only a post card to guide them, together with dimensions supplied by the father. Those Indians could not read and were otherwise as primitive as could be. But they knew how to weave and they knew their colors and keen eyes gave them the proportions.

Let me give you a part of the fellow's pedigree, verified by a banker of good repute—if the latter is possible. He, his two brothers and his father are all graduates of West Point. His father was ambassador to the United States from Ecuador. And his paternal grandfather was a former president of the Republic of Ecuador.

The hazards of flight

Yesterday (Jan. 21) we flew from Panama City. It took all day. The going was bad enough all along, but over high ridges and mountains or deep valleys it overdid things way too far. Somebody said wind currents caused it.

Then too, I saw what I thought were three loose screws sticking up on the wing on my side. I watched them closely, what time I wasn't getting things back level or watching that infernal electric sign up ahead that advised, "Tighten seat belt." It was the only honest thing about the ship—it never overstated.

The loose screws worried me considerably, so I went over and looked at the other wing, but they had them over there too. All looked of the same size, spaced alike, and equally rusted, so I didn't move over. One side was as good as the other.

Gum for the ears

Going up and coming down they gave us gum to chew. In a place such as I was, I always obeyed the stewardess or anybody in a blue suit and white cap. Chewing gum would, along with yawning, keep our ears from stopping up—maybe. Something went wrong. All of a sudden it came to me that everything had become absolutely quiet, like walking around in new snow. I listened for the roar of the motors. They had stopped. We *were* in a pickle. I turned to Aura May and said something, but I couldn't hear what I said.

It took a lot of gum chewing, yawning and calisthenics at the next stop to get partially unstopped. And my jaws are tired and sore. I'm not a regular gum-chewer.

We got off the ground early in the morning, circled over Panama City and the ocean, then back over land and a densely forested area. The tree tops looked like closely packed mushroom buttons, only the colors were varying shades of green. I couldn't see a field, road or house, and only rarely a stream.

Our first stop was at Managua, capital of Nicaragua. We went over Lake Nicaragua, a big lake.

We set down next at San Salvador. We approached it over comparatively level terrain. Thatched houses and cultivated fields were thick. The airport was as neat and nice as I have seen. It served coffee and shoeshines free. But I almost got caught.

Alligator bags are the vogue there. Aura May rather liked one. Just to test the man I asked the price. To my amazement he said $18. I said too much. He said, "What you give?" I said, $10. Before it was over, he was down to $12.50 and I was getting panicky. He was too close. I shook my head. He shook his. I left without looking back and never did go around that part of the building thereafter.

Palace and market

We next set down at Guatemala, with a two and a half hour wait. We hired a taxi and went to town. Enroute we passed two small coffee plantations. The driver told us Guatemala coffee was the finest in the world. They said the same thing at Santos and everywhere else, particularly Buenaventura and its mocha coffee.

We went to the presidential palace and got in. It's a fine place for the size and wealth of the country. Particularly the tile and stained glass murals depicting historical scenes of Guatemala. Splendid features were enormous glass chandeliers with prismatic glass tassels, and mahogany woodwork and floors of the banquet and reception rooms. The outside walls and windows had considerable bullet marks depicting the various revolutions the country had undergone. Also something to see is the one-piece table—top, sides, lower shelf and legs—with its intricate carvings, behind which the dictator of the day presides, listening to the wham of bullets outside.

The hillside Indian market took my eye. I yelled, "Whoa," and jumped out and got right in among them—kids, dogs, squatting women, tied-up hens, herbs, overripe bananas and other fruits, baskets, blankets, dolls, piles of yams, some pretty bony meats and a world of other things. To progress, you had to step over, through or around whatever was in front of you. I was making fair progress when our wild-eyed driver caught up and told me it was no place for me to be. My English caught the ear of a nearby fellow who had lost his wife and kid somewhere in the market. He was a House of God missionary from near Abilene, Texas, and had been down almost a month. We hit it up fine. The driver shrugged his shoulders and followed along. For my part, I had a pretty good time. The trip cost me five dimes and three nickels. I kept the quarter, had a good following, and everybody was on my side except the driver.

Just sign on the line

At the airport I ran into more trouble. The manager was paging me in an accent I never heard before. Aura May caught it. He told me a bottle of whiskey had broken in one of our bags and had leaked all over everything near. They didn't know what damage had been done or how I had broken the bottle.

"How *I* had broken the bottle?" I said. "Besides, I had no whiskey in any bag. Are you sure it was whiskey? Where is the bag?"

"It smells like whiskey," he said. "The bag has been transferred to the Mexico City plane. It is about time to leave. We admit the liability. We have made out the form. Just sign here."

"What amount did you fill in for the damage?" I asked.

"We left that blank to fill in later. We will do that for you."

We finally agreed he would radio their representative in Mexico City, and when we go through customs there we could all have a look.

Up from Guatemala we ran into higher and higher mountains and rougher and rougher land below. In time, Mt. Popocatepetl, 17,500 odd feet high, loomed in the distance, as did Mt. Ixtaccihuatl, a trifle lower. Now, you don't pass old Popo like you do an unattended traffic light on a bright Sunday morning. She stays in sight for a long time.

We grounded just before dark. In customs we opened up for all to see and smell. People would go by, catch a whiff and raise their eyes just like they were experiencing a sensation of "My Sin" toilet water. It was a broken bottle of Chilean wine some stranger had put in the wrong bag—maybe.

Years ago, I learned something. Our railroads never kill anything except thoroughbred stock. That bottle of wine was nestled inside my brand new tuxedo, next to my brown suit and one of the Haspel tropicals and two or three of Aura May's dresses. Kindly tell Central Insurance Agency.

Back to "cold" weather

Saturday, we flew say 1,500 miles here from intense heat to comparative cold. We are 7,500 feet up. This room in the Geneva Hotel is none too hot. It has heat of course, but they don't turn it on enough. Electricity is rationed or something.

Today, Sunday, Aura May went to see the people she lived with when in school here three or four years ago, and they had quite a reunion. These Mexicans are that way if they like you.

I hunted up another native market and had another good time. Two or three blocks of sidewalk have been partly boxed in with old corrugated metal roofing and partly left open to walk along. Hot tamales, fruits of all kinds, women cooking rather dirty looking meats and foods over rusted, greasy home made charcoal burners. I saw sheep heads with the wool on at one place and stood around to learn what disposition of them was being made, but no customers came along.

We had been warned to drink no water or milk and to eat nothing like lettuce or strawberries, in fact to eat nothing that does not have a peeling on it. Anything out of a corked bottle is all right.

Insider tour of Mexico City

To The Graphic,
Greencastle, Ind.

In Mexico City, we thought our string of rare good fortune had at last run out. But no. On Monday morning the manager of one of those heart-warming two corporations called to say he had just returned to town, and that a car and driver were at our disposal day and night for the one-week period of our stay.

That was the third time I had heard the combination "day and night" inserted in the conversation. It made me wonder whether some of my predecessors—old buzzards in their late 30s like me—had come down and vainly attempted to rejuvenate their youth with a pop gun burst of night life activity, or whether it was just a Latin American way of expressing an all out attitude toward guests. I found them a good deal that way as I went along.

Driver knows his way around

That afternoon our driver showed up—capless and uniformless—but whatever he may have lacked in uniform, he made up for in ability, knowledge and intelligence. He was a wonder. He seemed to know everybody and what their weaknesses were—custodians, policemen, lottery ticket vendors, car watchers and parking place attendants. Known and liked by everybody, he probably hadn't a single enemy in town.

For instance, the cap of my shoe and the rest of the shoe had parted company. Did he know where a shoe sewing machine could be found? That may sound trite to you as we were in a city of 3 million people, but in Mexico City machines are as rare as bad women in Greencastle. Everything is hand work. All he said was, "We go." We did, a mile or two. The price was 50 centavos—a trifle over five cents in our money.

10% off on 60 roosters

We looked around a big jewelry store. I happened to see a little sterling silver fork, the sort of thing you use to spear out olives and cherries or jab into canapés. The thing that caught my eye was that on the end of the handle was a rooster—good old Democratic stuff. It seems that a rooster in Mexico means something national—at least not political as we know it. I asked the saleswoman the price. She told me. I asked how much by the dozen. She multiplied by 12. Six dozen? She multiplied the last figure by six. I said, "Thank you," and turned to go.

Back at the car, we were talking about the forks and the design on them. Our trusty driver evidently caught the drift, because he said, "I think I know silver factory, Cheaper. We go?"

We did. How could I pass up a silver factory? There they were by the hundreds—roosters and all. Our driver went in with us. The price? It was considerably less for one than the other place. How much for a dozen? It was some less than 12 times the price of one. How much for five dozen? Some less than five times the dozen price. Fortunately, some people from Evansville came along just at the right time and I moved off.

In due time our faithful driver sidled up and said, "I get you 10% off your price."

My main idea had been to see a silver factory, but there is always a time to quit bluffing, even though you started out more or less in fun. I said, "Go buy them."

And so, I have 60 roosters. Even so, they're much cheaper than 60 roosters on the hoof.

Enrique is the name of our driver. He is a Colombian. Where and how and when he acquired his knowledge and information is probably a mystery even to his employers. Enrique is a philosopher too. His hobbies are art, fine homes and buying lottery tickets.

Churches and pyramids

Enrique is thoroughly up on his churches, and there are lots of them in Mexico as well as all South America. He said the Basilica of Guadelupe was the richest in the New World, and one of the oldest. It is in the old part of town. We arrived during Mass. Hundreds were attending that afternoon. The altar is a massive structure, and evidently of tremendous value. In back is a mural the Pope gave the church for its success in extending the faith. Enrique got hold of a boy who unlocked the doors of a big wall case and showed us the gold service of the church.

We had parked the car at the side. When we left, Enrique gave some money to a man, not exactly a policeman, but somehow connected. I asked what it was for. He shrugged and said, "Graft. If I had not given him money he would have spotted the car and the next time he would have damaged it in some way. These fellows are bad that way."

We drove next day to the pyramids—quite a distance from town. The temple or shrine to the snake gods is something to see. Made entirely of stone masonry, the outside is adorned with those famous protruding gargoyles, still in a reasonably good state of preservation. The masonry is excellent. On top was a sacrificial altar where Enrique told us thousands of human beings, mostly women, were beheaded from time to time to appease the snakes. Troughs led down and to each side, where two sizable wells at last stopped and held the flow of blood.

The high stone walls of the fort enclosed an area of a good many acres. The walls are more or less hollow because the priests lived inside and thought up new and more vicious ways and means of torturing a simple people.

No one seems to know who built the pyramids, or when. They were erected prior to the advent of the Aztecs, 1,500 to 3,000 years ago. The Pyramid of the Sun is 200 feet high and big around in proportion. Its building entailed millions of man hours. The Temple to the Moon is much lower and smaller, but at that was no after school hours chore.

Thieves Market, private serenade

One afternoon Enrique suggested he show us some fine homes, but I suggested we go out among the Indians and the poorer peoples' markets.

He said, "Maybe you like to go to the Thieves Market, where they sell stolen goods and pick your pockets." . . . We could drive slowly, and stop now and then, and see from the car. . .

The street was crowded. Everything that wasn't old was shoddy. If all that stuff had been stolen goods, it would have taken the entire population months to have actually stolen the articles, and when they got done the value of the whole thing would have been in the low thousands of dollars. No the Thieves Market in my opinion is a part of the "dress" of Mexico City. The words sound mysterious and dangerous, and give the tourists a shot in the arm. Still I was glad I had taken Enrique's advice and kept to the car. Six or eight dirty hands in my pocket could have left enough germs to have contaminated everybody west of Stilesville.

We also encountered a singer and serenader and his band who assembled around our car and played for us for five pesos (less than 60 cents) a song. We had five fiddles, one cornet, three whopping big guitars, two regular size guitars and one mandolin. I was asked what I wanted. I suggested "The Fire Scene" from Wagner or Lilly Pon's latest song, but they didn't know those so I told them anything purely Mexican. . . It was what I would call a big Carnegie Hall success. We left amid profuse thanks.

Treasured homes

I thought a change might not be a bad idea. We drove into what he said was the finest residential district—very fine and elaborate homes. The proportion will not equal that of any American city. The proportion of poor and poverty stricken people is high here. The most striking feature of these homes to me is the extravagant use of wrought iron grillwork in the openings in the walls surrounding the premises and the framing of all windows and gates. The designs are intricate. These homes are built with the idea of exclusion. It is hard to see the grounds unless a gate or doors are left open. Enrique would stop very candidly where there was an opening. What we saw was always immaculately kept. Labor is cheap.

Enrique saved "the three finest homes in Mexico" for last. They were really fine homes. And they were big of course. One was built by a rich Spanish merchant, the other two by politicians, both of whom at one time or another had been connected with the Treasury of Mexico. Quite a coincidence I thought—best two out of three.

Pap in La Perricholi's bathtub in Lima. Peru. (La Perricholi was
mistress of the first Viceroy of Peru.)

Pap's legal tradition continues. Pap's granddaughter, Margaret Durham McGaughey (Isaacson), Assistant U.S. Attorney General in the District of Maine, with Attorney-General Janet Reno at the U.S. Department of Justice in Washington on the day Margaret was presented with a Citation "For Outstanding Service" in 1994. On Margaret's left are Carol di Battista (head of executive field of office personnel) and Jamie Gorelick, second in command at the Justice Department.